"Thinking is drawing in your head."
Alan Fletcher, *The Art of Looking Sideways*

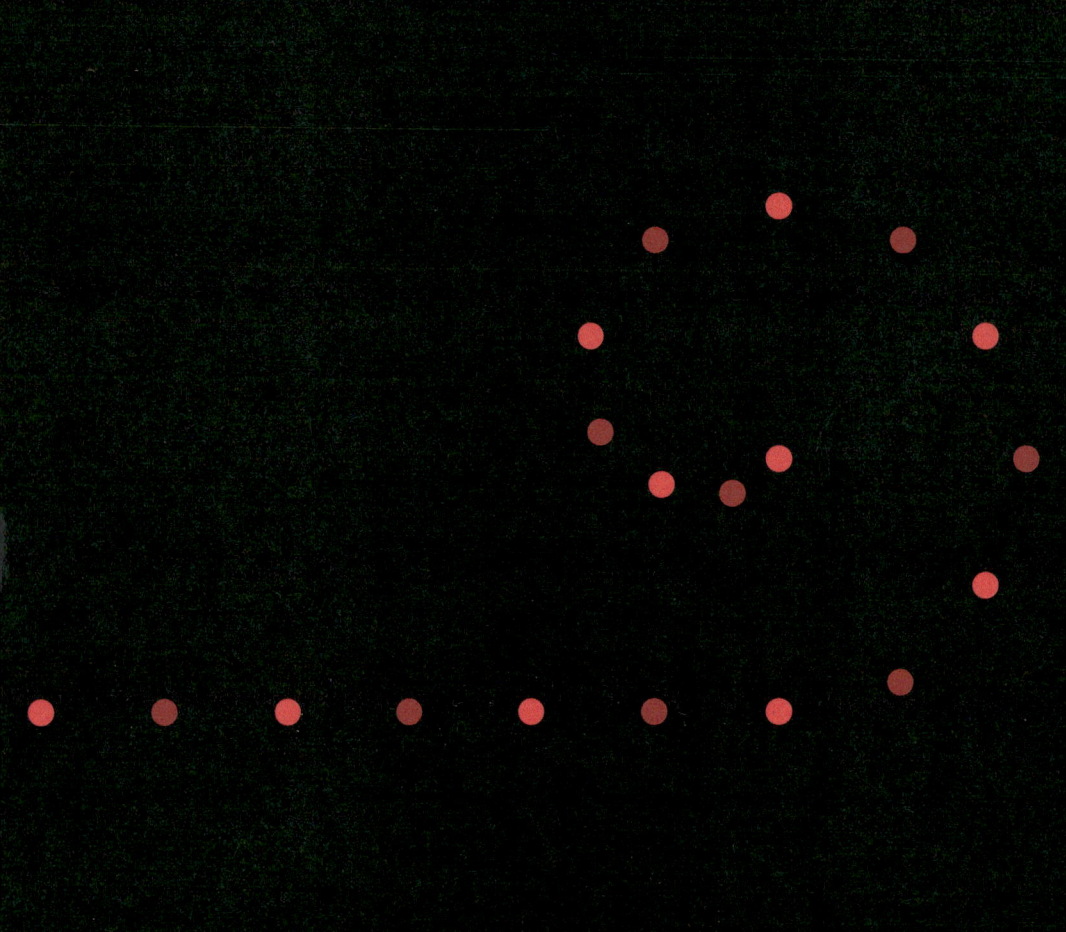

"We can think of the world as made up of things. Of substances. Of entities. Of something that is. Or we can think of it as made up of events. Of happenings. Of processes. Of something that occurs. Something that does not last, and that undergoes continual transformation, that is not permanent in time."

Carlo Rovelli, *The Order of Time*

THINK IN 4D

Design brilliant user experiences and valuable digital products

Erica Heinz

Contents

INTRO

11 **About This Book**

FRAMEWORK

17 **The 4D Thinking Model**
Product experience phases: TIIM • Layers: 2D/3D/4D • Areas (12) • Using the model

23 **The Method**
Prototype • Lower the fidelity • Work backward • Work in circles • Use principles • Use metrics • Co-create

PRACTICE

	THREADS	IMPRESSIONS	INTERACTIONS	MEMORIES
2D	41 **Words** Create content strategically Make a navigable place Refine language contextually	83 **Layouts** Lead the eye Set readable structures Add breathing room	125 **Symbols** Define design principles Refine functional details Reduce cognitive load	173 **Images** Find the right feeling Show the value Represent appropriately
3D	55 **Inclusivity** Include diverse perspectives Adapt to varied constraints Build in redundancy	95 **Flexibility** Refine the hierarchies Build fluid containers Prepare for live content	143 **Usability** Select easy input formats Communicate constraints Give good feedback	185 **Personalization** Use relevant, ethical data Have a real-life presence Build human connections
4D	69 **Relationships** Model ideal behavior Make it easy to reconnect See and support change	107 **Patterns** Reuse functional patterns Fill the in-between states Streamline repeated use	155 **Paths** Choreograph the steps Inspire and assist action Prevent exploitation	197 **Moments** Map the mental model Define unique value Turn value props into UI

CRAFT

213 **Prototyping**
Write • Sketch • Wireframe • Play

227 **Thinking**
Deconstruct • Frame • Research • Diverge • Converge • Differentiate • Think in 4D

OUTRO

239 **Acknowledgments**

Practice principles

	THREADS	IMPRESSIONS	INTERACTIONS	MEMORIES	
	WORDS	**LAYOUTS**	**SYMBOLS**	**IMAGES**	2D
	Five hat racks	Z pattern	Mapping	Picture superiority effect	
	Framing	Proximity	Aesthetic-usability effect	Iconic representation	
	Wayfinding	Gestalt	Garbage in, garbage out	Face-ism ratio	
	INCLUSIVITY	**FLEXIBILITY**	**USABILITY**	**PERSONALIZATION**	3D
	Empathy	80/20 rule	Visibility	Endowment effect	
	Progressive enhancement	Expectation effect	Forgiveness	Signal-to-noise ratio	
	Redundancy	Flexibility-usability tradeoff	Performance versus preference	Availability bias	
	RELATIONSHIPS	**PATTERNS**	**PATHS**	**MOMENTS**	4D
	Precommitment	Modularity	Inertia	Peak-end rule	
	Control	Consistency	Progressive disclosure	Isolation effect	
	Parity	Mere exposure effect	Loss aversion	Fundamental attribution error	

Practice exercises

	THREADS	IMPRESSIONS	INTERACTIONS	MEMORIES
2D	**WORDS** Press release Card sort Click-through test	**LAYOUTS** Square dance Text measures Squint test	**SYMBOLS** Design principles UI styling Iconography	**IMAGES** World building Visual storytelling Art direction
3D	**INCLUSIVITY** Empathy map Alternative modes Operability test	**FLEXIBILITY** Priority list Content blocking Null/full states	**USABILITY** Touch target test Task completion test Flowchart	**PERSONALIZATION** Data boundaries AEIOU research Swimlane diagram
4D	**RELATIONSHIPS** Interaction metaphor Retention hooks Privileges plan	**PATTERNS** Components Interstitials Loops	**PATHS** See/do lists Incentives Ethics check	**MOMENTS** Journey map Value propositions Experience model

Key exercises

THREADS	IMPRESSIONS	INTERACTIONS	MEMORIES
CREATE	**CREATE**	**CREATE**	**CREATE**
Links	Screens	Flows	Concepts
CRITIQUE	**CRITIQUE**	**CRITIQUE**	**CRITIQUE**
☑ Forward ☑ Backward ☑ Zooming out ☑ Diving deeper	☑ Hierarchy ☑ Functionality ☑ Flexibility ☑ Style	☑ Format ☑ Order ☑ Quantity ☑ Feedback	☑ Impressions ☑ Utility ☑ Distinction ☑ Memorability
Navigation	Layouts	Content	Value

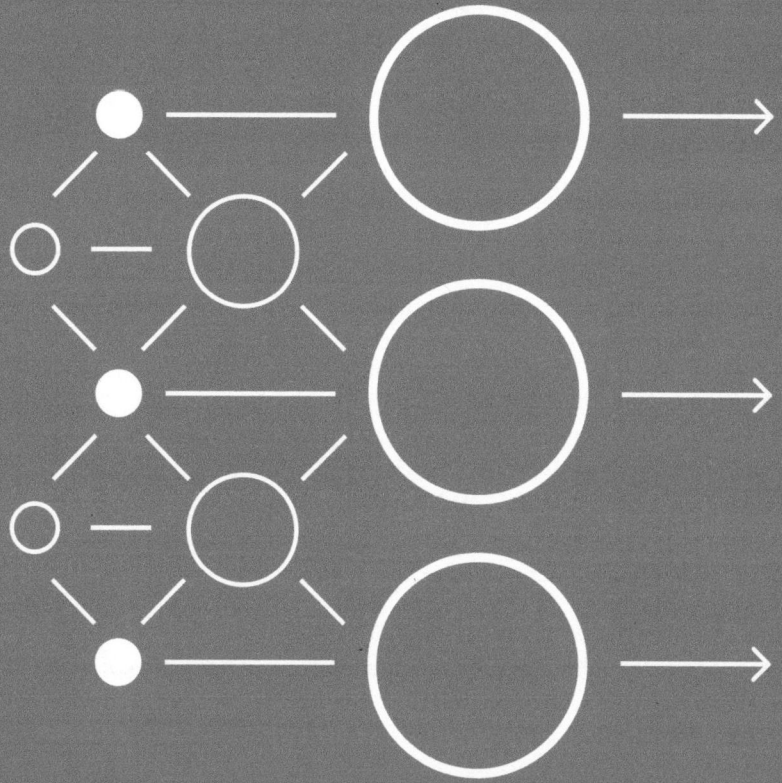

Threads

———————————————→

Threads are the connections to and through a product. They are the first part of each interaction: the assorted touchpoints users encounter (from official marketing to word-of-mouth stories to functional links) that shape the context for each visit. Good threads build interest, engagement, and relationships over time. Designers must create clear, accessible, adaptable navigation to and around an experience.

Threads create the web. Links were the foundational innovation of the internet, connecting formerly isolated ideas and eventually the people behind them. Product experience doesn't have to be any more complex than links between screens. Craigslist has barely changed since its launch in 1995; Wikipedia's value lies in the access it provides to information, not in its design.

Words are a key tool in this phase; language shapes expectations and behavior. If a link says "Feed," what do you expect to see there? What if it said "People" or "Read" or "New!" or "Posts"? Each word carries connotations, both culturally and in the history of digital interfaces. Clear language will increase understanding; inspiring language will increase participation.

Finding the right connective threads requires inclusive design practices that take the time to understand a variety of cultures and constraints. Accommodating diversity (creating more accessible or customized threads) increases a product's resilience and supports organic growth. All the threads we weave together create usable architecture for information and easier relationships with the product.

In this phase we'll look at words, inclusivity, and relationships. This section is intersectional, focused on broadening access to an experience. The chapters in this section are micro and macro; they zoom in to consider each little connection and zoom out to examine long-term impacts.

PRACTICE

2D words: Be strategic with language to make navigable content that's appropriate to its context. Carefully consider and refine the words that frame, categorize, or label each small element or larger experience.

3D inclusivity: Include diverse perspectives and accommodate varied constraints to create many methods of access. Use empathy, progressive enhancement, and redundancy to increase user access and product resilience.

4D relationships: Define the interaction metaphor, make it easy to reconnect, recognize how visitors change, and support their growth. Understand how the product fits into peoples' minds, and provide prompts or controls that fit each proficiency level.

Links: Sketch the navigation to or through an experience. Evaluate the impact of each word, and refine the containing information architecture. Use appropriate metaphors and controls to build long-term relationships.

INTRO

About This Book

• The concept

Digital designs do not exist. There's only a screen, with pixels changing color in patterns that convince our brains and bodies to believe or do something. Digital design is a psychological craft; the designs are only impressions in time.

Pixels might convey familiar shapes or invent new ones. They might reflect a viewer's physical environment or conjure cyberspaces. They might fade in soothing rhythms or pop in surprising bursts. If all these tricks connect systematically, they create a symbolic language people can interact with.

Interactive systems are logical, emotional, visual, and invisible at the same time. And because they are so complicated, product design has to split ideas into workable parts, refine each microsystem, and then see how they combine.

Abstraction helps us handle digital levels of complexity. When we reduce fidelity visually, we can focus on a few details at a time. When we synthesize many insights into a single theme strategically, we can keep that big idea in our short-term memory and use it with other things. This book works entirely at low fidelity to show what a focused, abstracted design process looks like.

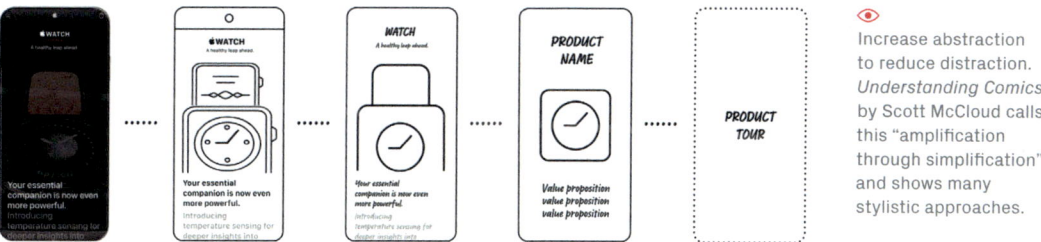

Increase abstraction to reduce distraction. *Understanding Comics* by Scott McCloud calls this "amplification through simplification" and shows many stylistic approaches.

Think in 4D turns this conceptual viewpoint into a practical handbook. It's a book about product experience design: how to think holistically, creatively, and critically to design savvy strategies and valuable products. It pushes you to think beyond 2D designs and 3D devices to 4D impacts.

• The outline

Part 1 of this book, FRAMEWORK, outlines the 4D Thinking model. I define product experience as consisting of four phases (threads, impressions, interactions, and memories) that occur in three types of dimensional space (2D, 3D, and 4D). This easy-to-remember model splits product design into manageable parts and helps us recall related nodes throughout the process.

Part 1 also supplies a method of working with the model: for best results we prototype, lower the fidelity, work backward, work in circles, use principles, use metrics, and co-create.

Part 2, PRACTICE, takes the 4D Thinking model into usable design guidelines. The three chapters in each of the four phases include key questions, principles, examples, and exercises for that topic. Each phase also ends with a larger design challenge (creating concepts, flows, screens, or links) and critique outline. I suggest doing the exercises while reading to increase your absorption of the material; they should expand your thinking and your design toolkit. If you're building a design portfolio, the exercises will also help you develop a solid process and show the deep thinking that hiring managers love to see.

Part 3, CRAFT, wraps up the book with ways to advance your creative and conceptual skills. Prototyping is the tangible craft; we build our executional skills by refining how we write, sketch, wireframe, and play. Thinking is the invisible craft; we improve our strategic skills by learning to deconstruct, frame, research, diverge, converge, differentiate, and think in 4D.

This book will not cover the details of user interface design; visual design systems are definitely their own specialty at this point, and style guidelines quickly become dated in print. You don't need to master color, motion, or high-fidelity design software to do great product design. You *do* need to leverage hierarchy, contrast, and patterns, so I've included those visual foundations. As you advance your practice, you can layer on skills in UI (or research, or coding, or writing).

For additional resources and updates, subscribe to my newsletter at thinkin4D.com.

• My experience

This book draws from more than twenty years working as a design consultant in New York City. I got my first paid web design job as an art school freshman and have stayed in the field ever since. I've gone from the era of designing and coding entire websites and apps myself to strategizing multiyear, multimillion-dollar products with executives. Product experience became my core focus; I love its combination of problem-solving, systems thinking, visual composition, and human behavior.

As a near-lifelong consultant, I'm sharing an adaptable approach drawn from common principles across many industries and applications. I've done strategy and design for agencies, small businesses, early-stage startups, nonprofits, and Fortune 500 companies. This material is not specific vocational training to get a job at a large tech company (though I think it would help you do that too); rather, it is a guidebook for the type of strategic thinking that large companies hire consultants to do.

This book also builds on my courses for Parsons School of Design, the School of Visual Arts, Skillshare, and various clients. I taught undergraduate interaction design and graduate product design at Parsons, helping develop the curriculum for their master's degree in the latter. I taught summer intensives for SVA's MFA in interaction design and did thesis advising for their MFA in design. I've led UX workshops in multiple NYC startup accelerators and launched three top-rated prototyping classes on Skillshare. And, working as part of the Runyon Design studio, I taught the UX portion of an accelerator program at a Fortune 100 company.

Think in 4D shares the lessons I have learned along the way.

• The problem

Teaching interaction design and product design made me aware of recurring gaps in how students thought about digital experiences. Art students fixated on the graphic design aspects, career changers struggled with the flexible thinking required, and experienced professionals still just seemed to copy existing sites and apps instead of being strategic and developing unique solutions.

The learning experiences I saw did not address these issues well. UX bootcamps provided formulaic processes and boring portfolios; corporate programs were vocational training for their particular deployment structures; video lessons focused on software and surface details; and a flood of articles rehashed familiar concepts for SEO or personal brand-building without any awareness of how the topics fit together.

I saw the need for a solid and practical conceptual model for creative and strategic thinking, a clear and memorable structure that could also adapt to a wide variety of digital projects.

• The goals

Think in 4D is a strategic practice manual for the product design community: those looking to enter it, and those already shaping its features. It shares ways to make design work more impactful for audiences, businesses, and designers. The 4D Thinking model will help you generate many ideas from valuable perspectives; as I was finishing up the second draft of this book and also kicking off a new project, I came up with twice as many concepts as anyone else (and the final product was extremely well received).

If you're learning or practicing digital design, this book will help you…

- Plan effective, valuable design initiatives
- Apply cognitive and visual principles at appropriate times
- Design memorable concepts, enjoyable flows, clear screens, and useful links
- Advance from reactive production to strategic leadership
- Retain learning within a solid conceptual model

If you're managing a product or design team, this book will help you…

- Frame productive design discussions and initiatives
- Strategize valuable experiences for audiences
- Prioritize design initiatives and iterations
- Critique experience designs from many angles
- Differentiate products for success in the marketplace

● The book

This book takes a postmodern approach: it attempts to recognize its influences while also building new ideas from them. It is full of connections to other sources for continued learning, but tries to remain as useful as possible on its own. This book is:

As visual as possible
I don't think it makes sense to use a lot of words to teach product design, so I try to show rather than tell. The book's 500+ illustrations will feed and build the visual or experiential parts of your brain. They are prompts to pause and think. Use your imagination to build on them. ◉

As short as possible
There are plenty of 700-page design bibles you'll never finish. This book is a collection of stand-alone sections for busy schedules and modern attention spans. Try a page at random or skim through the whole thing.

As challenging as possible
This book asks a lot of questions and doesn't always provide the answers. That may feel frustrating at first, but deep thinking is a core skill to practice. Interacting with information helps you develop your own point of view and become an independent creative professional. Respond to, riff on, or argue with the prompts.

A companion, not a lecture
You can't learn design just by listening; have paper or software on hand so you can practice. Applying the ideas to a project as you go along will prevent information overload and increase retention. Take breaks to jot down notes, try the exercises, or sketch your thoughts.

A perspective, not a dictionary
Our field does not have a standard vocabulary for many processes and deliverables, which is kind of a problem. People use the same term to mean different things, or different terms for the same thing. This book labels and groups ideas using the terms I've heard most often and a structure I find most useful. Refine and redefine as needed.

A resource list, not a checklist
No project will need every step in this book; use what's relevant and skip what's not. Workflows to create new marketing sites vary hugely from those to refine existing apps. Each of the four practice phases has nine exercises before the final design challenge. As in real life, do as many or as few exercises as feels right for you.

"'What is the use of a book,' thought Alice, 'without pictures or conversations?'"
Lewis Carroll, *Alice's Adventures in Wonderland*

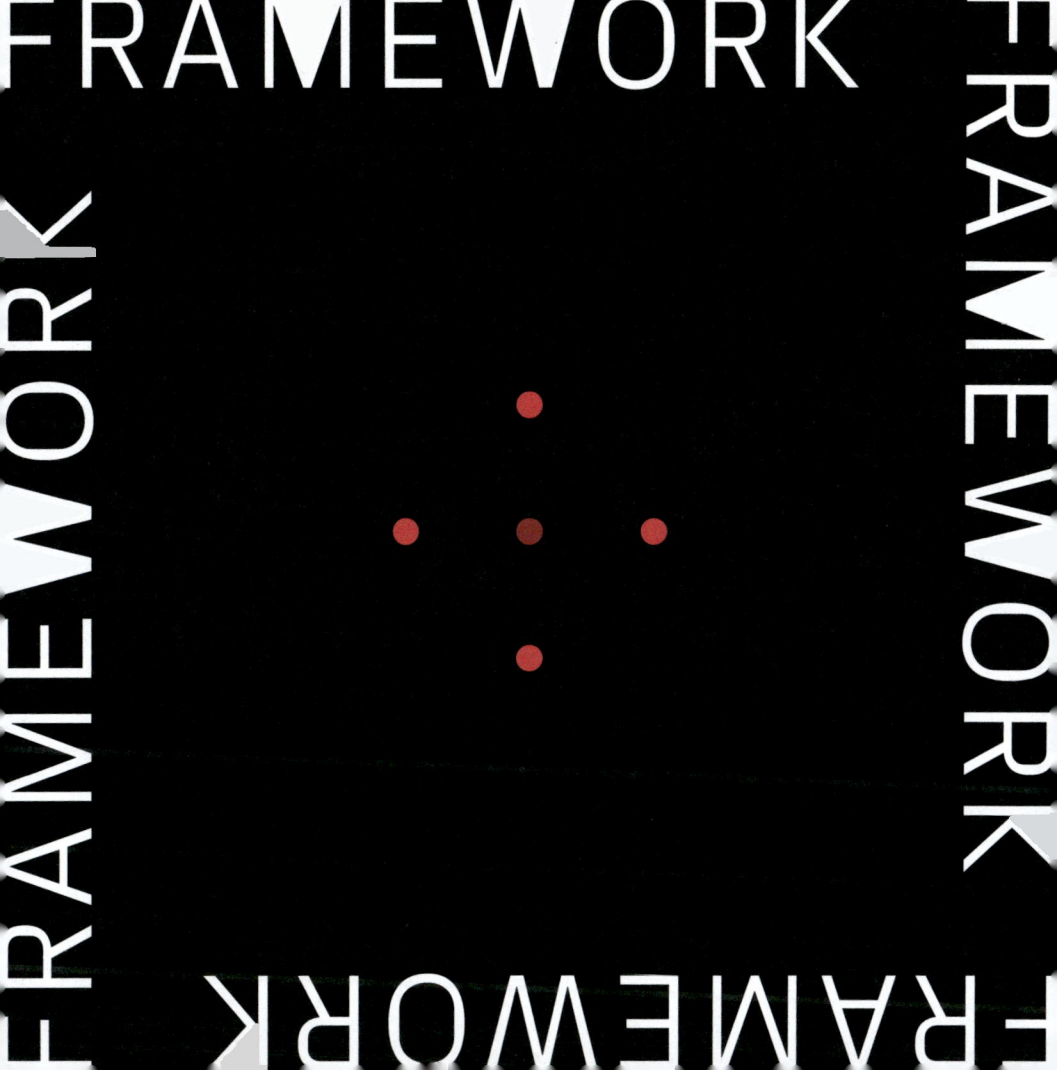

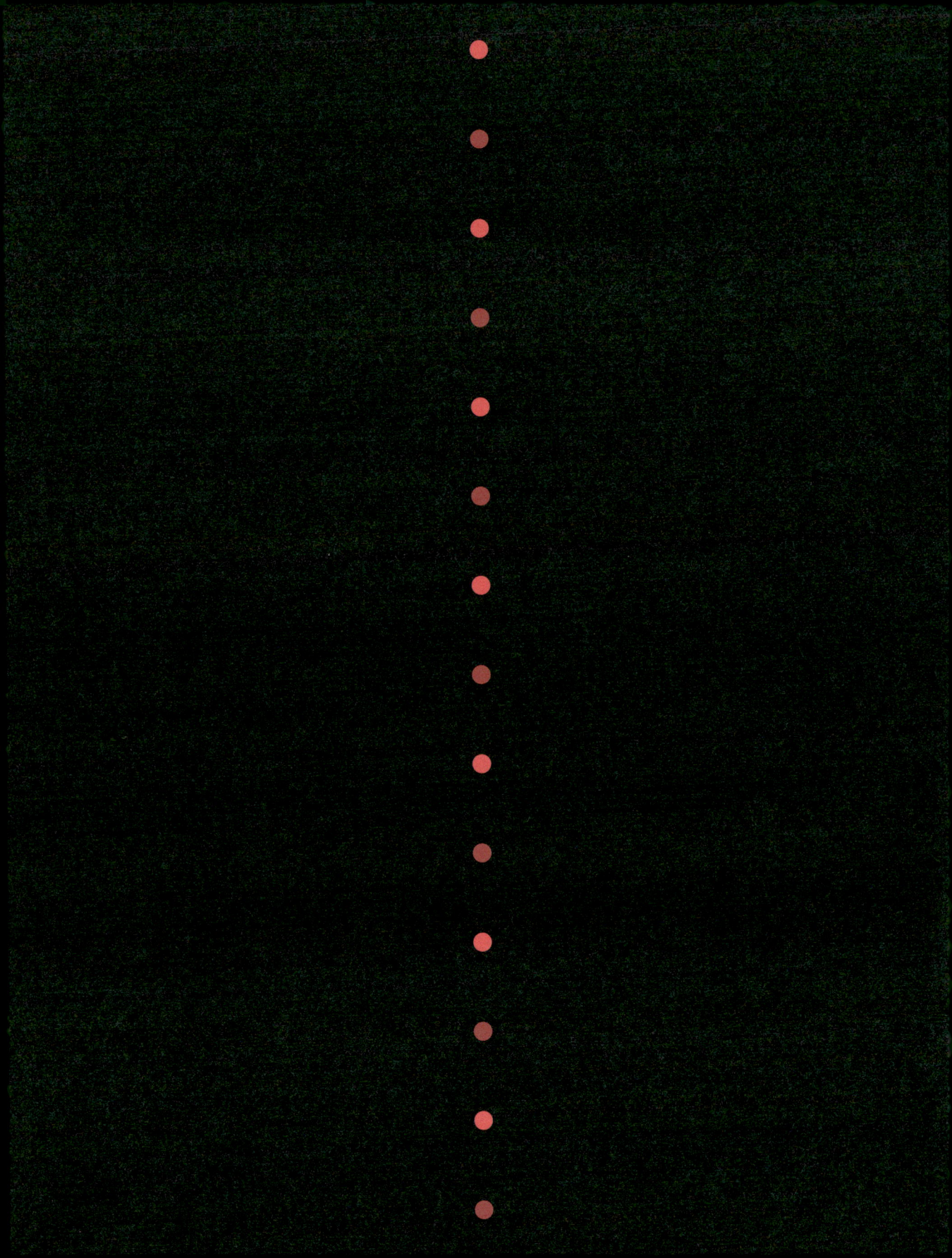

The 4D Thinking Model

Product design is a slippery beast. The medium is complex and dynamic; the experiences are subjective and ephemeral. To grasp and shape all the interconnected parts, we need a mental model that's modular but manageable, a definition that's memorable and practical. The 4D Thinking model defines product experience as the threads, impressions, interactions, and memories a product provides in two, three, and four dimensions. Let's look at why that definition is useful, and how.

Note: this approach builds heavily on the practice of user experience design, taking a holistic viewpoint similar to Don Norman's original definition of UX. However, I use the phrase "product experience" instead of "user experience" to create a stronger connection to the intertwined fields of product design and product management, to avoid the negative connotations of the word "user," and to emphasize the material qualities of digital experiences in people's minds.

"User experience [is] everything that touches upon your experience with the product. And it may not even be near the product. It may be when you're telling somebody else about it. That's what we meant when we devised the term 'user experience'."
Don Norman, "The Term 'UX'"

• Product experience phases: TIIM (time)

While teaching the user experience portion of an accelerator program at a Fortune 100 company, I wondered how to explain UX to a corporate audience in an actionable way. What would prevent them from fixating on graphic design and start them on the path to experience design? What would discourage them from copying existing products and help them create unique ones?

One key piece to the puzzle was *context:* visitors come to your site or app from somewhere, and they're carrying that baggage when they arrive. They've heard stories and have clicked links that then frame their interpretations of the things they see when they land in your world.

A second, larger piece was *interactivity:* digital design crafts not only things people *see,* but also things they *do.* Screens aren't meant for passive watching; they're built for actions and reactions.

The final important piece was *memory:* visitors leave, and experiences are ephemeral, so the imprint those experiences make determines any return. It also provides the context for the next cycle of experience.

These pieces implied four key phases of product experience—context, impression, interaction, and memory—and conveyed a desired focus on timelines, not screens. As I refined the idea, my colleague Sam Raddatz said it could use a memorable acronym, so I framed it as TIIM (conveniently pronounced "time"): threads, impressions, interactions, and memories.

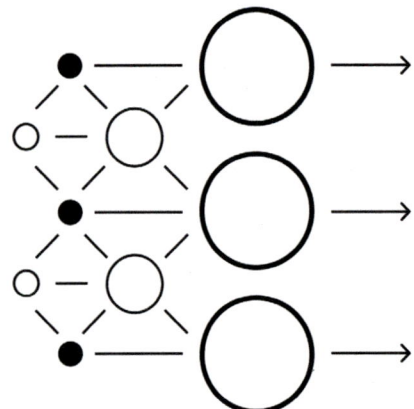

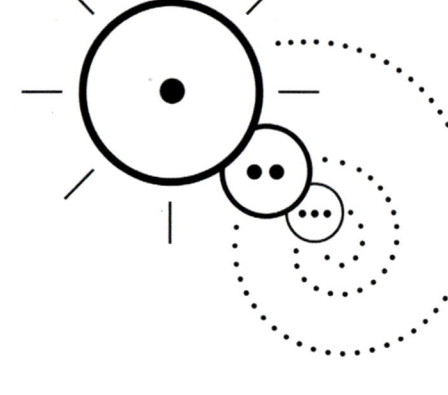

Threads provide the channels for people to visit, as well as some context. Official stories and social touchpoints create links that encourage visitors to investigate, act, and build relationships over time. Designers must create easy and inclusive navigation to and around the experience.

Impressions flash across visitors' retinas on their first visit and any future ones. Each screen must lead their eyes through space and time, adapting to a variety of devices and content. Designers must create clear, consistent, compelling, and flexible layouts.

👁 The TIIM model for product experience.

👁 Product experience and product design occur in opposite directions.

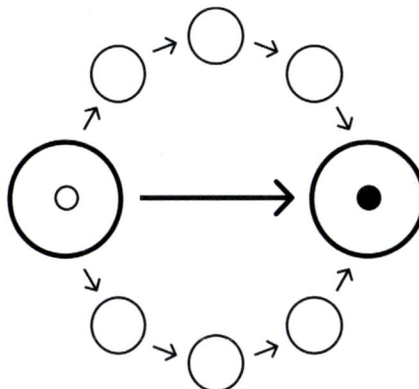
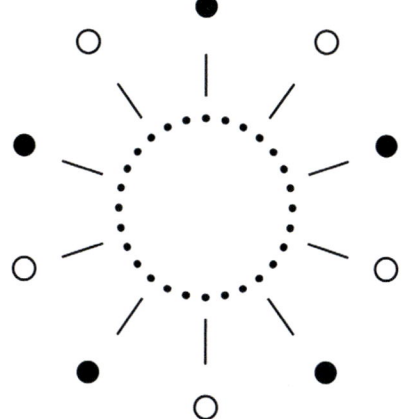

Interactions make up the bulk of visitors' time with an experience, and provide the unique constraints of interactive designs. Familiar or innovative systems of symbols help make actions efficient and enjoyable. Designers must create inspiring, ethical, usable flows.

Memories reveal the most valuable or impactful parts of the experience. Emotional moments, personalized interactions, and evocative images help visitors retain and share that experience. Designers must create human-centered, empathetic, differentiated concepts.

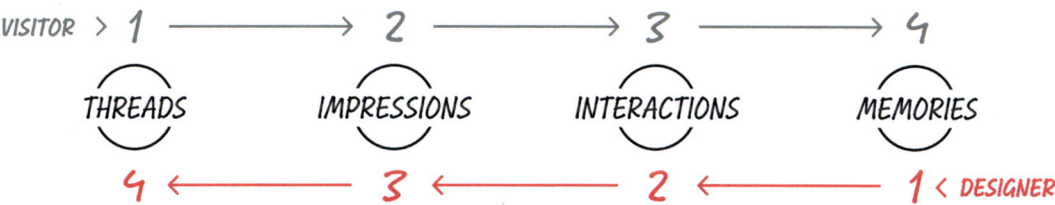

A final twist is the experiential process versus the creative one: product *experience* versus product experience *design*. To ensure that design processes lead to a certain point, we have to work backward from that goal. In my process, I tend to start by finding and designing memorable moments, structuring the interactions to and from them, refining the impressions at each step, and building lots of threads at the end. I'm presenting these phases in experiential order so the model is clear, but I actually see the creative part backward (and wrote this book backward too).

• Product experience layers: 2D/3D/4D

My second goal for the model was to include both the visible and invisible parts of experience design. I often found myself twitching in design critiques when stakeholders wanted to change colors or features without understanding the ripple effects of those decisions. I needed a way to help teams not only think about the layout designs they saw, but also remember the physical devices and sequential events that surrounded them. I started to think of product experiences as multidimensional.

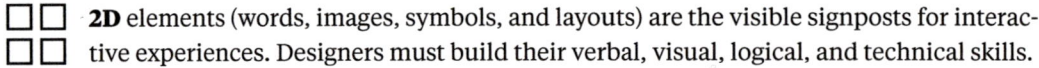 **2D** elements (words, images, symbols, and layouts) are the visible signposts for interactive experiences. Designers must build their verbal, visual, logical, and technical skills.

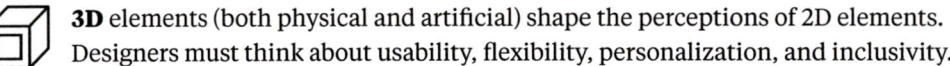 **3D** elements (both physical and artificial) shape the perceptions of 2D elements. Designers must think about usability, flexibility, personalization, and inclusivity.

> *Physical 3D* (devices and environments) creates complex tactile or cultural considerations: big fingers on small phones on a bus; tiny hands on giant phablets in the dark; screen readers and microphones in an open office.

> *Artificial 3D* (layers and depth effects) brings real-world interaction models into digital interfaces: shaded buttons that seem to depress if a mouse is clicked; popup layers that appear to float over less important ones; scrolling windows that imply more content is hidden outside a frame.

 4D elements (sequence, duration, and repetition) are the core of experience design versus visual design: the moments, paths, patterns, and relationships that occur over short or long time frames. Designers must work with stories, logic, and timelines to be choreographers, party planners, and urban planners.

When I introduced this model, people got it (with only minor pedantic arguments about the scientific or mathematical definitions of the fourth dimension). They started to loosen up on layout design and think more deeply about system design.

As with the TIIM phases, it's easiest to understand these layers progressively but often smartest to design in the opposite direction. Think through the 4D strategy, adapt it to 3D contexts, then design any needed 2D representations. In college you learn by advancing sequentially from 100-level to 400-level classes, but once you understand the higher-level ideas you can start there.

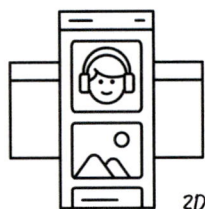

Consider 2D layouts, 3D devices, and 4D scenarios.

Product experience areas

Combining the four phases and three layers of the 4D Thinking model provides twelve key areas of experience design. This practical arrangement makes it easy to remember all the topics and intelligently connect future learning to the scaffolding. (In academic terms, this is known as a *construct theory,* which is intended to be useful; as opposed to an *event theory,* which is intended to be measured or proven.)

	Threads	Impressions	Interactions	Memories
2D	**Words** — tell stories or provide links that inspire action.	**Layouts** — create visual hierarchies of info, plus a gestalt.	**Symbols** — communicate the possible actions.	**Images** — deliver eye-catching or iconic ideas.
3D	**Inclusivity** — ensures that all people can enjoy an experience.	**Flexibility** — accommodates varied content and screen sizes.	**Usability** — helps visitors start and finish actions effectively.	**Personalization** — makes experiences more relevant and valuable.
4D	**Relationships** — model the cadence and intimacy of connections.	**Patterns** — build familiarity and ease through consistency.	**Paths** — connect specific steps to serve a specific goal.	**Moments** — provide anchors within streams of action.

COMPARE Twelve areas of product experience

Working phase by phase, we can use each layer to add more depth to each design. Threads can increase connection if we refine words, broaden inclusion, and model relationships. Impressions can increase understanding if we refine layouts, add flexibility, and leverage familiar patterns. Interactions can increase engagement if we refine symbols, check usability, and create pleasant paths. Memories can increase value if we refine images, personalize experiences, and make moments that matter.

Working layer by layer, we can use each phase to prompt more thoughtful and impactful designs. Sketch in 2D, from initial words-of-mouth to memorable images. Test in 3D, from initial access to memorable personalization. Think in 4D, from initial encounters to memorable moments.

For ease of understanding, this book presents topics in chronological order of experience and ascending order of complexity. But once you understand the framework, work in any order that makes the most sense for a given situation. (For new projects I usually work backward, starting with Moments.) This book provides the dots; the connections depend on the context.

Using the model

Okay, so we have a whole new mental model for product experience! How do we use it?

Different initiatives will need more or less breadth or depth, and different practitioners will have more or less capacity to use the whole model. Andy Hunt, in *Pragmatic Thinking and Learning,* cites studies saying that most people, for most skills, never get past "advanced beginner" proficiency (the second of five levels): "performing the tasks they need and learning new tasks as the need arises but never acquiring a more broad-based, conceptual understanding of the task environment." With the 4D Thinking framework, designers can tackle individual topics as standalone opportunities for improvement and work toward integrating the whole model.

Feature refinement
Students or junior product designers should be able to deliver clear improvements to existing product design structures in one or more areas. They might read and get a lot of value from a single chapter in the PRACTICE part of this book. Look for the area with the largest opportunity for improvement based on your particular product, team, and context. Iterate from lower to higher fidelity.

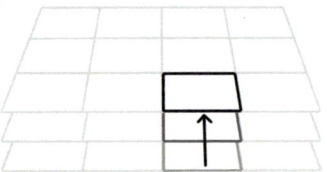
◉ Choose one area to improve and spend an hour in sketches, a day in wireframes, and a week in mockups.

Product refinement
Mid- to senior-level product designers should have a general understanding of all the areas in this model and be able to iterate features or products with a holistic view. They might skim the bulk of this book, reading only the sections of greatest relevance, or use it as a checklist as they work through iterations.

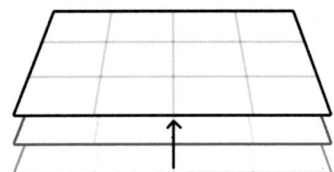
◉ Take a four-week journey and iterate a product experience from sketches to wireframes to mockups.

Product vision
Principal or staff-level product designers should have a deep understanding of all the areas in this model, and how they relate to one another. They might understand and enjoy all the topics in this book, and should be able to start from scratch to create a unique product vision. In my practice, this process goes backward (from a strong memory to integrated threads) and upward (from 4D strategy to 2D expressions). It doesn't always have to happen in high fidelity.

◉ Do a four-day sprint at low fidelity, one day per phase: create and critique memories, interactions, impressions, and threads.

Now, let's get a bit more specific about those methods.

The Method

A holistic approach to experience design requires a collaborative, adaptable, goal-oriented method that focuses on the strategic questions at hand. Product design is interactive, so we make prototypes to reveal the interactions. We work in low fidelity for as long as possible to answer specific questions and reduce business risk. We work backward from a goal, in small circles that repeatedly polish the most important elements. We use design and cognitive principles plus growth and satisfaction metrics to help us generate and evaluate ideas. Throughout the process, we co-create with the audience and other subject matter experts to make sure the outcome is valuable and sustainable.

• Prototype

"The thing holding us back as designers is that we still identify our individual value with the type of documentation we create. Design is not a sketch, or a written description, or a piece of code. These are just various ways to document the design. The design is the thinking."

Erika Hall, Twitter

When we say "experience design," what do we expect to see or make? It can honestly be anything from scribbles to code. But visual designs, no matter how polished, are not the product; they're just visual aids that facilitate conversations or document them. Digital products are made from decisions and code. So the most useful designs are prototypes, a word that can mean any sort of working model or simulation.

Good prototypes have three key attributes:

Good prototypes are fast

The point of prototyping is to test an assumption or hypothesis and reduce a project's risk. The right prototype is one that will answer crucial questions as quickly and as clearly as possible. Some people love visual design so much that they resist making "ugly" things. But don't invest so much time that you bias the test with your own sunk costs. Get your idea in front of people sooner, not later.

Good prototypes are interactive

As soon as we have anything visual, we can look at what we're really designing: interactions. We're designing behaviors, not objects, so prototypes should help us observe actions and reactions. Turn the ideas in your head into a form that other people can use, not just see. Help them shift out of hypotheticals and into more tangible situations. Using paper or screens, make the design touchable so that people lean forward rather than back.

Good prototypes are throwaway

Prototypes cannot be precious; they are tools for answering questions before you set up more serious structures. After you learn from a prototype, you throw it away. That's sometimes hard to do, especially under time pressure like a sprint or budget pressure like a small business. But you need to have the mindset of churning out ideas as if they're firewood, not fine art. The value is what you learn through the process. Practice nonattachment; stop when the idea feels clear but not final.

Make a prototype, not a drawing.

EXERCISE: Button test

Grab a piece of paper and write your name on it. Draw a small rectangle underneath your name and write "Contact me" inside. Congratulations! You've prototyped a website, complete with information and functionality. Show it to a potential visitor and you can already gather insights.

1. **Is it clear?** What do visitors expect to happen if they tap the button?
2. **Is it usable?** Does their finger fit in the button? Their thumb?
3. **Is it helpful?** Would they prefer to see an email address, a phone number, a social media handle?
4. **Is it satisfying?** What else do they want to know, feel, or do?

• Lower the fidelity

Product experiences are very complex; we can't figure everything out at once. On screens we can prototype hi-fi mockups or code, but this book works with its own simple materials (ink and paper) to demonstrate how to make brilliant designs and valuable products with just lo-fi writing, sketching, and wireframing. Reducing design fidelity increases the quantity of iterations and strategic changes possible. Abstraction focuses the work and its viewers on essential elements.

> "The more 'done' something appears, the more narrow and incremental the feedback."
>
> Kathy Sierra, "Don't Make the Demo Look Done"

• Avoid distractions

C. Northcote Parkinson's law of triviality says that people spend a disproportionate amount of time on trivial issues. To illustrate this, Parkinson gave the example of a nuclear power plant, where people were so overwhelmed by the decision of approval that they spent the bulk of their time discussing the attached bike shed (leading to the term *bikeshedding*).

Parkinson's law of triviality states that people get overwhelmed by big decisions and spend disproportionate time on small ones.

Understand behavioral psychology. If participants feel lost discussing workflows or value propositions, they'll zoom in on a minor thing like a button they feel confident having an opinion on. Feedback on styles, layouts, or images may seem useful, but it can obscure larger issues like participants avoiding the awkwardness of saying the feature is useless to them.

Focus on the input you must get within the cadence you've set. Take away the candy of beautiful high-fidelity mocks. Lower fidelity forces research participants to read the headlines, consider the idea, and react to the strategy. Those are big-picture things that are much harder or more disruptive to change later. Figure them out now, before you spend months or millions on branding and code.

"Unfinished" designs also mean research participants don't feel as bad giving you critical feedback. With hi-fi mocks, research participants can tell you spent a lot of time on it so they can't help but be nicer. Don't waste your product development time getting lip service. Show something lo-fi enough that people can imagine serious edits. Give them a marker if it helps.

• Select the lowest fidelity that can answer key questions

It's tempting to jump into beautiful mockups. And in some areas, like editorial design, the look and feel *is* the design challenge. But there is great value in going lo-fi. You can generate more options and more iterations in the same amount of time and you'll get more conceptual feedback. If the design looks done, participants often see the idea as untouchable, and you'll get more nitpicky comments on colors and fonts.

Focus on the biggest, riskiest assumptions first; find the simplest way to test them. Are you sure people want the solution you're proposing? Test a headline. Are you sure the interface you've envisioned matches their mental model? Test a sketch. Are you sure they want slider controls and not input fields? Test a wireframe. Work from large questions to small, from concepts to details.

Certain loops of product design will also require you to consider the particular audience for the research and the practical constraints of the business. A prototype that's also going to executives may need a higher level of polish. A prototype that needs to be done in one week by you alone might need to stretch but not overwhelm your skills. Be practical.

Each form of prototyping has its own benefits, attachment levels, requirements, pros, and cons.

COMPARE
Five fidelity levels

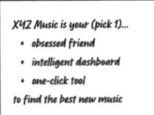    

Fidelity	Words	Sketches	Wireframes	Mockups	Code
Benefits	Clarify the concept and its communication	Illustrate and rapidly iterate the idea	Plot content, functionality, and layout	Visualize the interface, feeling, and impression	Demonstrate how things work (or don't work)
Attachment	**Low** (revisions are instant)	**Low** (obviously not final)	**Moderate** (depending on complexity)	**High** (danger: they feel very real)	**Moderate** (depending on complexity)
Requirements	Fluency, diversity	Steady hand, courage	Layout software or skills	Design software and skills	Programming skills
Pros	Super minimal, tool-agnostic, unbounded	Fast, unbounded, approachable, lo-fi interactive	Realistic enough, easily editable, mid-fi interactive	Crystal clear, familiar, exciting, hi-fi interactive	Responsive to screen size, modular, truly interactive
Cons	Super minimal, only verbal, least interactive	Non-modular, limited remote access	Easy to do poorly, can be boring or repulsive	Fairly precious, harder to maintain, distracting	Very logical, more complex, often expensive

⊢——— Good place to play ———⊣

• Weigh the benefits against the attachment level

Words are the lowest-fidelity medium, but they're extremely powerful. They help define a concept and its possibilities. We could test a statement like "XYZ Music is your obsessed friend for finding the best new music" to see if our target audience even *wants* to find new music, and what value a product that acts like a music-obsessed friend would have. Companies like Amazon are known for using a narrative document as the backbone of each project, iterating on it in each meeting. You can test an idea with an audience using a simple headline on a page. This is design, too: you're designing with words. Words are extremely easy to revise or throw away, although they can last all the way to the final interface.

Sketches help us illustrate and rapidly iterate on ideas. They can happen on paper, whiteboards, or digital equivalents. If you have trouble making sketches legible, slow down. Anyone can draw a rectangle or a smiley face; go line by line. Sketches are easy to throw away *if* you remember that you're visualizing concepts, not making art. You're putting ideas in a format where people can work with them, not crafting drawings to be judged on artistic merit.

Wireframes may range from abstract arrangements of labeled boxes to detailed outlines of user interfaces. They help you plot the content, functionality, logic, and layout for each screen. Both paper and digital versions can be interactive, but they're still simple enough that you won't feel sad throwing them away if they don't resonate. Larger projects benefit more from digital versions: symbol libraries, text editing, and copy/paste save a lot of time.

Mockups communicate a finished future interface, including many visual details that add up to some kind of feeling. For editorial or other content-heavy experiences where visual design details are the primary variables, mockups may be the best place to play. Certain stakeholders may also need a pixel-perfect mockup in order to get excited, but that's usually a sales tool and not a true prototype. Proper mockups take a chunk of time, but the bigger danger is that people (including you) see them as finished designs, not throwaway prototypes.

Code helps you see how things work (or don't work). If an idea has a large technical risk, it's wise to see if a solution is even possible. It's also the most dynamic and interactive form of prototype. Coding can be super fast if you have the skills, and the license to write trash code that's not going to production is very liberating! A danger is that stakeholders want all engineering effort to be shipped; it can be hard to convince them that an expensive engineer's work is throwaway. But newer tools make basic coding easier and easier.

- Weigh the requirements against the pros and cons

Words only require fluency in a language and diversity on a team to consider the varied connotations of specific choices. They're super minimal and tool-agnostic—you can write in pretty much every app. They're unbounded; there's no structure you have to use. This minimalism is also a con, though: visual or kinesthetic learners and creators may struggle with purely verbal thinking. And words are not interactive (unless you count click-through tests).

Sketches only require a steady hand and the courage to draw in front of coworkers. They're fast and they have no boundaries. They're charmingly unfinished and therefore approachable. And they're lo-fi interactive "devices" at a real, finger-friendly scale. The major cons are that they're non-modular (you can't copy and paste them), and remote access is limited (although there are ways of getting around that, such as taking photos and dropping them into shared folders or collaboration apps).

Wireframes require skills and some kind of layout software, though you can totally use whatever awkward presentation tool your office requires. Wires are more realistic in terms of the size and look of text and interface elements. They're easily editable, and can be made moderately interactive. But they often prompt overly logical approaches—they can make it harder to loosen up and play. And if you're just dragging gray boxes onto a screen, wireframes can be boring or hit the "uncanny valley" of design that actually repels viewers.

Mockups require special software and skills, but they're crystal clear and familiar. They're exciting and give you the pride of feeling like you really made something. They can be super interactive—the tools to make them just keep getting better. But beware! They are fairly precious, they're a pain to maintain, and they frequently distract people from focusing on larger strategic questions. Unless you're testing editorial or interface concepts where the visual presentation is the idea, take a long pause before moving to high fidelity.

Code is the final frontier. Even though technical prototypes require coding skills, they can be the most modular and flexible. They are the only forms that are truly responsive to different screen sizes, shrinking or stretching designs like a real digital product would. And they're hi-fi interactive, using the exact medium of the final product. But the cons are that they frequently trigger overly pragmatic thinking, can easily get fairly complex, and often cost a lot in terms of the time or salaries they take.

• ## Play with paper

Sketches and wireframes are great places for strategic thinkers to play. Start with a focus on ideas (sketches) and evolve into models for interactive value (wireframes). Then, if needed, build the visual, verbal, or technical skills to work in more formats.

Five fidelity levels and the questions they help answer.

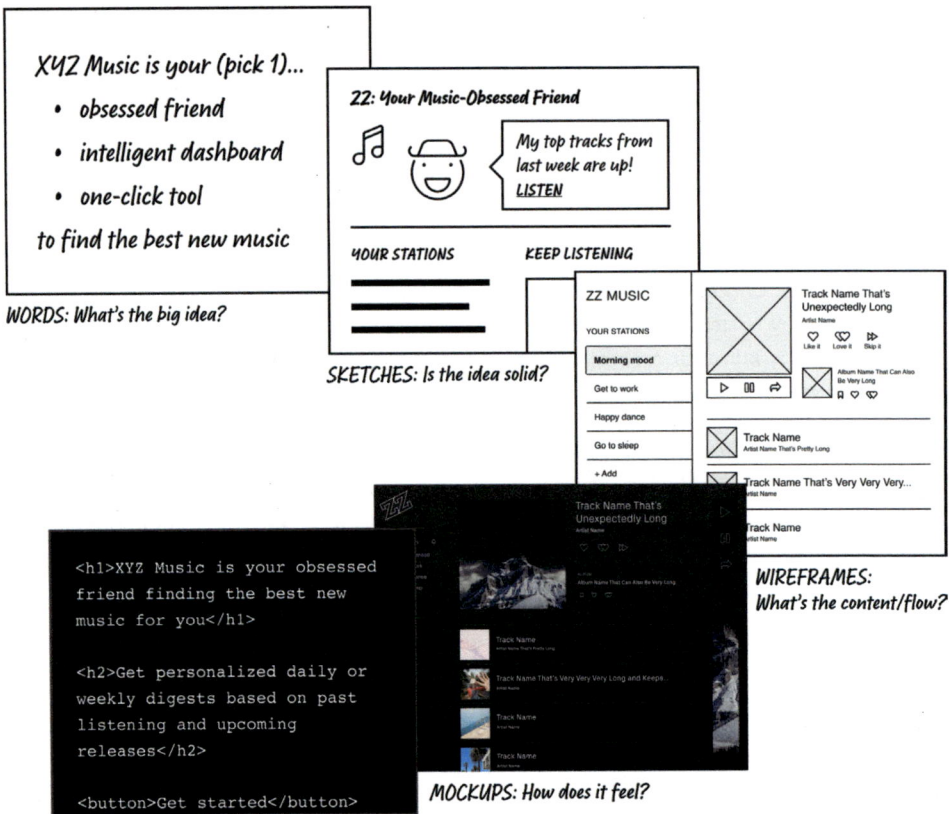

• Work backward

Visitors proceed from first step to last, but designers can start at the end. This is the principle of working backward. Large companies use it when they start a project by writing a future-state press release. Human-centered organizations use it when they focus on solutions that excite the audience, not the designers. Product teams use it when they prioritize a valuable deadline for a key question and reduce design scope or fidelity to meet it.

Working forward is a progressive exploration with infinite branches. It's a way to take things step by step and adapt as needed. Working backward boxes things in, forcing a structure and a scope. It's intensely practical, finding a backward path from the must-have to the currently-have and deprioritizing everything that prevents us from getting there.

The only definite way to end up exactly where you want is to start there.

4 ← 3 ← 2 ← 1 < DESIGNER

> "[Pragmatism] is the attitude of looking away from first things, principles, 'categories,' supposed necessities; and of looking towards last things, fruits, consequences, facts."
>
> William James, *Pragmatism*

EXERCISE: Fidelity selection

Consider the purpose for a prototype, the deadline, and the audience for it. Choose the lowest possible fidelity: whatever will force a focused discussion but still provide enough detail to produce valid decisions.

Choose a fidelity level that suits the question you need to answer.

Example Question	Timeline	Lowest Fidelity
Which of these ideas should we pursue?	Hours / Days	Sketches
What order might the steps of this flow occur in?	Hours / Days	Sketches
What states or decision points have we not considered?	Hours / Days	Sketches / Wires
What are the content and functionality requirements?	Days	Sketches / Wires
How do colors, fonts, or styling affect the experience?	Days	Mockups
How will this content reflow on different devices?	Days	Mockups / Code
How fast will this idea load?	Weeks	Code
?	?	?

• Work in circles

"It isn't 10,000 hours that creates outliers, it's 10,000 iterations."

Naval Ravikant, Twitter

Digital products are never done. Unlike printed materials, they can still be changed after going to production. They're also incredibly complex; it took me years to admit there is absolutely no way to get everything right on the first try. Working in small loops helps us learn faster and reduce wasted effort. We course-correct sooner, avoiding long journeys in the wrong direction.

Linear, "waterfall" processes may sometimes support needed deep thinking (e.g., "sprint zeros" to develop initial strategies), but as larger structures their inevitable delays cause later phases to suffer. Smaller sprints reduce risk and accelerate learning. Prioritize multiple iterations, not individual perfection.

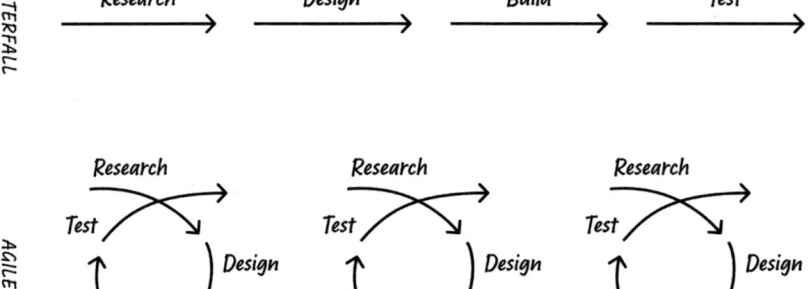

Waterfall versus agile processes.

Get used to shipping "unfinished" work. Break ideas down into smaller pieces; ask and answer a few key questions with each prototype. Expect surprises; be ready to learn and adapt. Like the Agile Manifesto, we need to place less value on codified processes and plans and more value on individual interactions, customer collaboration, working prototypes, and responding to change. Expecting and allowing many loops means we can hear and use more feedback.

Iterating may feel like working in circles, because it is.

• Use principles

All these circles of iteration create many, many decision points. To make better guesses, use principles.

Design principles are creative guidelines and executional patterns that hold true in many different contexts. They can help us generate ideas or evaluate them, providing thought-starters and options when we're stuck. They also buttress design choices in debates, giving stakeholders comfort that an approach is already validated. (You can justify a design with something other than the golden ratio!) Out of context, principles may seem abstract and hard to apply, like corny adages. But put into regular practice, they become the logic behind creativity; they're the DNA of unique and consistent brands.

Cognitive principles (or cognitive biases) are similar patterns based on psychological research. They provide reminders of and warnings about how people tend to think and act, which is often less rational than we might imagine. Effective product design requires deep insight into an audience's mindset and behavior to support or spur specific thoughts, feelings, and actions over time. Designing in a psychological arena means that we must be aware of the funny ways the mind behaves.

Each chapter in Part 2, PRACTICE, starts with three of the most relevant and impactful principles for that topic. Try using them in the exercises; as you refine your practice, you can add to those lists or develop your own cheat sheet. (There are hundreds of cognitive biases and design principles out there; if you're hungry for more, try *Universal Principles of Design* by William Lidwell, Kritina Holden, and Jill Butler; *Laws of UX* by Jon Yablonski; *Pocket Biases* by Buster Benson; or Wikipedia.)

"As to methods, there may be a million and then some, but principles are few. The man who grasps principles can successfully select his own methods. The man who tries methods, ignoring principles, is sure to have trouble."

Harrington Emerson, *The Twelve Principles of Efficiency*

Example use

Use case	Relevant Principles	Example Decision	
Where should I put this image?	Alignment, Consistency, Figure-ground relationship, Golden ratio, Hierarchy, Picture superiority effect, Progressive disclosure, Proximity, Rule of thirds, Storytelling, Symmetry	I want this image to reinforce the page's headline, so I'll use the principle of **Proximity** (things that are close together seem related) and snuggle it next to the text.	
What should happen if this form has an error?	Confirmation, Consistency, Forgiveness, Framing, Garbage in, garbage out, Iconic representation, Mental model, Operant conditioning, Progressive disclosure, Redundancy, Visibility	I think this error could be avoided altogether, so I'll use the principle of **Garbage in, garbage out** (input quality determines output quality) and add hint text on the field to help people enter good information.	

COMPARE
Putting principles into practice

• Use metrics

"Generating numbers is easy; generating numbers you should trust is hard!"

Ron Kohavi, Diane Tang, and Ya Xu, "Trustworthy Online Controlled Experiments"

Another way to make decisions is with metrics. As with principles, they can help us generate or evaluate ideas.

At data-rich companies, product designs will be responsible for pushing very specific numbers, and so every initiative may start and end with success metrics. But even teams or projects with no data can use data-driven strategies to prompt creative or critical thinking about audience behavior and business sustainability. The key is choosing the right focus.

• Consider growth and satisfaction measures

What metrics are most important to improve at this moment in time?

Growth is a foundational goal for new ideas; it doesn't matter how brilliant an idea is if no one ever encounters it.

Entrepreneur/investor Dave McClure created a great shortlist of growth metrics for startups, hilariously called Pirate Metrics because the acronym spells out "AARRR!!!" I use them all the time for idea generation; you'll see them referenced in many places throughout this book.

COMPARE
Pirate metrics

Acquisition	Activation	Retention	Revenue	Referral
New visits (from organic or paid channels)	Acting, not bouncing (clicking or viewing more)	Repeat visits (ideally quickly and frequently)	Contributing money, content, emails, or other sustaining input	Telling others (with or without incentives)

User satisfaction is another obvious goal, but measuring it may seem more fuzzy.

Google's HEART metrics offer a scalable method: "a framework and process for defining large-scale user-centered metrics, both attitudinal and behavioral." The framework has five high-level categories, each with useful submetrics.

COMPARE
HEART metrics

Happiness	Engagement	Adoption	Retention	Task Success
Subjective satisfaction with visual appeal and ease of use	Interaction depth, frequency, or intensity during a time period	New users during some specific time period	Users from a time period who are still present later	Usability ratings for efficiency, completion, or lack of errors

To use either of these frameworks with actual data, break them down: define the categorical goals of the product or feature, develop specific metrics to track, and identify signals of success. For example, the "Activation" category may include a "Happy First Visit" metric, defined as visiting x pages, staying y seconds, and clicking z times.

We can also use metrics as inspiration by flipping them into framing questions: How might we increase activation, happy first visits, or pages visited?

• Find industry-specific signals

Growth and satisfaction metrics are useful for just about any company, but industry-specific metrics can refine your understanding of a product's value to users. Tech writer Lenny Rachitsky asked his Twitter followers who work on consumer subscription products about the key performance indicators they watch. The answers varied depending on the business.

Which metrics give the best signals for our particular service?

- *Jonathan Korn:* "We're Aaptiv + Headpace. We measure 'WorkoutFinished' (a metric that shows the user is extracting value from the app) and then slice it accordingly. WorkoutFinished retention, time to WorkoutFinished, WorkoutFinished conversion…"
- *Mat Yurow:* "[At TripAdvisor it was] active days/month. Habit formation is key to most subscription businesses. Frequency is a better indicator of habit than other metrics like time spent."
- *Victoria Young Idol:* "Whichever metric was the strongest indication of product / market fit and engagement. For uberPOOL it was request rate and match rate, at Facebook video it was watch time and watchers, at Netflix it was 30 day watchers for success of a show."

Notice the specific design questions that specific metrics inspire: How might we help people finish more workouts? How might we increase the frequency of visits? How might we increase user requests or matches? How might we increase watch time or watchers? Find metrics that highlight troubling trends (like incomplete sessions in a therapy app) or win-win behaviors (like regularity of savings in a banking app).

• Gather and interpret data carefully

Good metrics inspire good designs, communicate user activity, and provide clear signals of progress or danger. But there are many ways to use data poorly. Beware of "vanity" metrics that go steadily up but have unclear sources; pull apart correlation and causation. Watch out for the downstream effects of setting metrics; don't accidentally incentivize unethical user or business behavior.

"It is clear that metrics should not stand alone. They should be triangulated with findings from other sources, such as usability studies and field studies [...] and are not a substitute for early or formative user research."

Kerry Rodden, Hilary Hutchinson, and Xin Fu, "Measuring the User Experience on a Large Scale"

Take metrics as inspiration, not gospel; data can easily be mishandled through naivete, bias, or happenstance. I've heard of large companies that ran the same design on both sides of an A/B test and got significantly different results. "Data-driven" is kind of a misnomer: all data comes from some human drive to collect it; there's not some wellspring sorting itself into spreadsheets. Include qualified data analysts throughout the process, and follow up with user interviews. Remember that quantitative data can tell you the *what,* but qualitative data tells you the *why.*

Overreliance on metrics can also create a reactive culture, where nothing is done until the data exists. Airbnb CEO Brian Chesky has spoken about the need to worry about things proactively, before they become larger problems; and about the need to craft digital worlds using thinking from the humanities, not just the sciences. Use data well, but use other information too.

• Co-create

> "We should embrace the subjective nature of what we do and allow for the multiplicity of responses to thrive, because the mixed pool represents the diversity of human perspective. That diversity fortifies us, makes us strong."
>
> Frank Chimero,
> *The Shape of Design*

The final essential piece of a 4D Thinking method for product design is co-creation.

Design programs often sit within art schools, so it's easy to confuse design with art. Design has elements of self-expression, but it is a service industry. The target audience is *not you*. We serve people with very different goals and preferences. And the best way to design for them is to design *with* them.

Human-centered design, popularized by IDEO, deeply involves other people at every step: internal stakeholders, external audiences, and niche experts. As I will continue to repeat, digital design is so complex that it's just not possible to think of every issue and answer yourself. Target audiences understand details and scenarios it would take designers hundreds of iterations to guess. Subject matter experts know about issues or solutions you've never seen. Business stakeholders have insights and connections that help make a project sustainable.

I was resistant to extra voices on a project until I heard them. While designing the Sahana Foundation's Community Resilience Mapping Tool, which helped people in Los Angeles prepare for an earthquake by mapping resources and logging inventory, the board asked me to interview target users across LA county (which ranges from Venice Beach to rural canyons). I had imagined that people would map places that would be most essential after an earthquake, like grocery stores and gas stations. Farmers had a different priority: mapping all the cow paths, so they had routes to get their livestock out. I never, ever would have come up with this use case myself.

Inviting non-designers to participate throughout a creative process can add some confusion or stress. Are we giving ourselves additional bosses? What do they know about design? A key mindset is to see the input as insider information or special access. Human-centered design is *not* other people telling you what to do. They're telling you what they need; you can imagine different ways to do it. Appropriate craftspeople are still responsible for the execution. As my brilliant friend Jodi Leo says, you still hold the marker.

Respectful labels will improve the collaborative spirit. Consider the connotations of "human" or "person" versus "user" or "consumer" or "target." The field may be "user experience," but I tend to refer to users as *visitors* to emphasize the responsibilities of a good host; or *audience* to emphasize the expectations for a great entertainer; or *customers* to remind myself of their personal investments; or just *people* to reiterate our commonality. When I'm working with clients or stakeholders, I tend to say *partner* or *subject matter expert* to give respectful weight to their perspective. I've also avoided saying "your designs" or "your project" throughout the book to minimize ideas of personal authorship and ownership.

Throughout this book, I've tagged each exercise with some suggested collaborators. These extra voices will expand the depth and breadth of insights shaping the designs, and will save rounds of revisions down the road. Other people can identify obstacles and opportunities we simply can't see on our own.

UXer · Strategist · Researcher · Subject expert · Writer · Visual designer · Engineer · Generalist

Typical product design collaborators.

Great collaboration also requires thoughtful timing. Bring people in early enough that their feedback can be heard without resistance, and often enough that opinions evolve in parallel. Early access and input help teammates feel more invested in the success of a project. You're building a bigger support network for the initiative right from the start.

Co-creation is a secret weapon for design. Accelerate your design process, avoid entire rounds of revisions, and achieve success in the market by including the right people at the right time.

REMEMBER:

The 4D Thinking Framework

Product experience is the threads, impressions, interactions, and memories that a product provides in two, three, and four dimensions. This holistic view requires a collaborative, adaptable, goal-oriented method for product design.

• The model

Choose a phase, dimension, or area with the biggest potential for impact.

	Threads	**Impressions**	**Interactions**	**Memories**
2D	Words	Layouts	Symbols	Images
3D	Inclusivity	Flexibility	Usability	Personalization
4D	Relationships	Patterns	Paths	Moments

• The method

Use a focused, strategic approach that answers the key questions at hand.

| Prototype | Lower the fidelity | Work backward | Work in circles | Use principles | Use metrics | Co-create |

Now that we have a solid conceptual model and strategic working method for product experience design, it's time to put it into practice.

PRACTICE · PRACTICE · PRACTICE · PRACTICE · PRACTICE · PRACTICE

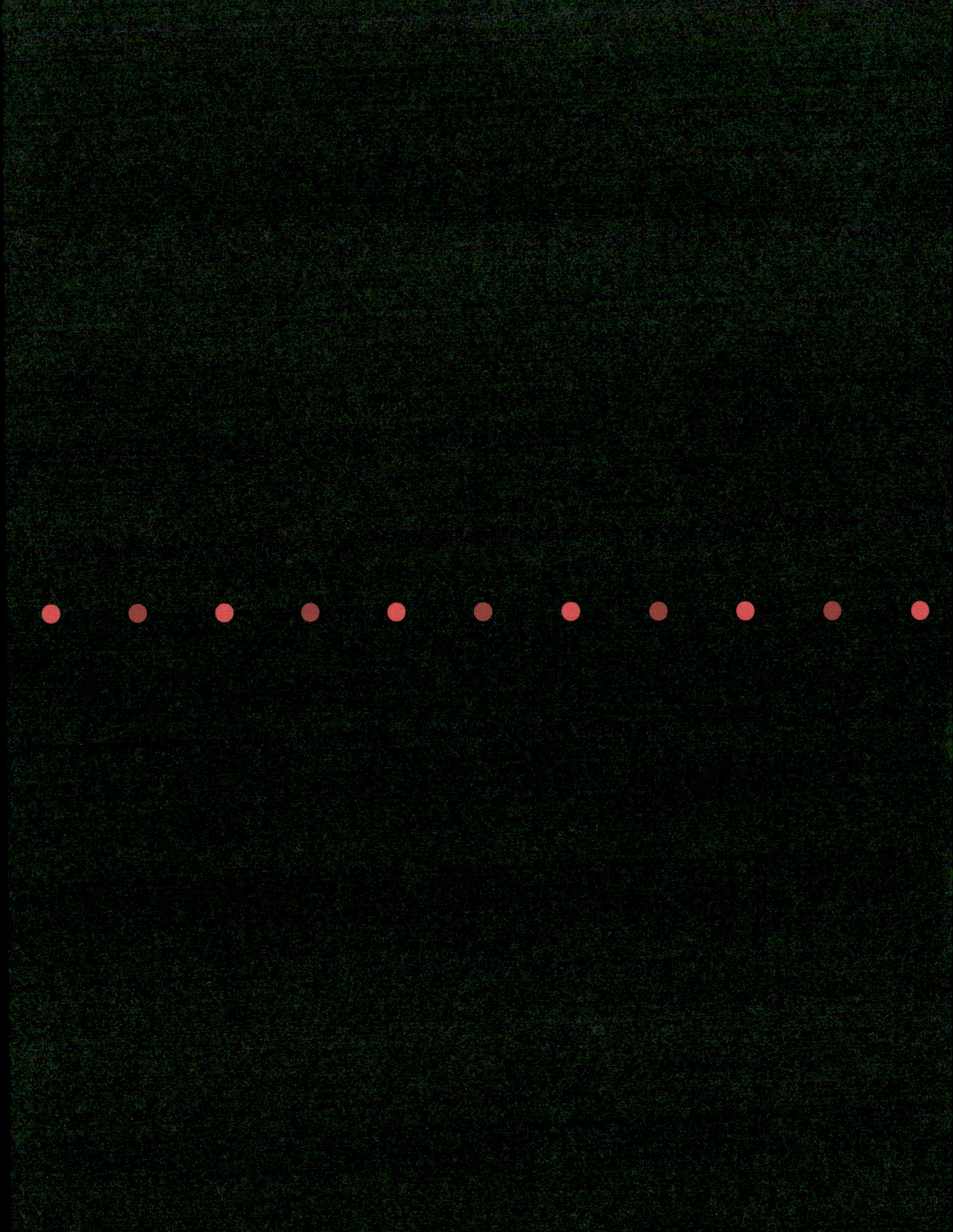

Words
2D THREADS

Words are the most fundamental layer of communication design, from practical labels and links to evocative metaphors and stories. This book is made mostly of words, and those little squiggles making up the words somehow create thoughts, feelings, and images in other people's minds. The possibilities of language are powerful, but the connotations are very individual; make sure that interface writing speaks to audiences appropriately, conveys clear mental models, and helps them navigate their own path. Successful product design has words that work well at the micro and macro levels.

KEY QUESTIONS	EXERCISES
Story: What is the most compelling expression of the big idea?	Press release
Labeling: How do people get oriented and find their destination?	Card sort
Voice: Which words inspire understanding and action?	Click-through test

COGNITIVE PRINCIPLES

- **Five hat racks**
  There are five major ways to organize information: alphabetically, categorically, chronologically, comparatively, or spatially (hat tip to Richard Saul Wurman).

- **Framing**
  The way information is worded, and whether it has positive or negative associations, has a dramatic impact on people's decisions.

- **Wayfinding**
  All navigation processes have four stages: orientation, route selection, route monitoring, and destination recognition.

• Create content strategically

We can design an entire product just with words; they're the simplest and fastest technology around.

Designing *well* with words requires strategy. Content strategy can be an entire role or department, but it's also a key skill for product designers to practice. Story, format, and SEO are all part of the puzzle.

> "It's a complicated and noisy world, and we're not going to get a chance to get people to remember much about us. [...] So we have to be really clear about what we want them to know about us."
> Steve Jobs

• Have a clear story

Why do people need this product?

> "We are the storytelling animal."
> Salman Rushdie

Storytelling is a helpful exercise at either end of a design process. Starting a design project by writing a future press release tests the value of the idea to the audience and helps build internal buy-in (Amazon is especially known for popularizing this strategy). Ending a design cycle by writing a celebratory announcement socializes and evangelizes the new idea, adding more momentum to its success.

Stories help us clarify and remember why the product needs to exist. Good stories help us validate good products; if we can't talk about the idea without the audience's eyes glazing over, it may not need to exist.

Compelling stories are user-centered. It's easy to write about our team's technical or creative accomplishments, but most people don't care how the sausage got made. Focus on the problem a product solves for a person, and how it improves their lives.

Compelling stories are also sticky. We live in a crowded world; even great ideas are easily forgotten. In *Made to Stick: Why Some Ideas Survive and Others Die,* researchers Chip and Dan Heath note that people remember simple, concrete, credible, unexpected, and emotional stories. Include clear or surprising details and human touches.

Think about the three elements of typical narratives: the characters, the conflict, and the resolution. Think about the inverted-pyramid approach in journalism, which presents the most newsworthy information (like a hook or an anecdotal lead) first, then the supporting details, and finally the supplementary information. Try the exercise at the end of this section to practice your storytelling skills.

What's a simple, exciting story that communicates real value for an audience?

• Choose supportive formats

How should the story come to life?

Once we have a compelling story about why the experience exists, we can think about other content that would demonstrate or support the story.

Smart content strategy chooses forms that match the idea's function: Is the product intended to inspire, persuade, entertain, or educate?

Experiences can be 100 percent words, or 0 percent. Those words can be mostly static (like company bios) or highly interactive (like wikis). Lists and paragraphs can be left as is for audiences who love to read, or converted to other forms for audiences who prefer to look or listen. Imagine information as an article, video, photo, cartoon, diagram, chart, email, e-book, podcast, discussion, or something else entirely.

It's important to pause and make sure we're not defaulting to our own preferences. For example, I hate the time it takes to watch long videos—I'd much rather go at my own pace through an article. So, I have to constantly prompt myself to reconsider long-form text (no matter how beautifully designed) and ask whether the audience would rather lean back and watch a video instead.

What forms of content make the story most absorbable and believable?

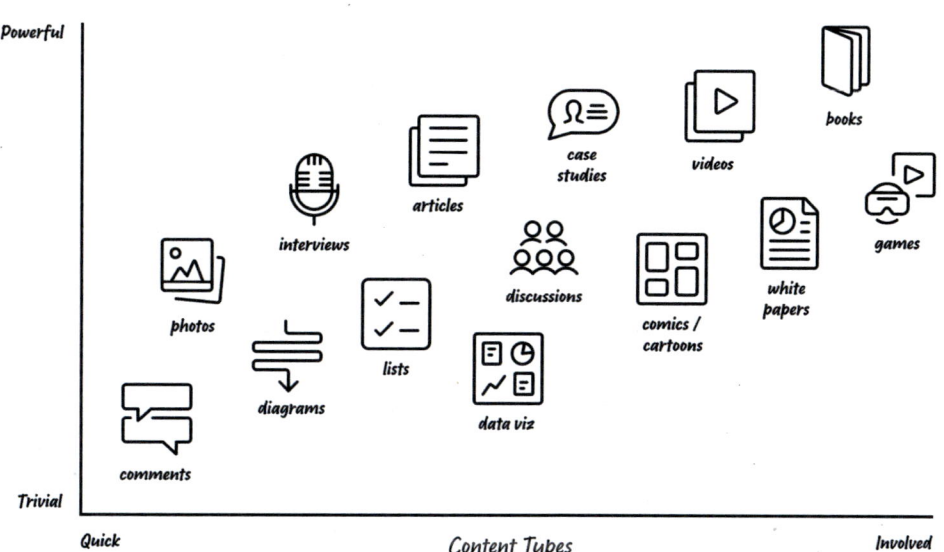

Find content types that are both valuable for the audience and feasible for the business.

- ### Know your keywords

As we get deeper into the details of the content, we might shape and sharpen the words even further.

What are people searching for?

Search engine optimization is a behind-the-scenes skill that can inform each phase of design and improve the eventual success of the product; designs are useless if no one finds them. SEO is another massive field of expertise that exceeds the scope of this book, but even a small bit of applied knowledge can help boost a site's visibility.

Guidelines constantly change to keep up with the algorithms, but some SEO methods have stood the test of time, and overlap with accessibility and usability principles too.

Here are three core SEO strategies to elevate the eventual visibility and sustainability of a product.

Know what the audience is searching for.
Take each of your target use cases and imagine (or research) people's pre-site activities as they pursue a particular goal. What phrases would they type into a search engine? (Be exhaustive in your research and imagination; people type all sorts of funny things into search fields.) If you already have a site, how well is it currently ranking for those search terms?

Fill headlines and links with keywords.
Search engines rank each page based partially on the number of links to that page and the text for those links. "Click here" gives bots no information about why a page was linked. "See the best cameras for travel" gives spiders specific verbs, adjectives, and nouns to match. Page titles need to look compelling in page designs, but also in search results next to competitors' links. Visualize those search results, and see which one the audience would click on.

Create focused, user-friendly screens.
Luckily, great experience design often yields great SEO. Content and navigation that are easy for people to use will also be easy for spiders to crawl. Consider splitting multitopic pages into separate ones; if a page is too complex, search engines won't know how to categorize it, so it may not rank as highly in results. Don't try to game the system; search engines long ago started penalizing tactics like keyword stuffing.

What are the natural words and targets of the people you're serving?

EXERCISE: Press release

Explain the value of the experience in one page, paragraph, or sentence.

Writer
Strategist

Writing a press release helps us work backward from the future experience and make sure the product being created will be exciting and valuable. Writer and content strategist Nicole Fenton's Tiny Content Framework shares a helpful checklist for product marketing pages that's a great start.

1. **Gather facts:** Name, purpose, features, use cases, ingredients, pricing, specs, availability
2. **Tell your story:** Purpose, history, process, differentiation, reputation, use cases
3. **Arrange and revise:** Most important things first, concrete benefits throughout
4. **Read it out loud:** Remove awkwardness, improve the rhythm

Make a navigable place

Once we have a story or experience, people have to get through it. A complement to storytelling is *placemaking*. And one form of this is *information architecture* (IA).

IA is the process of organizing all possible flows and content into a navigable system. One of the hardest aspects of experience design is that people have minds of their own. You may craft and gently push an optimal path through an experience, but visitors will constantly surprise you with their own adventures into the bushes. Good IA creates many paths to a goal, giving visitors more agency. This is one of usability expert Jakob Nielsen's classic usability heuristics: "user control and freedom." Game designer Hannes Seiford has called this "'Swiss cheese' design": players have multiple ways to go through each mission, with no dead ends.

IA involves both invisible structures and visible signposts: it defines the buckets that information sits in and provides the labels people use to get oriented and explore.

Consider Wikipedia: it has millions of pages of content and billions of possible paths, but it's easily navigated.

"The objectivist criteria for being in the same category is having common properties. But there is no objectivist criterion for *which properties* are to count."

George Lakoff, *Women, Fire, and Dangerous Things: What Categories Reveal about the Mind*

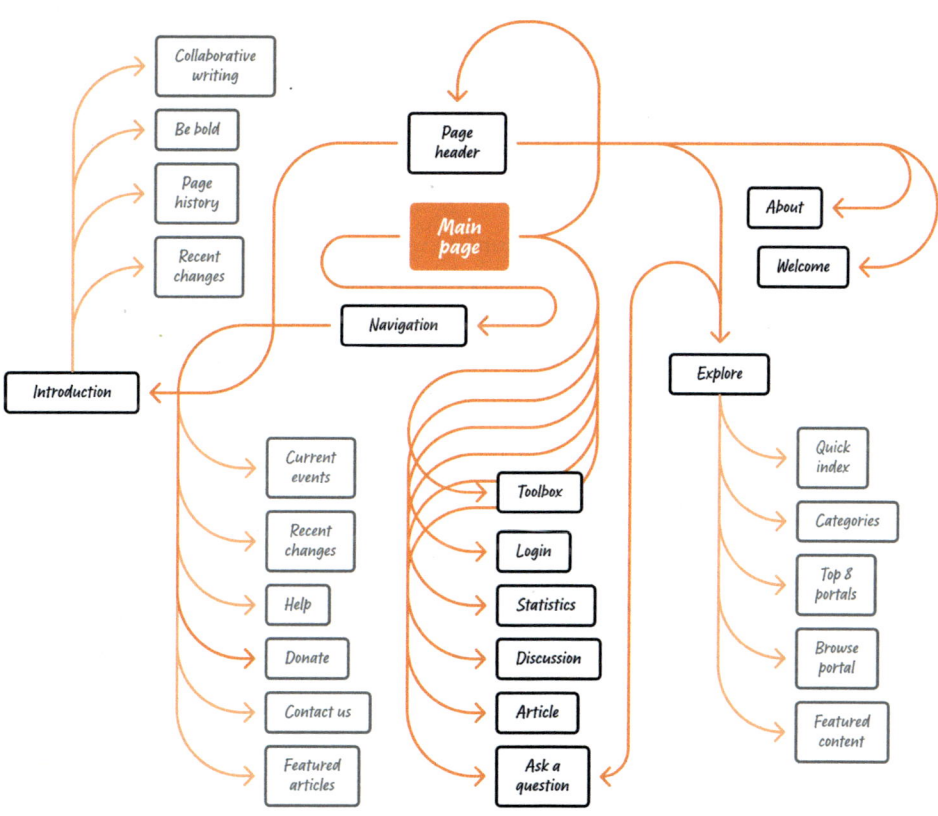

Wikipedia uses category links, inline links, featured (or random) content, and search to increase discoverability.

Consider IKEA: it has one long and comprehensive path to browse each giant store, but also has time-saving shortcuts for people on more specific missions.

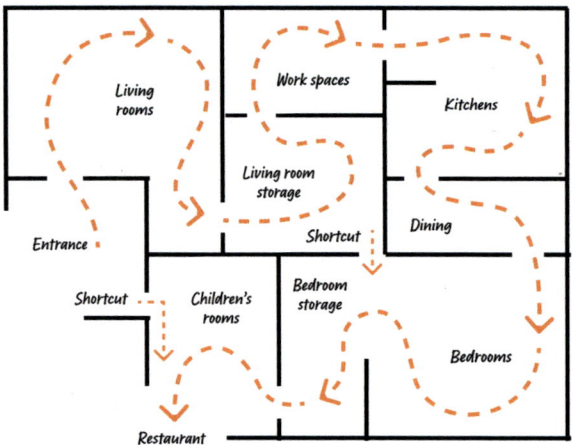

IKEA has one all-purpose flow, but also special shortcuts with clear signage.

"At one end of the spectrum, the little information architect may focus solely on bottom-up tasks such as the definition of metadata fields and controlled vocabularies. At the other end, the Big Information Architect may play the role of 'an orchestra conductor or film director, conceiving a vision and moving the team forward,' as described by Gayle Curtis."

Peter Morville, "Big Architect, Little Architect"

I see IA as a subset of product experience (and the ancestor of UX, though some people see IA and UX as the same thing). Title-wise, people who call themselves IAs often focus on logical, systemic thinking with artifacts like maps, taxonomies, and usability analyses; UXers often extend into emotional or psychological considerations and provide detailed holistic recommendations like annotated flows; product designers usually add on aesthetic and brand strategy considerations and deliver pixel-perfect high-fidelity designs. But the scope of a project greatly shapes each role. It's always a good idea to clarify the assumed responsibilities.

Experience design processes may begin or end with IA. Revision or expansion projects often need to start by auditing and organizing existing information; zero-to-one projects might end with navigation systems once the content and product strategy are done. When you have a huge pile of content, a confusing sea of links, or an inconsistent scramble of flows, it's time to zoom out and build some architecture.

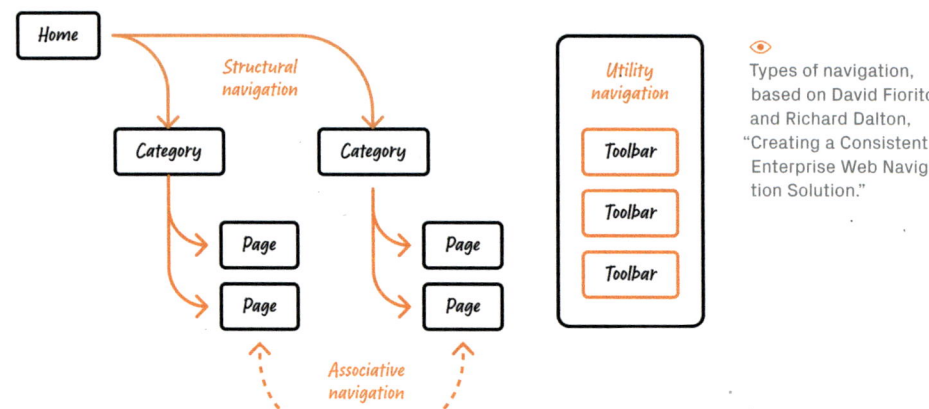

Types of navigation, based on David Fiorito and Richard Dalton, "Creating a Consistent Enterprise Web Navigation Solution."

IA is a huge subject. This section focuses on navigation design because it's the most visible, usable experience. We combine semantics, utility, frequency, and space to create primary routes, supplemental shortcuts, or directive guides. Navigation implementations will vary depending on the scope and content of the site, and how much space is available (see the Patterns chapter for more ideas). Here's a good list of navigational improvements to consider.

• Improve one-way roads

A simple starting point for IA improvements is within user flows. They usually focus on moving people forward, but easy enhancements are links in the opposite direction, and smaller or larger increments. Consider stepped navigation refinements.

Can the route go the way I want?

Pagination / progress indicators
Simple "Next" and "Back" actions are table stakes, but full control might let people skip to the end, jump to a certain step, or start over.

Media controllers
Video and audio content has other standards, including defaults like fast-forward and rewind, but also nice custom elements like "10 seconds back" or "bookmark this spot."

Wizards / guides
Many visitors don't fully read instructions or explore apps on their own, so wizard patterns highlight sections of a screen step by step to guide users through each thing in a caring way (often increasing initial activation metrics and future engagement).

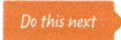

• Build hierarchical paths

A next level of architecture creates parent/child relationships, providing links up or down a hierarchy. Unless the flow is an isolated tunnel, it usually belongs to a larger category of screens. Consider multidirectional navigation.

Can I widen my lens just a little?

Breadcrumbs
Companies tend to obsess over the homepage, but visitors often land on an article or product page and go sideways or up. Breadcrumbs instantly tell users how deep they are in a site and give one-click ways to go up levels and expand the lens of focus.

Home → Adopt → Dogs

Local navigation
Sibling screens or flows are often useful links for visitors. Local navigation components index each section to aid speed and comprehension. Elsewhere, these links are less relevant, and can usually hide in secondary menus.

• Build shortcuts

Can you take me straight to what I want, or what I might want?

Structures and hierarchies often take a lot of time to understand and use. Google's simple-seeming search engine blew past Yahoo's careful categorical architecture for the web, and our mental models haven't been the same since. Consider direct paths.

Search

Search is the most user-centered form of navigation: tell me what you want in your own words. Adding a search icon is simple; designing the full experience is not. Ideal inputs may be text or multimedia; patterns like autocomplete and recent searches may be required to speed the input experience; results screens may be overwhelming without sorting, filtering, or faceted search.

Inline links / associative navigation

Return policy

Associative navigation creates paths to related content in more distant branches. (For example, if someone's shopping for clothes, they often want to know the store's return policy and might also like to know about a clothing recycling program.) It can take the form of inline text links, "see also" menus, or special callouts.

Indexes

1. Our story
2. Our products
3. Our oatmeal cookie recipe

An index is a linked list of every single important page. It can be helpful for users who prefer to skim or use a browser's "find" command, and also very valuable for search engine crawler bots. More visible indexes might be sorted by category, time, location, alphabet, or magnitude. A mini version is often helpful in the footer of screens.

• Build special places

Can you provide useful arrangements for me?

Like anyone else in a creative field, product designers can make stuff up. Navigation systems often benefit from collections of ideas that match the audience's particular routines or mental models. Which items might make a nice home together?

Work triangles

☆ *Dashboard*

A "kitchen work triangle" is an architectural idea that increases ease and comfort by arranging a kitchen's three main tools (sink, stove, and fridge) to create an efficient triangle. This is a made-up idea of place, defined only by patterns of action. Digital architects should look for similar constructs of action or information, whether that's "My Dashboard," a "Settings Panel," or something custom.

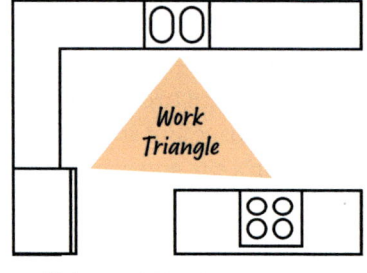

👁 Kitchen work triangles are constructs for efficiency.

Metadata

♪♪ *Slow jams*
♪♪ *Marathon pace*

Invisible statistics can also be made visible or usable. For example, songs could be sorted by beats per minute (BPM) and divided into tempo groups like "Slow Jams" or "Marathon Pace." Recipes could have an "Is it worth the dishes?" rating, with links to "Easy Cleanup" or "Great but Complicated." Mine or create valuable metadata.

- ## Build steady landmarks

    The thorniest type of navigation is structural. Fully representing a site's information architecture takes a lot of space; accurately matching it to the audience's mental model takes a lot of time. Structurally sorted navigation is also really boring; story-telling approaches can be much more interesting. Find and highlight site landmarks that give the clearest sense of the place.

    What are the must-see features?

    ### Global navigation
    Some designers say that global navigation is a last resort for users—inline links should provide all the navigation needed in each experience—but content-heavy sites may beg to disagree. Top-down categorical links provide practical access to most key sections, as well as a skimmable overview of a product.

    ### Utility navigation / toolbars
    One-tap access to the most valuable or frequently used resources saves users time and confusion. Common utilities include font-styling palettes, chat buttons, legal pages, or "buy now" links. Toolbars can be fixed or movable, static or customizable, ever-present or toggleable.

- ## Build worlds

    Design has patterns and standards, and also freedom. Think about what kind of world you're trying to build and then dream up some matching navigation.

    > "Taxonomies, controlled vocabularies, those are just tools. Metadata is just a material. Information Architecture is about making meaning out of piles of facts. Who cares how you do it, or in what medium?"
    > Christina Wodtke, "Towards a New Information Architecture"

EXERCISE: Card sort

Create an index card or digital equivalent for each screen, section, or topic in the experience. Consider nouns, verbs, or even phrases. Have blank cards ready for new screens, and different-color cards ready for labels.

Find content groupings and navigation labels that make sense to the target audience.

✘ Writer
🐶 Researcher

1. Decide whether the card sort will be open or closed (to develop IA, or to test it).
    - *Open:* Let participants group cards freely and label each group at the end.
    - *Closed (a.k.a. a tree test):* Have participants group cards under preexisting labels.
2. Ask the participant to arrange the cards into groups that make sense to them and their workflows or habits. They can do subgroups if needed.
3. To get extra hints for navigation design, have participants sort the groups by importance or frequency of use.

• Refine language contextually

> "Grammar is a piano I play by ear."
> Joan Didion, "Why I Write"

Even the most strategic, visionary stories and places still need some adaptations for various digital contexts. 2D spaces, 3D environments, and 4D scenarios should all inform the chosen voice, grammar, style, tone, timing, and length of words.

• Have a voice

What product voice serves both brand and interaction strategies?

Voice is the way a product expresses itself verbally. Undefined product voices lead to muddy brands or outdated brand identities that feel out of place on the web.

Voice choices should build on brand principles, but may require some back-and-forth between brand strategists, writers, and interface designers to reach a style that works strategically (for the audience and against the competition) and functionally (for the specific interface metaphor and element size). Consider the experiential effects of each stylistic choice, from reading level to sense of humor. All the bits of language affect visitors' expectations, comprehension, efficiency, and retention.

Reading level

- Access prospectus
- Get the PDF

Accessibility guidelines recommend writing at a lower secondary-education level (grades 6–9) and providing supplementary explanations for anything above that. Technical topics and audiences may require more academic language.

Energy level

- totally unemotional
- extremely excited

Values and energy come through in word choice, so a brand may want to be quieter and more factual, or livelier and more expressive.

Punctuation

- Traditionalist.
- teenager!!!!!!

The use of punctuation varies greatly by age and personality. For heavy texters, exclamation points indicate friendliness more than excitement. Periods can come off as unnecessarily serious for sentences that already end in a chat bubble.

Contractions

- do not use them
- can't <3 'em enuf

Formal or professional brands may spell out all words; fun or friendly brands may prefer brevity and more casual forms of speech.

Slang

- off-limits
- omfg yesssss

Language constantly changes, and more fashion-forward sites may want to reflect their audience's words (and emoji). But corporations using slang often sound awkward or tone-deaf; make sure it's appropriate, not appropriated.

Sense of humor

- I'm serious
- I'm actually a dog

"Surprise and delight" is such a common design goal that it has become cliché, but few companies are actually bold enough to make jokes on a business website. If your audience is fun-loving, unexpected humor can add a boost of energy to an experience.

Use consistent grammar and typography

The structure, syntax, and styling of text in an interface affects its interpretation. Design guidelines should codify the particular words and styles that reinforce desired mental models and feelings.

Dialect
Clear wayfinding systems use the natural language of the visitors; you may call it a "boat," but the audience may be looking for the "ferry." Do user interviews to find the right words, and card sorts to find the right groupings. Familiar language will be more usable and feel more personal.

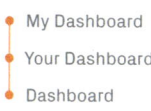

Point of view
First-person voice often matches the way users refer to experiences ("my page"), but it's frequently inconsistent with marketing or support materials that write in an explanatory tone. Second-person voice creates a consistent conversational style in which the site always speaks *to* the visitor, not *as* the visitor. Third-person voice communicates structures most minimally—but also most impersonally.

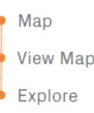

Part of speech
Interactive text might use nouns or verbs, single words or phrases. Establish a default and a rationale for any diversions. Nouns present tangible things to use; verbs reinforce action; phrases mirror natural conversation patterns. Specific noun/verb/phrase choices may also be worth testing for their effect on metrics: "Next" or "Go" or "Get Started" or "Register" could have very different impacts on whether people click that button.

Capitalization
Text transformations change the perception of words. Designers and writers should agree on standards that express the right personality visually and grammatically. Consistency is key.

ALL-CAPS CREATES A MINIMALIST STRIPE. IT MAY ALSO SEEM LIKE SHOUTING.

lowercase letters have a bumpy silhouette, so they're more legible (squint at this). all lowercase seems super casual and quick like you didn't have time to press shift.

Title Case Is a Classic Emphasis Style but I Can Never Remember What to Capitalize

Sentence case looks like a thoughtfully edited conversation, sir.

Implications
Consider the downstream effects of language; even verb choices can snowball. Facebook started with "like" as the main action, and it became a feed of people sharing their most likable moments. Cowbird (a social network by artist Jonathan Harris) let you "sprout" or "dedicate" stories, and it became a collection of people sharing their most vulnerable moments. Think through the systemic impacts of labels.

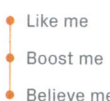

- **Allow the tone to adapt to the moment**

Voice and copywriting guidelines exist to serve real people having real problems. Messages aren't standalone artifacts; they exist within a certain context. 2D layouts need to remember the 4D flows in which they sit. Where did the visitor come from, and what are they trying to accomplish? What are they feeling right now?

How is the visitor feeling right now?

Consider the emotional impact of each word. The energy of messages can range from celebratory excitement to reassuring professionalism.

Successful?

Be excited by success
Confirmation pages and success messages are great places for humor and fun; it's a mutual celebration. Extra emphasis and energy can make a positive experience more memorable and shareable.

Productive?

Be useful for usability
Interactive elements need to help visitors realize they can do something with the text, and then do it. Labels and other explanatory text need enough familiarity and detail to be clear; accessible inputs require constraints, responses, and corrections that are readable, predictable, and helpful.

Uncertain?

Be motivating as needed
Energy levels tend to come up a notch on marketing pages that have to convince busy visitors to take a chance on yet another service, or product pages that have to give a waffling shopper confidence to pull the trigger. Statistics and stories may need to get a bit more impressive and inspiring. *Calls to action* (CTAs) often benefit from more active or assertive tones.

Unsucessful?

Be gentle with corrections
Error messages and warnings are micro-stressors. People react disproportionately strongly to negative feedback, so corrective messages must be extra empathetic. Unknown jargon can be especially frustrating, so explain it. Humor can seem out of place or confusing, so avoid it in this context. Try not to blame the user: errors may always be a system issue.

Upset?

Be reassuring during issues
Frustrating problems like spotty internet, annoying moments like customer service queues, and serious issues like account fraud create times when reassurance is appreciated and humor is tone-deaf. People want to know that their situations are being handled with gravity and urgency. A calm tone shows empathy, not apathy.

Interaction design is half user action and half system response. As with in-person conversations, thoughtful reactions will keep the relationship going.

Tone adaptations for language, based on Tangity's tone spectrum.

• Be sophisticated with timing

The feeling of a message is also affected by its visibility and timing. Imagine a 4D storyboard for each little piece of text, and how it might be animated or responsive. Prototype and refine the exact lengths of time that a brand takes to speak its messages.

When will words be noticed and welcomed?

Static
Text that's always visible feels stable and secure, but may be overlooked by skimmers.

Dynamic
Text that fades or slides in feels alive (just make sure it's not delaying action or reducing readability).

Immediate
Visible options and instant feedback can increase understanding and efficiency. For example, hint text that updates based on each keystroke in a form field (getting more positive for great input or more directive for less-than-great input) improves data quality.

Delayed
Hiding some text until it's needed can reduce visual clutter and make interfaces feel simpler. Small delays can increase drama or attention and feel more conversational (e.g., the small pause and animated ellipses in chat windows create a feeling that someone is thinking).

• Get to the point

> "Get rid of half the words on each page, then get rid of half of what's left."
>
> Steve Krug,
> *Don't Make Me Think*

The final context is the digital world altogether. Product experiences are active; product design is more like environmental design than print design. People aren't slowly paging forward through every word of a good book, they're swiping and scrolling and zooming and tapping a virtual space or tool, looking for action. Web text generally needs to be much shorter than printed text, allowing easy skimming.

Interface elements also require brevity because of space constraints. Expressive desktop layouts often have to take it down a notch on mobile screens; conversational buttons or menus might look messy or stop working if the text wraps.

If there's an unavoidable pile of information to communicate, try a one-two punch. Stakeholders or casual browsers often just want the gist of an idea, but technical or invested audiences often want and need all the details. Consider a clear headline or visual that everyone will grasp, then additional info for the detail-oriented people who keep scrolling or digging.

The shorter the sentences, the lighter the layout. Be brief.

EXERCISE: Click-through test

Make sure text and functionality are readable, predictable, and assistive.

 Writer
 Researcher

1. *Quant option:* Use an A/B testing tool or a search engine ads platform to set up a test with two different headlines. Filter the recipients to match your target audience. See which message triggers more action (and if it's statistically significant).

2. *Qual option:* Recruit 6–10 members of your target audience. Show them a few headlines, and ask them which message (or part of the message) they prefer, and *why*. Also ask them what they'd expect to see if they clicked on it in search results, so you learn if the headline accurately conveys your idea.

REMEMBER: WORDS

Create content strategically

 Press release

 Five hat racks

Make a navigable place

 Card sort

 Framing

Refine language contextually

 Click-through test

 Wayfinding

Inclusivity
3D THREADS

Digital designs serve a wide range of perspectives, environments, cultures, and capabilities. Empathetic and inclusive design practices take the time to co-create with varied voices and build more resilient systems. We're all distracted, dysfunctional, or disabled sometimes; inclusive designs increase access and ease of use for everyone. Start with simple, low-tech connections and add refinements, settings, or modes for additional contexts; redundancy increases reliability. Successful product design includes and accommodates diverse audiences.

KEY QUESTIONS	EXERCISES
• **Biases:** What personal preferences must be acknowledged?	Empathy map
• **Context:** What are the environmental constraints?	Alternate modes
• **Access:** Are all people receiving equivalent experiences?	Operability check

COGNITIVE PRINCIPLES

- **Empathy**
The deliberate and active effort to see the world as other people do, understand their feelings, reflect those feelings, and remain free of judgement.

- **Progressive enhancement**
Delivering content and functionality using the most basic technology possible and then layering on additional improvements as a device or internet connection allows.

- **Redundancy**
The duplication of critical components or functions of a system in order to increase its reliability.

• Include diverse perspectives

> "Software, like all technologies, is inherently political. [...] Code inevitably reflects the choices, biases and desires of its creators."
>
> Jamais Cascio, "The Singularity Needs You"

Designing for other people, not just ourselves, is a first accomplishment in digital design. Designing for a diverse array of people—including minority populations, not just the majority—is next-level.

Inclusive design recognizes differing levels of power and access, and attempts to bring all experiences up to parity. It considers physical and cognitive abilities, as well as personal differences like culture and gender. The practice helps us check our privileges, understand other perspectives, discover more assumptions, design more resilient products, and broaden access.

Inclusivity is not just a conceptual skill; it's also a working method. In my opinion, you can't do truly inclusive design without including the audience in the process. Yes, thought exercises will build your mental muscles, but there's no one to tell you when you're wrong! Many tone-deaf features have been launched because corporations didn't get input from the communities affected. Include the audience in creation, not just consumption.

Principles of inclusive design overlap principles of human-centered design and usability (covered elsewhere in this book). As with HCD, we want to create audience-oriented value. As with usability, we want to be consistent and give users control. Then, for inclusive design, we also need to include diverse perspectives, accommodate varied constraints, and build in redundancy. Let's start by analyzing our own angles.

• Acknowledge the inevitability of personal bias

Why is inclusive, human-centered design so important? Aren't we smart enough to decide what a good experience is?

Nope, we're all biased. We have personal motivations and preferences; we have values and behaviors we learned (or didn't learn) from our families; we have communities and cultural icons that influence us. We bring this background to our designs. A good question is not *if* we are biased, but *how*.

Personality bias

How does a design deal with someone who's shy, someone who's aggressive, someone who lies?

👁 Personality models like "the big five" (developed in the US in the 1980s) may not be universal, but helpfully remind us of the wide spectrum of behavioral tendencies.

A first issue comes from the huge natural variation in people's personalities: we can't possibly imagine all the ways visitors will perceive and use our designs. Other people are more or less open than you, more or less honest than you. Resilient designs must serve and protect many personality types.

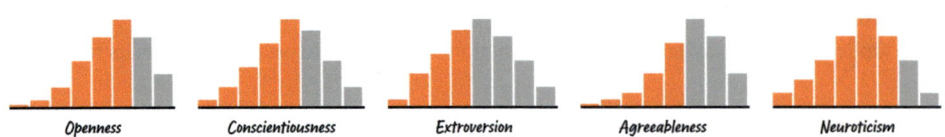
Openness — Conscientiousness — Extroversion — Agreeableness — Neuroticism

The Malkovich bias

The Malkovich bias, coined by technologist Andres Glusman, is the tendency to believe that everyone uses technology as you do. (It's inspired by the movie *Being John Malkovich,* where the characters enter a portal into John Malkovich's mind.) If you never read long articles, you think no one does. If you don't have a tablet, you forget about them. Our assumptions are not always obvious until we talk to someone with a different perspective.

What personal habits might you be assuming?

White savior complex

A similar situation happens frequently in civic work or volunteering. Well-meaning individuals gain their first awareness of a societal issue, think of a "quick fix" solution, and jump in to play the Hollywood hero (or design a feel-good portfolio piece) instead of finding and supporting the local experts and community members working on nuanced, long-term, sustainable initiatives. There can be a profound lack of respect for the people involved and an underlying self-centeredness. Don't play the hero, find the heroes. Be a supporting character.

What is your deeper motivation?

Tech solutionism

Tech workers also jump to create tech solutions because that's their skill set. I can make apps, therefore this cause needs an app! At hackathons for disaster relief, the amount of brain power used creating yet another "matching people who have stuff with people who need stuff" app is sobering. Before I learned human-centered design, I spent an embarrassing number of months volunteering on civic projects or creating impulsive side projects that had little input from the intended audience and no long-term impact. As the saying goes: if you have a hammer, everything looks like a nail.

Does this project really need to exist?

The Dunning-Kruger effect

The Dunning-Kruger effect is the tendency for people with little ability in a field to overestimate their skills: people gain a few insights and quickly see themselves as adept. We're dangerous designers at that first peak, because we don't realize we don't know what's going on. But if we expect our own ignorance, we can plan for the time needed to build real understanding. Do user research (with an open mind) to reveal gaps and fill them with experienced voices.

Where might you have more to learn?

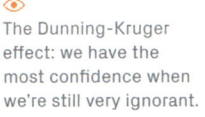

The Dunning-Kruger effect: we have the most confidence when we're still very ignorant.

● Recognize the value of diverse perspectives

Diversity builds resilience in teams and in products. We all want projects to succeed; inclusive design gives them the qualities that help them do so. (That increase in value may also help convince reluctant partners to budget more time for inclusion.)

Breadth
Accommodating multiple cultures increases the number of people who can join in. When I was designing a checking account for children, one culturally Greek participant said that allowances were not a thing in his community (kids make individual requests for money), and he wouldn't want the app to create an expectation for one. If technology doesn't respect the cultural standards that people hold dear, they won't participate.

Relevance
Inclusive design can also make individual experiences more relevant and impactful. When we accommodate diversity in details, from images to navigation to UI controls (e.g., filtering skincare products by skin type or hairstyle images by texture), we reduce noise and increase efficiency. The experience becomes more personal and powerful.

Safety
Inclusive design practices can also reduce abuse, danger, or cruelty; not everyone wants to receive comments from strangers or remember Mother's Day. I'll never forget the launch of a new social networking app that connected people based on their immediate and recurring locations. Every woman I talked to stopped when she got to the "turn on location information" step; the men didn't see a problem. Listen to more vulnerable audiences.

Longevity
Projects that include diverse perspectives from the beginning will be more resilient and long-lasting. They're connected to more communities and stress-tested for more scenarios. Single-author design projects can be self-serving and even colonialist. Sustainable solutions live and evolve with the end users and their knowledge, so we should bring that in as early as possible.

Design must be a service, not a gift.

> "Study after study shows that diverse teams perform better. [...] It 'forces group members to prepare better, to anticipate alternative viewpoints and to expect that reaching consensus will take effort.'"
>
> Sara Wachter-Boettcher,
> *Technically Wrong*

● Take the time to empathize

The final essential element of inclusivity is empathy. It's one of those skills that nearly everyone thinks they have, but empathy is a practice and not a trait. Nursing scholar Theresa Wiseman suggests that there are four defining attributes of empathy: seeing someone else's perspective, understanding their feelings, refraining from judgement, and communicating understanding. These are active verbs, not innate qualities.

When and how will you hear and imagine other perspectives?

Can *everyone* be empathetic? We probably all know people who are distinctly not. In one study, though, scientists tried to teach empathy to people with high levels of narcissism. Those given specific prompts to empathize ("Imagine how Susan feels. Try to take her perspective in the video, imagining how she is feeling about what is happening.") reported empathy levels or showed heart-rate increases similar to the control group; those left alone did not. So even narcissists are probably capable of empathy.

It's one thing to know a principle; it's another to make the time to practice it. Pause your internal monologue and imagine someone else's.

EXERCISE: Empathy map

Empathy maps are research-based summaries of what users say, do, think, and feel (originally created by Dave Gray). They're "10-minute personas": quick research summaries, or first steps to proper personas. I like to do one for each participant and/or each audience segment. I also have designers map themselves to unearth and neutralize their own personal preferences.

Summarize behavior and mindsets; synthesize needs and insights.

Researcher

1. **Identify:** Write the participant's name. Add a photo or sketch that helps you remember them.
2. **Summarize:** For the following categories, list the most important and relevant details from user research. Direct quotes from the person will make the document really come to life, but summaries are fine too.
    - *Goals:* what they're trying to do or be, how they measure success
    - *Barriers:* personal pain points, frustrations, anxieties, or challenges
    - *Activities:* routines, tasks, or behaviors the product may fit into
    - *Influences:* environments, people, or resources that shape their behavior
3. **Synthesize:** Look across all the sections for insights that could inspire or inform designs, such as surprising contradictions, interesting patterns, or deeper needs.

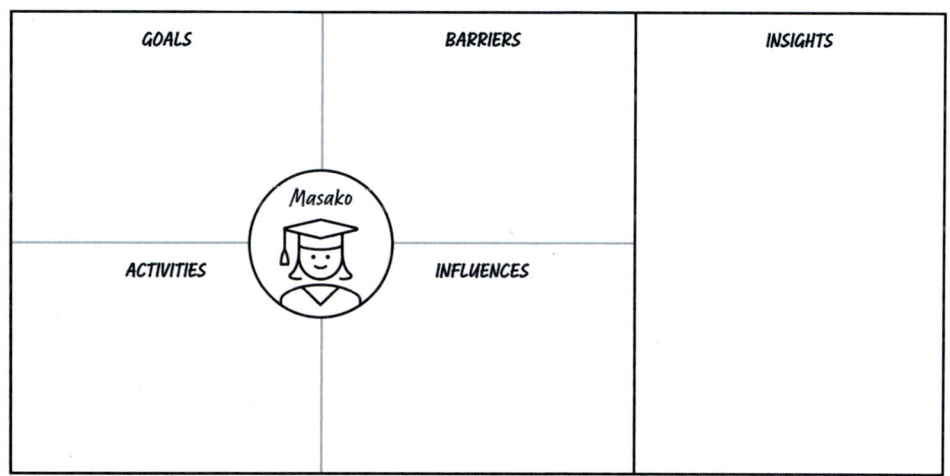

• Adapt to varied constraints

> "Inclusive design doesn't mean you're designing one thing for all people. You're designing a diversity of ways to participate so that everyone has a sense of belonging."
>
> Susan Goltsman, cited in Kat Holmes's *Mismatch: How Inclusion Shapes Design*

Now that we have the foundation of diverse perspectives in the room, we can consider another layer of inclusion: diverse constraints. These may be permanent, temporary, or situational; they may be environmental, social, physical, or emotional. Multiple constraints can occur simultaneously.

Accommodating designs often improve the experience for everyone, not just special visitors. A classic example is curb cuts: they're essential for people in wheelchairs, but are also appreciated by the elderly and enjoyed by anyone crossing the street. Another example is voice inputs: they're essential for accessibility, but make navigation easier for everyone. (My parents started using Siri long before I realized that it's often faster than tapping or swiping characters.)

Providing equal experiences to all people doesn't always mean the same experience. Adaptations can take a few different forms:

- *One design.* Simpler interfaces can be stress-tested and refined until they serve all audiences. Text, images, forms, and filters can all be more accommodating.
- *Custom settings.* Conflicting needs may be best served by customizable interfaces. Video games increased accessibility by adding controls for the experience's background, colors, contrast, flashing, magnification, and language.
- *Alternate modes.* Specific scenarios might justify an entirely different experience. One design may struggle to serve all situations: daylight and darkness, hands-free and hands-on, editing and viewing, colorblind and not. Multiple modes make each experience simpler and more polished.

Inclusive adaptations can shape a single structure or imply multiple experiences.

One Design

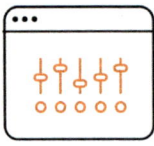
Custom Settings

Alternate Modes

As we go through different accommodations, think about how each one might be served by the default experience, a custom setting, or an alternate mode.

• Accommodate social constraints

Who is watching?
Who is being watched?

Interfaces may assume we're alone, but the people around us may affect what we want to see, do, or hear.

In public spaces

Libraries and other public spaces give people welcome access to services, but can also expose them to risk if they forget to log out. Public transit scenarios have prying eyes and listening ears in close proximity. Auto-logout and shielded passwords are smart defaults. Be very mindful of privacy and security risks.

What private details are risky in public?

With coworkers

In a professional setting, off-the-clock elements can range from party fouls to HR issues. Browsing history and "for you" selections can be irrelevant or embarrassing in a different context. (A Twitter friend was sharing his screen, pulling up a website that started with P, and belatedly realized what other history would come up.) Chrome launched browser profiles for each email address; Apple added a Hide feature that keeps private photos out of the main library. Think about segmenting experiences.

Is the experience safe for work?

With family and friends

At home or with trusted contacts, shortcuts and sensor-based experiences can be cool and not creepy. Yes, I'm happy to share my Wi-Fi password with my best friend! If my companions are minors, I may want ways to limit the full experience. Podcasts with bleeped versions save parents from precocious profanity; Netflix's multiple profiles saves me from my sister's taste in movies. Consider support for more intimate connections.

Is physical or social closeness relevant?

With emotional involvement

"Content" and "functionality" are vague, neutral words, but some breaking news or automated albums can be disruptive or devastating. Twitter's "muted words" feature is a key stress reducer; Google Photos' "hide this person" option makes their albums still usable emotionally by letting you look at certain photos if and when you are ready. Think about implementing need-to-know options.

Might the experience needlessly upset someone?

• Accommodate cultural constraints

We've talked about the importance of diversity in design teams and audiences. To move from default thinking to diverse thinking, keep investigating the assumptions in a design. Broaden its presentation and mechanics to serve a spectrum of participants.

	Default thinking	Diverse thinking
Language	Native speaker	Non-native speaker
Ethnicity	Majority culture	Marginalized culture
Gender	Same as those in power	Different from those in power
Sexual orientation	Same as majority	Different from majority
Sizing	A few simple sizes	Many sizing variables
Socioeconomic	More resources	Fewer resources

COMPARE
Default and diverse thinking

• Accommodate environmental constraints

Constantly designing on a laptop or desktop computer creates a bias to design for that same environment. Product designs exist in many environments; go feel these 3D factors and how they affect perception.

Does the interface work if it's shaking?

In motion

Screens are not always stable, so prevention and easy undo of errant gestures are important. Bumps in the road cause literal motor difficulties, and mobile screens may be a secondary focus. Helping people not crash their cars is a greater goal than any user flow conversion. Think of safe zones for usage in transit. For example, Spotify has an automatic Car Mode that reduces options and magnifies buttons for drivers.

Do the features still work with no signal or scripts?

In a low-tech area

Experiences that depend on videos or other high-fidelity media will not work in many locations or situations, and people often disable JavaScript, location services, or other technical features with some risk. Help people avoid slow load times, high carrier charges, and inaccessible services. Think of low-tech fallbacks for hi-tech elements. For example, my newsletter signup form was getting hidden by ad blockers, so I added a plain text link.

Does the brightness of the design match the environment?

In a dark environment

Bright white screens can strain eyes after long periods of use and glare like a floodlight in the dark. The blue light of screens can disrupt sleep patterns and brain chemistry. Consider adjusting colors for both usability and health. Dark mode and Night Shift were welcome additions to Apple's OS, for example.

• Accommodate physical/cognitive constraints

"Almost every one of us will be permanently or temporarily disabled at some point in life."

Margaret Chan, former director-general of the WHO

A final group of accommodations is physical and/or cognitive. According to the UN, 15 percent of the world's population (that's one billion people) live with disabilities, from mobility to cognition to hearing to vision. Do 15 percent of your research participants or personas have a disability?

It's not just "other people" who are disabled—contemporary organizations see disability not as an identity, but a state. There are permanent disabilities like blindness or deafness, but also temporary disabilities like injury or illness, plus situational disabilities like the cultural, environmental, and social constraints outlined above. Seen this way, inclusive design assists multiple billions of people worldwide.

Businesses are responsible for providing accessible experiences, but remember that the community can and should help, too. Twitter, for instance, was the first social network with prominent prompts to create alt text.

Sense	Permanent issue	Temporary issue	Situational issue
Touch	Paralysis Tremors	Hand injury	One-handed use Cold temperature
See	Blindness Colorblindness Low vision	Cataracts	Multitasking Dim lighting
Hear	Deafness Hearing loss	Ear infection	Loud office Poor connection
Speak	Non-speaking Speech impediment	Laryngitis	Library Auditorium
Think	Dyslexia ADHD	Sleep deprivation	Foreign country Caffeine deprivation

COMPARE
Spectrums of disability (based on Microsoft's Inclusive Design Toolkit)

The design solution for physical and cognitive constraints is, again, diversity: products need a variety of ways for people to act on them.

Each approach also needs a range of accommodations; personal constraints are spectrums, not binaries.

Let me touch

- People with motor difficulties may need larger clickable areas, or alternative ways to navigate interfaces.
- People with no motor control may need access via voice inputs, eye-controlled devices, or brain-computer interfaces.

Let me see

- People with trouble seeing may need higher or lower contrast, light or dark modes, scalable text and graphics, or custom settings for important elements. For example, Apple offers custom outline and fill colors on the cursor.
- People who cannot see need screen-reader-friendly captions or descriptions for images and transcriptions for audio or video.

Let me hear

- People with difficulty hearing may appreciate more distinct sound effects, or visual cues to indicate who's speaking in a group view.
- People who cannot hear need captions or transcripts for all audio content, ideally in real time and with accurate, sensitive moderation.

Let me speak

- People who have trouble speaking may need more time to add inputs to a voice system. Non-native language speakers may need specifically calibrated technology or additional clarifications.
- People who temporarily cannot speak may need formats that maintain silence. Those who cannot speak permanently may need text-to-speech options, including voices that represent their personal identity well.

Let me think

- People experiencing cognitive issues may need additional clarifications or fewer distractions on content. For example, people with ADHD tend to need clear instructions, plenty of time to complete them, and later reminders.
- People who cannot think under certain circumstances (those who get migraines from high-contrast text, for example, or seizures from strobe lighting) need up-front warnings and alternative experiences.

Let the bots

You know who else can't touch, see, hear, speak, or think? Spiderbots. A lot of accessibility work is also great for SEO. When you make experiences usable for screen readers, you also help the search engine crawlers.

EXERCISE: Alternative modes

Design an alternate mode to serve a particular use case.

 Researcher
 Visual designer
 Engineer

Interfaces don't have to serve every single audience in the same way; sometimes an alternative mode is the best way to serve a use case.

1. Research the audience's needs, and any modes that might help them (e.g., hands-free, large print, low bandwidth, no JavaScript, dark mode).
2. Create an alternative version of the interface for this mode, including the elements that let people select or switch modes.

Build accessibility

A final layer of inclusive design is accessibility. Inclusive design is a method; accessible design is a quality, an achievement of a specific set of technical standards. It's a subset of inclusive design that accommodates specific disabilities and makes sure affected parties can access the same content and functionality that everyone else gets.

Many accessibility requirements must be fulfilled in code, but product designers must do their part to meet these requirements throughout design processes. (If you're having trouble getting a team to prioritize the time required to do accessibility work, tell some scary stories about companies getting sued for noncompliance.) I've integrated accessibility practices throughout this book, since that's the most effective way to ensure it. Let's zoom in for a more detailed look.

Know the principles

The Web Content Accessibility Guidelines (WCAG) list four core principles for accessible interfaces (as of version 2.1). These principles form the acronym POUR: designs must be *perceivable, operable, understandable,* and *robust.*

Each principle has specific success criteria (with three levels of achievement: A, AA, or AAA), as well as detailed design recommendations. My summaries are below; for precise definitions and directives, read the full guidelines and latest resources online.

Perceivable

- Distinguishable in color, contrast, and audio levels
- Adaptable in purpose, sequence, and orientation
- Captioned with alt text for meaningful images, audio, and videos

Operable

- Pointer-friendly due to appropriate labels, targets, functions, and timing
- Keyboard-operable via headings, focus order (when tabbing), and shortcuts

Understandable

- Readable due to appropriate language, reading level, and explanations
- Predictable regarding inputs, context changes, and navigation
- Helpful with error prevention, communication, and resolution methods

Robust

- Compatible with current and future web browsers or assistive technologies

• Design operable, understandable UI at every fidelity

Operability and understandability are core accessibility concerns for product designs at all fidelity levels. (Perceivability is mostly relevant in hi-fi, and robustness in development.)

- Operable designs are friendly to fingers, mice, keyboards, trackballs, and styluses, as well as to assistive tech like screen magnifiers, screen readers, Braille displays, or sip-and-puff controls.
- Understandable designs are readable, predictable, and helpful (see the Usability and Layouts chapters for additional guidance).

Here's a checklist of accessibility questions to ask at each stage of design.

COMPARE
Operability and understanding issues at different fidelity levels

Low fidelity (sketches)
Consider multiple methods of operation when creating concepts.
- ☐ **Hover states:** What is the fallback behavior for touchscreens?
- ☐ **Gestures:** What is the fallback behavior for non-touchscreen devices?
- ☐ **Drag-and-drop controls:** What are the keyboard-only equivalents?
- ☐ **Interactive areas:** Are targets large enough for people with motor difficulties?

Medium fidelity (wireframes)
Consider multiple devices when plotting content and functionality.
- ☐ **Layouts:** Is each screen understandable when rearranged into one column?
- ☐ **Headings:** Do all sections have clear labels?
- ☐ **Links:** Is link text informative and its destination predictable?
- ☐ **Navigation:** Are options and shortcuts available for each input device?

High fidelity (mockups)
Check accessibility nuances when designing detailed mockups.
- ☐ **Layouts:** Does each screen present information in a logical order?
- ☐ **Color:** Are contrast levels adequate? Is color-coded information available in text too?
- ☐ **Animation:** Do blinking effects avoid physical reactions (no more than three flashes per second)?
- ☐ **Timing:** Are time limits long enough for people who read or type slowly?

Engineered fidelity (code)
Try these assistive tech checks from IBM's *Accessibility Handbook* when QAing code.
- ☐ **Screen magnifier:** Zoom to 200 percent to see if layouts still work with larger fonts.
- ☐ **Keyboard-only browser:** Try to access all content and functionality using only the tab, shift, arrow, enter, and space bar keys.
- ☐ **Screen reader:** Visit pages with a screen reader, disabling your mouse and using only your keyboard for input.

- ## Watch for the red flags

Accessibility standards can feel overwhelming at first. If you're wondering how to prioritize efforts, a February 2021 study by WebAIM listed the ten most common accessibility failures, grouped below into three core problems. Watch for these red flags whenever you're designing, and pause to think through accessible options.

Red Flag	Common Failures	Solutions
🚩 Minimal text	Ambiguous link text Missing/improper alt text Missing/improper headings	Check the text during strategy, design, and development phases. Make sure strategists, designers, writers, and developers all understand accessibility guidelines.
🚩 Complex layouts	CAPTCHAs Flash content Complex data tables Complex forms	Consider new formats or layouts for complex areas. For example, Excel added a separate navigation pane to let screen readers browse through its complex data tables.
🚩 Complex flows	Poor keyboard access Unexpected new windows Too many links Missing "skip nav" links Missing search	Test complex flows and navigation on multiple devices using multiple input formats. Include alternate, device-specific routes for speed or accuracy.

COMPARE
Three red flags for accessibility in designs

- ## Manage contrast levels early

Let's take a moment to highlight color contrast, since it's one of the most common accessibility discussions for designers. Color-contrast checks are mostly a higher-fidelity issue, but establishing good contrast in lower-fidelity designs is a prescient practice. Geri Coady's *Color Accessibility Workflows* helpfully notes that designs that are accessible in grayscale will generally be accessible when those values are converted into color.

Accessible text must meet certain levels of contrast (varying according to the text's size, boldness, and interactivity), but there's some nuance to this.

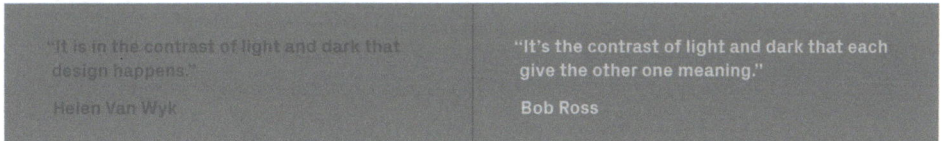

"It is in the contrast of light and dark that design happens."
Helen Van Wyk

"It's the contrast of light and dark that each give the other one meaning."
Bob Ross

👁 Contrast that's too low causes eye strain.

First off, the contrast calculations keep evolving (thankfully). Light colors like yellow and orange on white would fail the V2 math tests, but newer formulas are better matched to how humans see color. Always check the latest WCAG details.

A second issue: most accessibility tools only tell you when visual contrast is too low, not when it's too high. Maximum contrast (pure white vs pure black) can cause migraines for viewers, or a visual blurring effect called *halation* for people with astigmatism. Fight for very dark gray!

A third point is that contrast issues can be handled by some devices, so it may not be necessary to adapt to the most extreme cases. Research the audience's devices and see if low-vision users who need maximum contrast can toggle "accessibility mode" in their settings. Stay abreast of hardware and software improvements.

• Design redundancies

Accessibility is complex, but one simple way to think about it is in terms of multiple routes to the same goal. Redundancy may seem inefficient at first glance, but it's also a core principle of engineering. Things will fail somewhere; always have a fallback. A simple constant check is the I-N-G method put forth by landscape architect Susan Goltsman.

1. What "-ing" [verb] is most important here (e.g., reading, writing, conversing)?
2. How many ways can people engage in that activity (currently and ideally)?

EXERCISE: Operability check

Design for fingers, mice, trackballs, keyboards, pens, and more.

 Visual designer
 Engineer

Think about input devices other than the one you're currently using. Design equal access.

1. Design mouse-only equivalents for gestures and touchscreen inputs.
2. Design finger-only equivalents for hover states.
3. Design keyboard-only equivalents for drag-and-drop inputs and shortcuts for navigation.

REMEMBER:
INCLUSIVITY

Include diverse perspectives	 Empathy map	Empathy
Adapt to varied constraints	Alternative modes	 Progressive enhancement
Build in redundancy	 Operability check	 Redundancy

Relationships
4D THREADS

Over time, connections turn information architecture into relationship architecture. Consistent access patterns shape perceptions and feelings. Interaction metaphors may be spatial, prosthetic, or human, bringing people back for practical or emotional benefits. Off-site touchpoints and reminders can strengthen the connection. Visitors may evolve from new guests to repeat customers, reputable members, or expert admins, and the experience can change with them. Successful product design builds meaningful long-term relationships.

KEY QUESTIONS	EXERCISES
• **Personality:** What form or role does the experience take?	Interaction metaphor
• **Retention:** When and why will people return?	Retention hooks
• **Roles:** How does the experience evolve with use?	Privileges plan

COGNITIVE PRINCIPLES

- **Precommitment**
Self-imposed commitments or restrictions of choice increase people's ability to achieve longer or more difficult goals.

- **Control**
A system's level of control should match a user's level of proficiency (beginners need a gated experience; experts need a range of access and shortcuts).

- **Parity**
Physical or digital systems that replace mental processes are effectively part of the cognitive system (the "extended mind" theorized by Andy Clark and David Chalmers).

• Model the relationship

> "We live today not in the digital, not in the physical, but in the kind of minestrone that our mind makes of the two."
>
> Paola Antonelli, "Why I Brought Pac-Man to MoMA"

Interactions over time form some kind of relationship, whether it's steady and consistent or wildly unpredictable. Product experiences may feel like simple acquaintances, reliable friends, or intimate partners. They may have the tone of a nurturing parent, inspiring teacher, professional colleague, or multifaceted community. They play increasingly important roles in our lives, so it's worth our time to think about good relationship models.

An interaction metaphor can take many forms—spatial, prosthetic, or human—and can combine words, images, symbols, and timing into familiar models or otherworldly ones. It can mirror existing mental models or create new ones. An app that lets people curate playlists with friends could exist as a virtual room where characters play, a collaborative set list that everyone can edit, or a responsive DJ that takes requests on the fly. We can jump right into traditional interface designs, or explore more novel models based on connection frequency, strength, values, and metaphors.

• Imagine the frequency of visits

Is the relationship daily or occasional, short-term or long-term?

The metaphor for a product relationship should correlate with its frequency. If the product is a goal tracker, people might visit multiple times daily (and then not at all once they've reached their goal). If it's a tax assistant, they might visit only yearly, but forever.

Know when an audience's specific needs occur, and consider analogous service models. Existing habits are the clearest and least spammy entry points to an experience; consider interactions that piggyback on established behaviors. Creating new activities or habits is more difficult but is often part of the design challenge, and trusted brands can be more proactive with outreach. Find a healthy cadence for visits.

Yearly	Monthly	Weekly	Daily	Constant
Events, holidays, seasons	Bills, paydays, meetings	Chores, clubs, activities	Hygiene, meals, commutes	Thoughts, chats, distractions

• Analyze the strength of the connection

Is the relationship a simple pleasure or an essential need?

COMPARE
Connection strengths

The metaphor we build should also reflect the strength of the connection. Some products are used more casually than others, and shouldn't force a false intimacy (I don't want my library app to ask me a series of questions about my personal life). The VC world often talks about products as candy, vitamins, or pills.

Candy	Vitamins	Pills
Provides simple pleasures	Create tangible gains	Relieve specific pains
Weakest relationship: nice-to-have	Moderate relationship: should-have	Strongest relationship: must-have

Simple experiences can be delightful candy, but if a business-minded product is not a pill or at least a vitamin, it may be time to rethink the strategy. Review the audience's typical habits and look for specific use cases and pain points to serve. Build on the idea of service design, not product design, to reinforce user-centered thinking: the focus is on them, not us. Look for a must-have relationship.

• Define the shared values

Experience metaphors must speak to the audience's values, but also be authentic to the organization. Strong organizations have authentic and consistent values that are embodied in everything from interface design to employee conduct. Nike's core values include innovation and inspiration; this explains their fashion-forward interfaces filled with powerful human stories. Google's mission statement is "to organize the world's information and make it universally accessible and useful"; this supports their practical interfaces that follow and promote web standards. Solid relationships with customers come from mutual shared values. Find the overlapping ideals.

What overlaps exist between the audience's ideal experiences and the company's?

• Think in metaphors

Analogous thinking is one of the best routes to creative ideas (see the Thinking chapter for more). Once you understand the parameters for a connection, play with a variety of metaphors that capture the big idea and inspire designs.

Consider spatial metaphors
A sense of place creates instantly obvious navigation connotations—web "sites" have been the default digital metaphor for decades. It can also assist recall; orators and memory contest champions use "memory palaces" to plot information in space and retain it. Spaces can be industrial or organic: rigid academies or fuzzy clouds. They can be real, surreal, or hyperreal: futurist command centers or parallel universes. Designers turn into architects, balancing rich comforts with easy navigation. Imagine a space that serves the audience's organizational and interactive needs (a shopping mall, a garden, or a cloud, for example).

Is the experience a space or environment to navigate?

"The road to widespread internet adoption was paved with spatial metaphors, which helped non-technical people wrap their heads around this brand new technology. We drove down the information super*highway*, we visited cyber *space*, we navigated to web *sites*."

Aaron Z. Lewis, "Inside the Digital Sensorium"

👁 Spatial interaction metaphors are clear and common (see *Smart Things* by Mike Kuniavsky for more).

Is the experience a tool or resource to use?

"[A]ll technologies are extensions of our physical and nervous systems to increase power and speed."

Marshall McLuhan, *Understanding Media*

Is the experience a friend, an expert, a facilitator?

"[T]he user is not an operator. He does not operate the computer, he communicates with it."

Stuart K. Card, Thomas P. Moran, and Allen Newell, *The Psychology of Human-Computer Interaction*

Brand archetypes for core human needs (based on work by Margaret Mark and Carol Pearson)

Consider prosthetic metaphors

Technology can deliver new capacities, extend people's physical or nervous systems, and become a virtual part of cognition. Prosthetic metaphors are therefore apt and powerful. Digital contact lists and calculators replace the parts of our brain that used to remember phone numbers or do math; Google has turned us into all-knowing beings with massive memories. Mobile apps put advanced sensors and displays in the palm of our hands, while newer technologies replace graphic user interfaces (GUIs) with natural user interfaces (NUIs) that use the body as a controller. Imagine a tool that provides special or magical capabilities (e.g., a megaphone, a thermometer, an X-ray).

Consider human metaphors

People tend to anthropomorphize products, and so design choices create personality characteristics. Apple's auto-curated "Memories" feature feels like a loving friend; Siri is a literal concierge. Products can play simple roles or go much deeper. In their book *The Hero and the Outlaw: Building Extraordinary Brands,* Margaret Mark and Carol Pearson turned Carl Jung's work on archetypes into twelve brand archetypes serving four core human needs. For example, an "Explorer" brand provides adventure; a "Leader" brand provides order. (Remember that user-centered products don't possess the superpower; they provide it.) Design is a service, but wonderful service isn't just practical. Imagine a personality who connects on emotional levels—like a coach, a muse, or a provocateur.

Structure	Order	Innovation	Service		Connection	Belonging	Entertainment	Intimacy
	Leader	Creator	Caregiver			Friend	Joker	Lover
Freedom	Wisdom	Adventure	Purity		Achievement	Power	Triumph	Change
	Sage	Explorer	Idealist			Magician	Hero	Rebel

Define the times and ways that the experience fits into the audience's life.

Researcher
Strategist

EXERCISE: Interaction metaphor

Find a metaphor that captures the frequency, strength, and value of the product's relationship with people. Think about forms that could create a significant connection.

1. Outline a typical day, week, and year for the audience (so that you understand interaction frequencies and contexts). What regular habits, seasonal changes, or special occasions trigger the need for service?

2. Choose an interaction metaphor (spatial, prosthetic, or human) that inspires and unifies designs. See how the metaphor fits key moments or adapts to different contexts.

• Make it easy to reconnect

You can't build a relationship if people fail to return. At some point, successful products need to shift their design goals from the initial growth metrics of engagement and revenue (people interacting and contributing) to the later ones of retention and referral (people coming back and bringing others).

Are designs leading to relationships or leaving people cold?

Retention is a key indicator that a product is valuable and an essential ingredient in business growth; that's why websites bombard us with subscription popups. Consider retention in each screen's information hierarchy and each flow's success metrics. Does a design bring people back?

The flip side of retention is churn: the number of customers lost over time. This may appear as obvious account deletions or quiet abandonment. Reducing churn can be as valuable as acquiring new users; research the reasons people don't come back as well as the reasons they do. It's one thing to get a customer; it's another thing to keep them.

The core pieces of retention are *hooks, touchpoints,* and *notifications.*

• Ask for small investments

Sustainable products create regular habits of use; experiences must include compelling reasons to return. Nir Eyal's bestselling *Hooked* defined four parts to a behavioral hook: *trigger, action, reward,* and *investment.* (This formula was used to such terrific and horrible ends that Eyal wrote a follow-up book called *Indistractable.*)

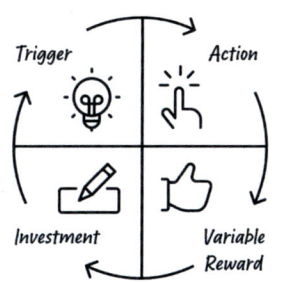

Nir Eyal's Hook model for habit formation.

Triggers and actions are the obvious components of a habit. The unique ideas of a hook are that rewards should be variable, not predictable, to increase chemical highs; and that investments are a necessary final step. Rewards may seem like the logical conclusion to an interaction, but investments create the anticipation of future rewards and increase commitment—even tiny ones can be enough to bring people back. Subscribing to a newsletter is an obvious investment, but investments can also be as simple as entering a username, liking a song, or earning a high score. Precommitment is a relevant cognitive bias: if people visibly state they're going to do something, they're more likely to do it. And investments proactively improve their experience on the next visit.

Hooks are definitely a place to spend extra time on ethics checks (see the sections on influence versus exploitation in the Paths chapter). Reminders and special prompts can help people finish things they start, get the most out of a service, or do more than they thought they could—just make sure investments are transparent, optional, and beneficial for the person involved.

Meet them where they are

Where would product reminders make sense?

A second part of retention is environmental. People leave a site or close an app and go on with their lives. Days are busy and attention is scattered; it's easy to forget that beautiful place or useful tool that was briefly enjoyed. Marketing and advertising are obviously out of scope for this book, but we have to think about other locations that bring people back to the experience we're creating.

Content and design don't have to sit alone on your little island; they should also appear on the mainland, where an audience is already hanging out. When I draw site or app maps for a brand, I include all relevant social media profiles because they're functionally and psychologically part of the same digital experience.

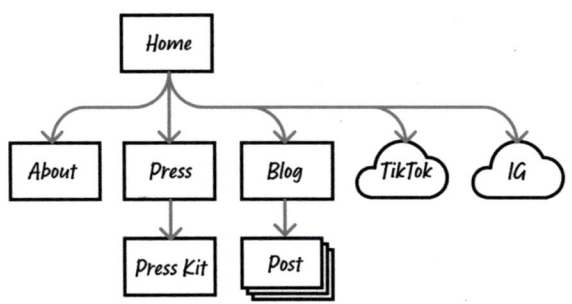

Include social profiles in site or app maps; they're part of the product experience in people's minds.

Maintaining a lively social media presence is no small task, but social media strategy dovetails with many product design initiatives. In addition, social media profiles are often the most-interacted-with parts of an entire brand, so the integrations must be considered. At the very least, meet people in their inboxes occasionally.

Think about the other sites, tools, or services that suit your brand and attract your audience. Then get visitors to smash that subscribe or follow button.

• Be proactive but not pushy

When would product reminders be welcome?

A final part of retention is timing. Notifications extend the product experience into channels of the audience's choosing, but designers need to think carefully about when and why those gates should open.

In my experience, the first week of product use is really important to nail, so it's wise to frame onboarding as a time period, not a flow. Consider *spaced repetition,* an evidence-based learning technique that can help build new behaviors: use shorter intervals between initial exposures, then increasing intervals over time. Marketers are very familiar with drip campaigns, and can easily set up outreach to drip drip drip out over the course of days, weeks, or months. Notification timing can then grow more refined and personalized as you see how each recipient reacts.

After the onboarding phase, the lines are fuzzier on when to connect with (or bother) an audience. Urgent issues like fraud are obvious notification reasons, but other time-sensitive issues like "breaking news" may require some judgment on whether they're worth agitating the audience's nervous system.

A nice construct for notification management is the Eisenhower Matrix for task management: if it's urgent and important, then do it (now). The interaction metaphor for an experience might also shape communications. A "news room" would be expected to blast updates constantly, for example; a "luxury concierge" would be expected to show restraint and good taste. Frequencies should match the brand's voice. They should also adjust to world events that affect people's lives and mental states.

"Like most relationships, communities don't form overnight; they take time to flourish. You'll need to stay invested in these people if you want to bring a community to life."

Bailey Richardson, Kevin Huynh, and Kai Elmer Sotto, *Get Together: How to Build a Community with Your People*

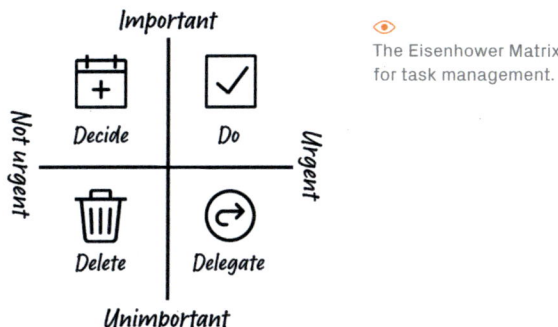

The Eisenhower Matrix for task management.

Increasing familiarity to increase retention is important, but I like to consider both the *familiarity bias* (people tend to choose options they're more familiar with) and the quite opposed adage "familiarity breeds contempt" (if you know someone too well, you can lose respect for them). Notifications and updates are an invitation to return, but also an opportunity to break things off. Influencer Kat Norton (a.k.a. Miss Excel) says she gets the most followers on days she *doesn't* post, because old content is still being shared with new people and existing followers aren't seeing any posts that might prompt them to unfollow. Doing nothing is a growth strategy too.

EXERCISE: Retention hook

Frequency of use is strongly correlated with the perceived value of a product. Adapt designs to spur return use.

1. What type of investment is most relevant for a particular audience (e.g., adding their info, playing a game, subscribing)?
2. When is the best time to ask for an investment? When will visitors feel most positive or least disrupted?
3. How could the interface support easy investments? Which design patterns make sense?

Make sure to include a next step for the relationship.

 Strategist
 Visual designer

• See and support change

> "Designing a product is designing a relationship."
> Steve Rogers

The final core element in product relationships is change. When designing new screens, it's hard not to see them like a new user. But if people do come back, they're not the same person they were before. They have history with the experience; they may have new goals or extra expectations based on their previous actions or some change in the world. Meaningful relationships will adapt.

People evolve in small steps, but workable models bucket change into larger stages.

- Novel experiences may focus on stages of understanding. Designers at Xerox called this the Experience Cycle: *connecting, orienting, interacting, mastering,* and *advocating*.
- Growth experiences often focus on conversion stages: *leads, prospects, customers, repeat users,* and *advocates*.
- Retail experiences generally focus on purchasing stages: *consideration, research, comparison, trial, selection, purchase,* and *loyalty*.

I'll focus on functional stages: *first-time guests, repeat guests, members,* and *experts/admins*. We'll also think about non-ideal changes: *disruptors*. Each level has different priorities and needs, as well as distinct success metrics to consider.

COMPARE
Relationship levels and needs

First-timers	Return visitors	Members	Experts	Disruptors
Need guidance	Need orientation	Need reciprocity	Need support	Need moderation

People may sit at one level for months or years, or progress quickly through the stages in one session. Successful digital experiences will empower people to achieve their goals at that stage and hopefully advance to another one.

• Guide first-time guests

What rules or information do novices need?

Brand-new visitors gather information and absorb a lot of material at once. They need to understand what this digital thing *is* to them, and what they can *do*. They often appreciate guided walk-throughs of the big idea or must-see highlights. They're usually juggling many options, and therefore need to know why this one is best for them.

Precommitment is a helpful principle here: people are more likely to finish actions that have structured follow-throughs or deadlines. Retention is also a key success metric: if new guests bounce, you may never see them again. Plan ways to continue the relationship. (Revisit the section on reconnection for ideas.)

- ## Orient returning guests

    Return visitors connect all the pieces of the experience to understand what's possible. They may appreciate ways to quickly pick up where they left off before. They may not need the same introductions, overviews, or calls to action.

    Activation is a good metric to watch for with repeat visitors: seeing what they're doing where, and how often. Trial periods for paid products (or simple interactive demos) may help people see value more quickly. Limited-functionality trials may help both customers and businesses: they prevent overwhelm by presenting an amount of functionality that matches users' expertise, and incentivize conversion to get the remaining features.

    What reminders or wayfinding would help return visitors?

- ## Reward members or customers

    Logged-in users can receive a more personalized, efficient, and meaningful experience (once they've contributed enough input). Special privileges are another way to reward their investment and optimize their experience. They may also like ways to reflect on past enjoyment, and repeat it. Remember that history and preferences can be an annoyance if you're past that stage or acting out of character (e.g., tiring of certain music, shopping for someone else); consider preference evolution or subdivision.

    Conversion is a key metric for any business, so it's essential to get a deep understanding of the needs or situations that get people over the line. The value of the member experience must correlate with the scale of someone's investment (whether of money, time, or personal information).

    How might investments be rewarded?

- ## Support the actions of experts

    Experienced users build their skills, master the product, and extend its use. To streamline their work, they might expect or need extra layers of functionality on each screen, as well as high-volume or high-frequency versions of features. Trusted users may also enjoy the responsibility of managing the site, product, or community. Editing privileges can improve the content or conduct in the product (and reduce the staff's workload).

    Referrals are a great indicator of customer satisfaction: people trust the brand enough to risk their own personal reputation, or like the place so much they want their friends there too. Supporting advocacy brings new people into the experience cycle. Make it easy and rewarding for people to refer, teach, integrate, or inspire others.

    What freedom or shortcuts do experts need?

- ## Moderate disruptors

What guardrails will hold back the trolls?

Problematic users can't be overlooked. Some people gently push boundaries for fun; others have serious malicious intent. Analyze each layer of access for both constructive and disruptive potential. Create safeguards as needed to protect the community. (See the Paths chapters for more ideas.)

EXERCISE: Privileges plan

Define levels of access and functionality.

Strategist
Engineer

Businesses must decide what level of free service is sustainable; developers need to know what content each group can access. Make a table that lists possible roles. For each level, identify the goals for the person and the business. What does the experience need to deliver?

Stage	User Goal	Business Goal	Experience Needs
First-time guest	?	?	?
Returning guest	?	?	?
Member or customer	?	?	?
Expert or admin	?	?	?
Disruptor (troll)	?	?	?

REMEMBER: RELATIONSHIPS

- Model the relationship
- Make it easy to reconnect
- See and support change

 Interaction metaphor

 Retention hooks

 Privileges plan

 Precommitment

 Control

 Parity

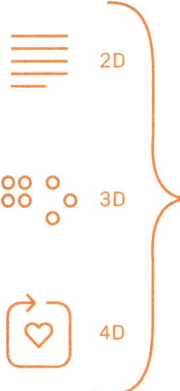

CREATE: Links

Even at low fidelity, we can start to create wayfinding elements that help people make sense of where they are in digital space and what they can do with this random assortment of pixels. Balance business directions with visitor priorities to create usable, successful sites.

1. **Where am I?** Make sure each screen has a clear title (whether it's styled like a headline or something else)—this is important for both humans and SEO bots.

2. **What's next?** Add emphasis to the primary call to action. If a screen supports multiple paths, figure out a visual hierarchy for the various calls to action so they're not fighting for attention. Remember to add send-off links at the "end" of a flow; there's always one more step.

3. **What's blocking me?** Consider the nonlinear or circular steps in a flow, like checking return policies or comparing similar products. Add inline links that could resolve any barriers or essential subtasks. Also consider linked help experiences like guides, wizards, chat, or search.

4. **What's related?** If a screen has siblings that might be useful and that don't distract from the main goals of the flow, consider a local navigation element that makes them one click away (a Movies visitor might also like links to TV Shows or Music, for example). If parent pages are also useful (going from Movies to Entertainment, for instance), consider adding breadcrumb navigation.

5. **What else is here?** Global navigation elements provide top-down ways to explore a site, but also a nice skimmable overview of what's there. They can be attention-getting headers or quiet footers, expanded areas or collapsed menu buttons. Also consider dedicated overview screens like sitemaps, indexes, or "about" pages.

6. **How will I get back here?** A growth-oriented designer always thinks about return visits. Create hooks, partnerships, or other threads that will lead people back to the experience. Consider inbound links on other sites.

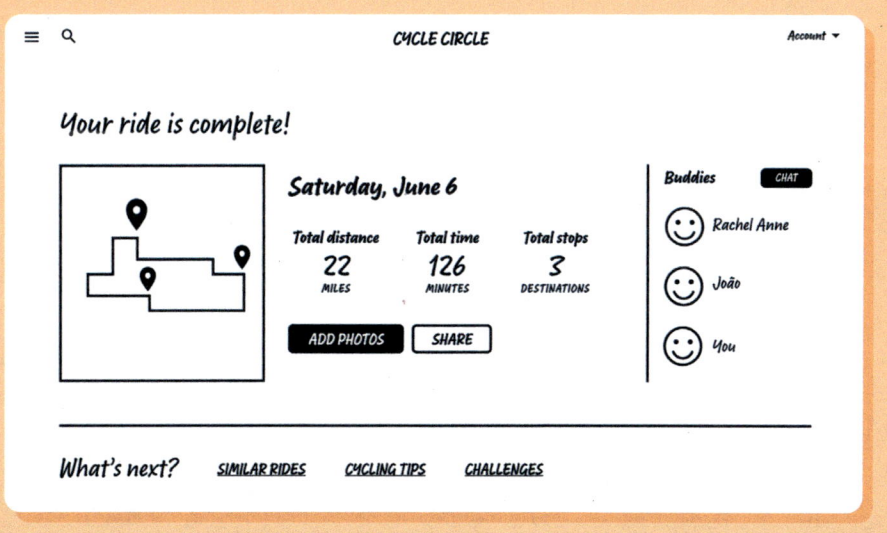

Provide routes and signposts throughout experiences.

CRITIQUE: Navigation

Navigation critiques help us zoom out from localized design considerations and see how all the elements fit together in a system. User-centered interfaces let visitors control the particular routes they take, but flexible and inclusive navigation designs require careful iteration. Check the format and the language of links with multiple audiences, for multiple paths.

Streamline paths and create additional routes between screens.

☑ Forward
— Take a goal-oriented lens to each screen, checking that the next step in each key path is clear.
— Are calls to action clear? Do they get people to their goal?

☑ Backward
— Take an error-prone lens to each key flow, checking that the previous screen or state is easily accessible.
— Can visitors quickly undo errors or change their minds?

☑ Zooming out
— Take a wide-angle lens to each screen, checking that brand-new visitors can easily get oriented.
— Each screen serves multiple flows. Are there clear wayfinding systems to help people find their route or change lanes?
— Is it easy for a visitor to understand where they are, and what else they can do?

☑ Diving deeper
— Take a focused lens to each screen, checking that hungry visitors can easily get more information or assistance.
— At each step in a flow, is there an opportunity to link someone to a deeper relationship?
— Are there easy ways to dig in, commit, and come back?

"Towering genius disdains a beaten path. It seeks regions hitherto unexplored."

Abraham Lincoln

REMEMBER: THREADS

To summarize: product experiences can be islands or hubs. Creating more routes to and through a design creates more opportunities for success. We need to think about 2D words, 3D inclusivity, and 4D relationships to create findable, navigable experiences.

Impressions

Impressions are the visual and verbal imprints that flash through visitors' brains. Each layout must deal with the dynamic nature of product design, flexing to fit a variety of hardware and content. Screens must also serve many different people simultaneously, as well as their evolving priorities on each visit. Strong impressions lead eyes, ears, or fingers through space and time. Designers must create compelling and adaptive, yet consistent, arrangements of functionality.

When you're doing online banking, when do you grab your phone and when do you turn to your computer?

The answer probably depends on the context—small screens are easy to pull up in any situation; large screens provide more information at once; in-between screens suit special environments or workflows.

But experience expectations will vary by context, too. If I'm reviewing transactions on my phone, I want thumb-friendly ways to expand or flag an entry. On my laptop, I want easy ways to compare data or download files. Modern products have to accommodate a mind-melting number of scenarios, balancing specific preferences on each device with consistency across them all. Designers have to manage hundreds of little details of what happens where, and how.

Hierarchy is our core tool for this phase, the solution to many messes (in screens, flows, and entire systems). Clear hierarchy guides viewers across space and time, turning masses of information into sequences of perception that reveal and support priorities. It's a universal tool for any design.

In this phase we'll consider layouts, flexibility, and patterns. This section focuses on arranging the content and functionality on each screen in an experience. The chapters in this section are more tactical, providing guidelines for interfaces that are technically informed, logically organized, and visually striking.

PRACTICE

2D layouts: Lead the eye with strong visual hierarchies, readable structures, and plenty of room to breathe. Arrange effective gaze patterns using proximity and emphasis, then zoom out to consider the gestalt effects.

3D flexibility: Refine the priorities for each screen size and build fluid containers that fit dynamic content. Consider each visitor's expectations, recognize that a small number of elements may take priority, and balance flexibility versus usability tradeoffs.

4D patterns: Find reusable design patterns, add transitions between states, and streamline repeated use. Use consistent, modular approaches to build familiarity and ease.

Screens: Sketch the content and functionality on each expected device. Evaluate the viability and value of various layout options, and refine the hierarchy of a chosen one.

Layouts
2D IMPRESSIONS

Layout design helps interfaces make an impression, communicating the information hierarchy in a correlating visual (and technical) one. Compositional tools like emphasis, alignment, and proximity convey relationships and structure the chronological perception of elements, leading visitors through space and time. Words, images, symbols, and space also combine into a gestalt that's perceived as a whole. Readable, usable layouts balance scales and combinations of elements and space. Successful product design creates a visual punch and a pleasant path.

KEY QUESTIONS	EXERCISES
• **Composition:** How do elements affect one another?	Square dance
• **Readability:** Do written elements read well on all screens?	Text measures
• **White space:** When are pauses or divisions needed?	Squint test

COGNITIVE PRINCIPLES

- **Z pattern**
In more complex layout designs, the eyes of Western readers scan in left-to-right horizontal sweeps from the top left to the bottom right of the screen.

- **Proximity**
People perceive elements positioned close together as more related than elements that are farther apart (and this connects to *chunking*: people remember small groups of items more easily than individual ones).

- **Gestalt**
The perception of objects as a whole, not a collection of individual parts.

• Lead the eye

Interaction design is a sequential art: each story has some starting point and some number of steps forward. But there are many options at each step, so the 2D designs must constantly balance competing needs. The initial visitor is trying to get oriented: What is this thing? What can I do here? The returning visitor is looking for signposts: Where's that thing I saw before? What's new?

Visual hierarchy sorts and simplifies experiences. It's storytelling: the order in which we introduce characters, make arguments, or present options. And it's extra important in digital design, where people often skim and scan, looking for points of interest rather than reading comprehensively. Information hierarchy clarifies relative importance; visual hierarchy determines absorption order.

Emphasis and composition are the primary variables in visual hierarchy: the elements that stand out on the screen, and the total gestalt. Strong layouts need a clear focal point, a pleasant path for the eyes, and an overall harmony. Start creating visual hierarchy by emphasizing the most important elements. Position, scale, eye contact, contrast, and repetition are key tools.

> **YOUR EYES HERE**
>
> then here
>
> *then over here*

• Choose a starting point

Position is the first design variable to use when establishing hierarchy.

Left-aligned elements are the most common for Western readers, who tend to start in the top left quadrant of the screen and proceed in a *Z* or *F* pattern through the remaining space. People skimming content are more likely to notice elements placed on the left, and left-aligned text is also considered most readable. (Note: all mentions of left and right in this section would of course be flipped for right-to-left languages.)

Centered elements are another popular starting point. Centering creates a clear, obvious focus for simple images or landing pages. But it cuts the screen into two halves, it's awkward in multicolumn layouts, it's less readable for long text, and it's boring for longer compositions (my professors called center-aligned pages a "tombstone" layout).

Flush-right starting points are unheard of, what are you doing???

Whichever starting point you choose, think about how you're going to maintain that alignment principle throughout the screen and flow.

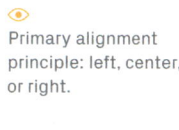

Primary alignment principle: left, center, or right.

• Emphasize the starting point

Position is often not enough to capture someone's eye; strong focal points need emphasis to get past the distraction of other elements on the screen. Traditional storytelling may be cinematic, slowly building suspense into a dramatic climax, but interactive design hierarchies often need to be journalistic, blasting key info before visitors bounce. Don't bury the lede: try some different ways to add emphasis.

Make eye contact

Images get perceived differently than other graphic elements. A circle filled with color and a circle filled with a headshot exert different forces on a composition. Eye-tracking studies show that users look at faces first; they'll even look next at what the subject is looking at. A photo with a face is a strong way to grab and direct viewers' attention (or throw the layout out of balance).

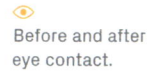

Before and after: eye contact.

Scale things up

A simple tool for emphasis is scale. If something is first in your information hierarchy, make it the biggest. Even if I hate to read, I'll still absorb at least part of a giant headline. If elements are less essential, reduce their size. Let them appear as the second beat or impression. Layouts where everything is the same size can feel like a crowded room or a wall of text.

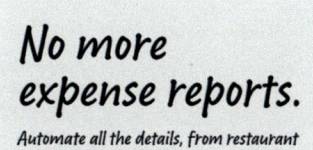

Before and after: scale.

Add tonal contrast

Another core tool for emphasis is contrast. If some text is important, make it bold. If an action is important, make it a solid button. Visual contrast is like the literal quantity of pixels colored: a solid button contains hundreds; an outlined button may only have a few dozen. Tonal contrast can be established even in early grayscale drafts, and then refined in each iteration. Give the most important elements the greatest contrast.

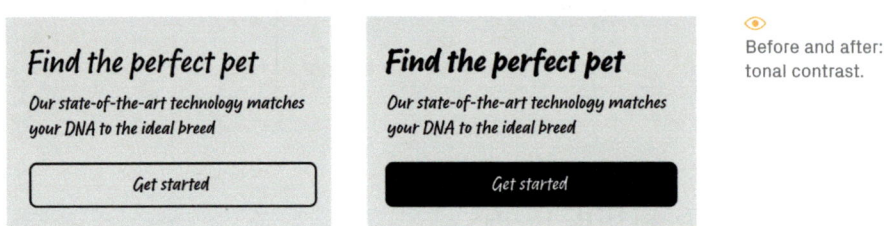

Before and after: tonal contrast.

Add chromatic contrast

Mathematically, the highest possible contrast is white versus black, but color contrasts can be even louder visually. Road signs often have yellow backgrounds with black text because it's maximally attention-getting and legible. Clashing colors like red against cyan can create visual drama or even vibrations. Play with color emphasis.

Add spatial contrast

Depth effects create contrast in artificial 3D, using techniques like overlapping to create obvious emphasis. Try spatial emphasis to increase clarity and usability.

Before and after: spatial contrast.

Add life

Even in 2D, we should remember our 4D tools of motion and transition. Pops of animation can grab attention instantly; fades between states can gently coach the eye across space. Imagine changes over time, and consider motion as an emphasis.

Before and after: motion.

Lead the eye to the next thing

Once you've established a focal point, lead the eye to the next thing in the information hierarchy. See which elements and arrangements create a clear path, and which distract from it.

Go right
The second destination for Western readers is often the top right of the screen (in *F* or *Z* scanning patterns). Second priorities may fit well there, but a pothole to avoid is banner blindness: people have learned that bold blocks on the top or right side of the screen are usually ads, and skip right over them.

Go down
Skimming and reading scenarios often proceed down the left side of the page, from scanning *F* patterns to skimming "layer cakes" to full reading "commitment" patterns. Placing secondary elements in a right-side column is a simple way to de-emphasize them, especially on wide screens.

Go dancing
Hunting or browsing scenarios often have a "spotted" pattern, where the eyes jump around the screen looking for a certain word or image. Alignment is less important in these screens, and creative arrangements can generate a sense of freedom and movement. Strictly aligned layouts can feel lifeless; curving or winding paths can feel more organic and fun, while overlapping or animated elements can feel more surprising or energetic.

"Most users will read very little from a wall of text; support them by chunking your content into sections and bulleted lists, by using meaningful subheadings, and by special visual styling for keywords."

Kara Pernice, "Text Scanning Patterns: Eyetracking Evidence"

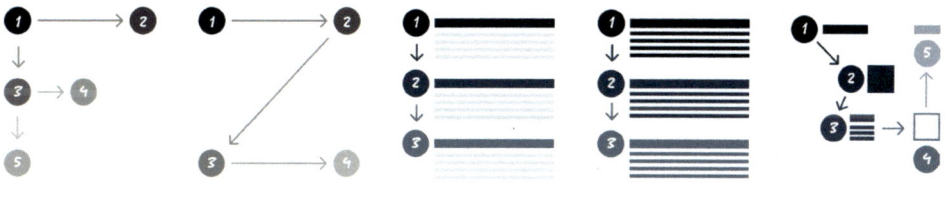

Common gaze patterns: F, Z, "layer cake," "commitment," and "spotted."

Reiterate the priorities

A final way to emphasize something important is to repeat it. Redundancy is a core engineering principle for successful, stable systems, and it's similarly valuable in design.

Consider multiple methods or locations for visitors to accomplish a key objective (e.g., repeating the main CTA at both the top and bottom of a screen). Repeat supporting points to make sure skimming visitors absorb them; repeat structures or visual themes to build a strong brand identity.

What is the main point to get across?

• Analyze the balance

If the layout were placed on a fulcrum, would it tip?

Once a nice path through the layout is clear, zoom out and consider the composition horizontally. Look at the weight of all the elements, as if you're summing up the total number of pixels they contain. More weight on the left is normal for left-to-right languages, but too much can make the design feel like it's going to tip over. Imbalance creates dramatic tension; asymmetrical balance creates harmony; symmetry creates calm.

Imbalance, asymmetrical balance, and symmetrical balance.

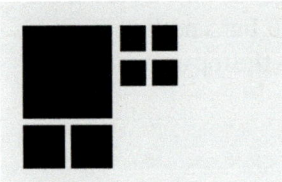 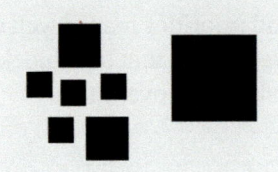 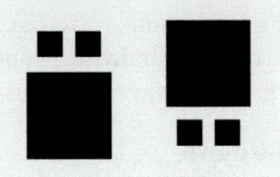

• Analyze the gestalt

Are elements competing for attention or creating a clear visual hierarchy?

The eye may wander around a scene from element to element, but the collection also creates a single impression referred to as the *gestalt*. This may be the imprint that remains in visitors' memories: a fuzzy flash, not an ordered list. Artist David Hockney played with this duality in his photographic pieces, collaging a variety of detailed shots into a shimmering whole. *Pearblossom Highway* (look it up) is not "a sky and a road and a stop sign and a cactus," it's "a desert highway."

A certain emphasis or alignment may be logical on a micro level but disruptive on a macro level. Design is an undulating process of zooming in to analyze the details and zooming out to analyze the gestalt.

EXERCISE: Square dance

Convey brand attributes with different arrangements of shapes in space.

Visual designer

Arranging squares is a classic design school exercise to build your composition skills. It helps you zoom out from design details and see the gestalt—the relationship the elements create.

1. Grab a marker and some sketch paper. Choose a feeling (or a brand attribute) like stability, surprise, happiness, or peacefulness.
2. Using only squares, lay out compositions that convey this feeling. If you want to be practical, lay out signup forms or other simple screens.

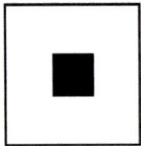 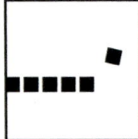 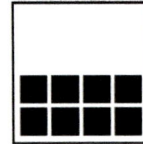 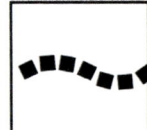  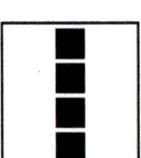

Set readable structures

This is not a visual design book, but we can't create decent screen or component structures without thinking about typography. Experience designers who don't know anything about typography will design layouts that don't work well for reading, which is kind of an important use case for most products.

Readability refers to the speed and ease of reading a piece of text (in contrast to *legibility,* which means that the individual characters are distinct and parsable). Text color, alignment, length, size, and layout all affect readability. These text adjustments also affect the space and shape that components take, so readability considerations need to fit into early iterations, if possible.

Ellen Lupton's books are a great place to start for detailed insights into typography, but also take a look at these five core readability guidelines:

Is the reading experience pleasant at all sizes?

Choose readable contrast levels

A basic test: Can you see the text? Even if we're working in grayscale, we can start to develop semantic, readable color-contrast levels. Accessible shades are often darker than we might expect; check the WCAG for the latest readable color ratios (calculations and guidelines keep evolving). Consider these levels to start.

15%: Non-text elements

30%: Text (absolute minimum)

45%: Large text (minimum)

60%: Paragraph text (minimum)

75%: Paragraph text (preferred minimum)

Use readable alignments

A second foundation is alignment. As mentioned in the last section, clear designs use consistent alignment principles throughout an experience (unless they're going for chaotic feels).

Left-aligned text is most readable in left-to-right languages; make it the default.	Centered text is readable in small quantities or simple layouts, but is more difficult to read in longer passages.	Right-aligned text is slower for Western visitors to read and comprehend, but it can give a poetic or creative feel to layouts.

Create readable line lengths

A larger issue is line length, or *measure;* a text block's width greatly affects its readability. As a reader's eye gets to the end of each line, it has to jump back and find the start of the next one. So line length and height can increase or decrease reading speed (as well as usability and appeal). Just because a container runs full-width doesn't mean the text should.

Traditional guidelines consider 45–75 characters per line optimal for readability, and WCAG AAA standards require line lengths of 80 characters or below. Try somewhere in the 45–80 character range; then see if each component's content feels easy and enjoyable to read at different screen or element sizes.

Readable line lengths: 45–80 characters.

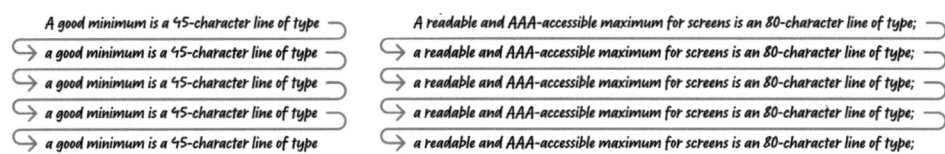

Use readable font sizes

"Use the old familiar [type] scale, or use new scales of your own devising, but limit yourself, at first, to a modest set of distinct and related intervals."

Robert Bringhurst,
The Elements of Typographic Style

Another important issue is font size. Big brands will have specific sizing guidelines for most text elements, but smaller design systems often fail to consider a variety of interactive scenarios. Ideally there will be a type scale (a set list of font sizes). Type scales give designs an overall feeling of cohesiveness and clarity. They build readability, hierarchy, consistency, and adaptability into systems from the start.

Paragraph font size is the most impactful choice for readability. 16pt has come to be the default size for web text, but product designers may need to step up or down the scale for different design scenarios. Consider these adaptations:

- Different typefaces at the same size appear optically larger or smaller. Do some tests in high fidelity to see if sizes are pleasant to read for a particular font.
- Different screen sizes create new line breaks and readability issues. Each text element may need to scale up or down as the screen or component does.
- Different layouts have alternate hierarchies that may require larger sizes for more visual emphasis, or smaller sizes for more density or quietness.

Find a readable font size that also considers hierarchy, screen size, and context.

Good type scales have an even slope.

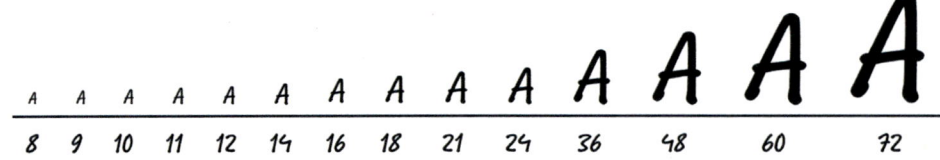

- ## Balance font size and line length

Product designs must balance the quality of the reading experience with the quantity of information displayed. A larger font size may be more readable but not fit much information on a small mobile screen; a smaller font size may be less readable but more usable if someone's trying to skim or compare. Our decisions should serve the particular content and context.

Here's how readability refinements may work in practice.

Let's say we have a 9-column or 1100px-wide layout grid, and the design system specifies 16pt Tiempos Text for body copy (paragraphs). A full-width text box is nearly 110 characters long.

To get the text within readability guidelines (45–80 characters), we could decrease the column width and increase the margins. This can add focus to the text, or leave space for marginalia (or thumbs).

We could also increase the font size. Larger type is usually more legible and readable (especially for older audiences), and often feels more approachable and friendly.

Another option is to narrow the text column. The layout could turn into a multicolumn design, or a main column with a sidebar.

Test a range of text types and scenarios; content is dynamic.

EXERCISE: Text measures

The width of a column of text is also called its *measure*. Designer Trent Walton shared a useful working method for setting a readable measure:

1. Insert an asterisk after 45 and 80 characters.
2. Resize your text box and confirm that the line length is still between the two markers.
3. See if any elements are going to break onto multiple lines; adjust the design accordingly.

Resize text sizes or measures for readability.

Visual designer

• Add breathing room

> "Interactions, both public and private, can be enhanced by a bit of a pause: intermission, the drumroll, the halftime show, the landing strip, the semicolon, interstitial ads, syncopated beats, Hadrian's villa, a moment of silence."
>
> Liz Danzico, "The Power of the Pause"

The final visual design element I insist on adding to this low-fidelity book is nothing: white space.

White space is the air flowing around the furniture, the cushions supporting focal points. It's easy to fill a whole layout with rectangles and feel like you've done something: the text is in a box, clearly a designer has been here! But visual hierarchy requires pauses for emphasis—adding space, not things. If the eye has less to process, the idea is more easily absorbed.

• Create pauses and divisions

What elements need a pause afterwards?

White space assists wayfinding, emphasizing the boundaries between areas. It's also a pause that gives people time to reflect on a section and prepare for the next one. It's a quiet form of emphasis, directing attention by removing distractions. Make layouts taller and give content plenty of room to breathe. A call to action can benefit from a rest afterward; a spacious gap between sections can let each one shine.

• Create closeness and groupings

What elements should be seen as closely related?

Reducing the space between objects creates associations without the clutter of container elements. The *law of proximity* says that things close to each other are perceived as related. Closeness pulls the eye from one thing to the next in an obvious path. Reduce the contrast between related elements. A subhead can nestle beneath its headline; an image can snuggle beside or beneath its description.

• Create rhythm and consistency

What spacing scales can be systematized?

Objects and spaces create a vertical rhythm as eyes move down a screen; the spaces are the pauses in the music. They can be systemized just like font and component sizes. A common approach is to pick a standard unit (e.g., 4 or 8 pixels), and make all vertical sizes and spaces multiples of that.

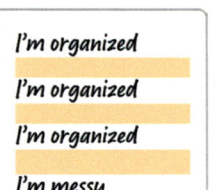

White space creates pauses, groupings, and rhythms.

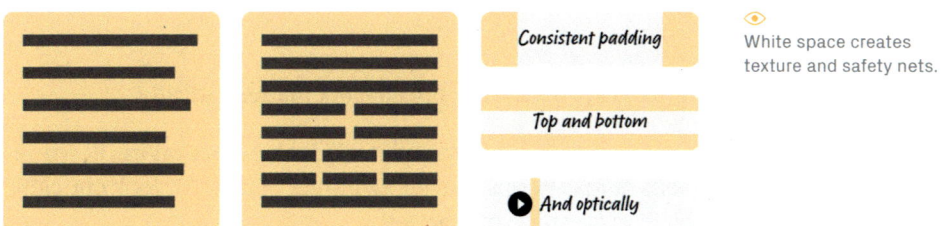

White space creates texture and safety nets.

• Create weight or texture

The quantity and arrangement of elements on a screen creates density or lightness. Full-width, justified arrangements create long gray tapestries, whereas sporadic, clustered elements blur into weighty blocks that pull the eye across space. Layouts can feel floaty with no clear structure, or anchored by grids and containers. But "clutter" is relative; cultures with logographic languages often prefer a much denser display of information. Find the right density for the particular audience.

How do elements fill up or cluster in space?

• Create safety nets

If I want to judge a designer's attention to detail, I look at their box and button padding—it's the smallest expression of their spacing system and their ability to see white space. Padding affects not only perception, but also usability. Well-padded buttons are more user-friendly; the larger the touch target, the faster it is to use (see Fitts's law). Print pages have left and right padding for thumbs to hold; mobile devices often need the same affordance. Look at the space inside each element.

Are similar elements consistently and usably padded?

• Remember readability

A final type of white space is the vertical space between the lines (known as *leading* or *line-height*). Wider columns need more leading to help the eye find the start of the next long line; narrower columns can be denser. Loose leading gives layouts an airier feeling; tight leading creates dense blocks. Sentence-case text may be more legible with more white space; all-caps text blurs into a nice block with less space.

How do spacing principles flow into text?

Tight leading makes text a darker element on the page, a dense block of information. It's better for narrow columns but if I wrote this whole book with tight leading, you'd read much more slowly because your eye would have to fight to find the next line. The font's ascenders and descenders could start to run into each other, yuck.

BUT BUTTONS AND ALL CAPS ELEMENTS LOOK CLEANER WITH TIGHT LEADING

Loose leading makes text a lighter element. The lines float individually; the eye has plenty of breathing room. It's better for wide columns; it's nice for minimalist sites without a lot of text. It feels a bit like a poem or a Hollywood script, with room for interpretation.

• Use your eye

> "Music is the space between the notes."
> Claude Debussy

> "Design is as much an act of spacing as an act of marking."
> Ellen Lupton,
> *Thinking with Type*

Sophisticated spacing systems are balanced optically, not mathematically.

Vertically center any element mathematically, and it will look like it's falling down the page (the splash screens of many apps provide examples of this). To look optically centered, items need a bit of extra space underneath.

Horizontally center an asymmetrical element mathematically, and it will look off balance (try centering the triangle in a "play" button). Optical centering will align the item's visual center of mass, not the center of the frame containing it.

Try to see white space as water and balance the amount flowing around the elements.

• Express the brand

All these spacing guidelines will vary according to aesthetic. Web designers tend to use looser leading than print designers; poetic brands will use more space than technical ones. Develop and return to design principles to maintain a consistent approach.

EXERCISE: Squint test

Check visual hierarchy and paths.

 Visual designer

To test the hierarchy of a composition, use the *squint test*. Yes, this is an actual thing taught in art school. Take a layout and squint at it. (For more details, also use eye-tracking tools.)

1. What do you notice first? Is there an obvious and appropriate starting point?
2. Where do your eyes go from there? Is it a smooth path or a jumpy one? Is it okay for the use case?
3. Does the visual hierarchy match the information hierarchy? If an element is popping out of order, count your styles. One or two levels of emphasis is enough to make a visual distinction.

REMEMBER: LAYOUTS

Lead the eye	Square dance	Z pattern
Set readable structures	Text measures	Proximity
Add breathing room	Squint test	Gestalt

Flexibility
3D IMPRESSIONS

Digital designs are moving targets; their environments, forms, and cultural contexts change constantly. People may use handheld or projected screens; experiences may happen on multiple devices sequentially or simultaneously. Containers are maddeningly uncertain, and so is content: designs may pull from databases that are empty, full, or overflowing. Scalable design systems will adjust priorities, formats, and layouts for each scenario. Successful product design makes a good impression at any scale, in any state.

KEY QUESTIONS	EXERCISES
• **Hierarchy**: What do the visitor and the business need most?	Priority lists
• **Structure**: How could containers arrange and rearrange?	Content blocking
• **Limits**: How minimal or maximal might the content be?	Null / full states

COGNITIVE PRINCIPLES

- **The 80/20 rule**
  80 percent of the consequences in a system come from 20 percent of the causes (and so it's wise to focus resources on that critical 20 percent).

- **Expectation effect**
  People's expectations for a person or thing change their behaviors toward and perceptions of it (from placebo to halo to Pygmalion effects).

- **Flexibility-usability tradeoff**
  The more flexible and less specialized a system is, the more complex and less usable it will be.

• Refine the hierarchies

"If there are too many seminal ideas, this is a sign that they are not seminal."

Umberto Eco, *Confessions of a Young Novelist*

Information hierarchy is the relative prioritization of elements on a page. If visitors only notice one thing, what should it be? If only two, what's the second?

Hierarchy is a universal tool for any device and any project; designers should check it constantly. Without clear hierarchy, design is noise.

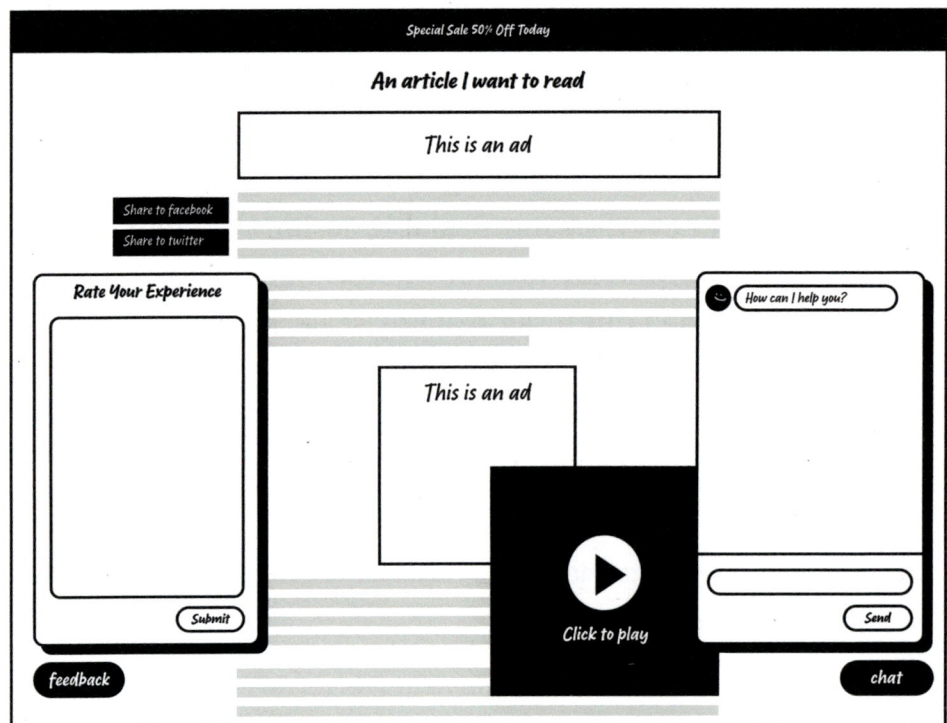

Complex commercial websites often have a horrible lack of hierarchy (see how-i-experience-web-today.com).

• Sort the priorities for each screen

A numbered list is the easiest way to organize information hierarchy, and a great first step for any layout. Sort the content from universal, valuable, and must-know to niche, supplemental, or nice-to-know. Get the team to agree.

Some industries have distinct storytelling patterns to leverage or leapfrog, so analogous research and audits can help with the content strategy part. Startups, for example, all need to explain their unique value and persuade visitors to convert, so their landing pages tend to have a common format:

1. **Unique selling proposition:** headline, supporting information, and CTA
2. **Hero image / video:** product demo, metaphor, lifestyle image, or data viz
3. **Benefits:** value to audience
4. **Social proof:** customer logos or stats
5. **Call to action:** repeated CTA for emphasis

Sometimes you have license to make things up; other times the work is to rearrange existing content. Here's a list I made to redesign a hurricane relief site:

1. **Urgent announcements:** e.g., "the Rockaways are closed to volunteers"
2. **Demonstration of need:** summary of disaster, photos or statistics showing scale
3. **Donation CTAs:** links to registries, list of supplies needed, map of drop-off locations
4. **Volunteer info:** instructions, map, signup form, training event schedule
5. **Retention hooks:** field for newsletter, follow buttons for social media
6. **News feed:** social media highlights
7. **Resources:** links for affected communities
8. **FAQ:** info to lighten some of the inbound email load
9. **Footer:** mission, impact, contact info, exit links

Note that information hierarchy does not always define the exact order things should appear in, just their importance. Graphic design will determine the visual hierarchy.

• Recognize the character of each device

Each device has certain strengths and limits that affect visitors' priorities at each step.

Unique hardware
Small screens have different hardware and software behind them, so each flow might need to be rethought to leverage specific native features. Mobile devices can easily ask users to connect their cameras, address books, photo libraries, or wallets, and people often expect to speak or swipe, not click or type. On desktop displays people often expect larger images, text, or data tables. Leverage device strengths.

What built-in features could I use?

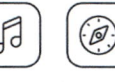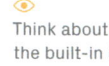

👁 Think about integrating the built-in hardware, software, and data of each device.

Standard systems
Each device has built-in capabilities and standard interaction patterns, but the flow will differ if it's following Google's Material Design guidelines on an Android device, or Apple's Human Interface Guidelines on an iPhone. Know the local language (and stay up to date with its evolutions).

What design language do people already know?

Perceived purpose

Why are people using this device?

Designing for one device or another is not just about screen size—people have different feelings about each one. Laptops and desktops may be "work stations"; tablets are often treated more like toys; mobile devices are the most intimate. But people may pick up their phone because it's close at hand, not because it's the "right" device for the experience. Know users' habits.

Multichannel tasks

Which steps might require a certain device?

People often start a task on one device but finish on another. For instant access they'll grab their phone, but if tasks require a lot of comparison or organization they often switch to larger screens. Think about the channels people might start in, and when they might switch to a smaller or larger device. Imagine cross-device transitions.

Companion devices

How might another screen complement a primary one?

Devices may serve as sister screens; people often use multiple devices at once (e.g., chatting on their phone while looking at something on a computer). A TV might serve as a background experience, a computer as a work experience, a tablet as a leisure experience, a phone as a conversational experience, a watch as an alert experience. And with the ever-expanding Internet of Things, a refrigerator or bicycle or wearable might provide a correlating experience! Imagine multiscreen scenarios.

	Look up	Explore	Compare	Organize	Purchase
Print catalog	Table of contents Index	Immersive photography	Flip pages back and forth	N/A *(flip pages back and forth)*	Order by phone Order by mail Order online
Website	Search box	Catalog-like browsing	Table view of selected items	Favorites Wish list / Gift registry	Standard checkout Expedited checkout Order by phone
Tablet app	Search box Voice input	Catalog-like browsing	Table view of selected items	Favorites Wish lists	Expedited checkout Standard checkout
Mobile app	Search box Voice input Barcode scanner	Browse by category	N/A *(impractical due to screen size)*	Save items Editing *(limited ability)*	Expedited checkout
Physical store	Clear signage Store map Helpful staff	Wander the aisles	Compare side by side Ask staff	Gift registry / Wish list	Staff assistance Self-checkout Scan-as-you-go
Shared assets	Product taxonomy *All channels powered by a single set of categories*		Compare engine *Web and tablet run by one component*	Universal favs *List shared by all digital channels*	Checkout flow *Universal process for digital channels*

COMPARE Channel-specific features and shared assets in each phase of retail flows (Tyler Tate's Cross-Channel Blueprint, CC 3.0)

- ### Use small screens to force prioritization

    When fitting content on screens, the most difficult scenario is usually a tiny phone. It's good to get that worst-case scenario solved first, and then use it to help you finalize the information hierarchy. On large screens you can keep adding elements to satisfy every stakeholder; on small screens that's simply impossible. Because mobile designs usually consist of one column, maybe two, proceeding in fairly linear order, they're a great way to force a conversation about priorities and creative solutions. Hierarchies are usually not identical on every device, but phones can help you force at least one.

What should we cut or add on a small-screen design?

Mobile layouts force decisions on hierarchy.

- ### Use large screens to inspire exploration

    Larger screens are different experiences, not just scaled-up ones. Consider the different goals and modes of a visitor on a tablet versus a laptop, a second monitor, or a TV.

How might we use extra space?

Bigger screens can hold different content (based on Vasilis van Gemert's "Logical Breakpoints for Responsive Design").

More content?
Responsive design is not just about restyling content; it's also about adding or removing it. Identify the must-have features (article text and navigation, for example), and focus on those in small screens. Save the high-bandwidth or less-essential ones (e.g., comments or related content) for more spacious places.

More navigation?
On larger screens, we don't have to hide all our submenus behind a button. Visibility increases clicks; showing more links by default often improves usability.

More images?
Larger screens can show more images at a time, which is super helpful if the user wants to compare things visually or browse reams of options. Swipeable slideshows may be fun on mobile, but image grids may be nicer on desktop. Ten images per page may be fine for a mobile gallery, but annoyingly sparse on a cinema display.

Larger images?
Extra space can hold larger images, so a viewer can see more detail. Fewer bandwidth constraints means it won't cost users to load a high-res image. If a company has invested in great photography, show it off! Fashion sites often pop a full-screen image if visitors show their interest with a click, or just fill extra space with larger images. This makes life easier for both the designers and the developers.

Larger fonts?

You can always use extra space to make the text bigger. It's a lot of fun to do huge chunky headlines on the web. Show off the nice typefaces you're licensing.

Larger margins?

You could also make your typography better with more white space. Add extra left and right margins to keep your body text at a readable line-length, or increase the line-height for a calmer vertical rhythm.

"We always design all screens simultaneously. Not mobile first or desktop first. The moment we have an idea for a component or a layout we try it on all screens at the same time and see if it makes sense across the board. Sometimes something that works on desktop does not translate well on touch devices and vice versa."

Design studio Anton & Irene

EXERCISE: Priority lists

Write a numbered list of the elements that must be on the screen, in order of importance.

 Researcher
 Strategist
 Subject expert
 Engineer

Listing information hierarchy is a simple but effective exercise to make sure everyone agrees on the priorities for each screen.

1. List all elements that must be included on the screen, in order of importance. Consider:
   - Audience priorities (the most helpful or valuable things for their goals)
   - Strategic priorities (key competitive differentiators)
   - Business priorities (the most revenue or retention-generating elements)
   - Brand priorities (visual and emotional hallmarks for brand consistency)
   - Engineering priorities (the fastest or smartest things to load first)
2. Create variations of the list for different hardware, software, or screen sizes. (For example, mobile visitors might want lower-bandwidth content or extra features like camera usage.)
3. Review the lists with stakeholders and revise until everyone agrees.

• Build fluid containers

Product design *always* involves a variety of phones, computers, or tablets, so we can't ever pick one single size for designs. But it's easy to slip into fixed thinking when viewing a single layout; one of the most common issues I see in critiques is precisely arranged layouts that shatter on smaller, larger, fuller, or less-full screens. Train your brain to look for flexible, fluid layout systems that adapt to any container.

"Disruption will only accelerate. The quantity and diversity of connected devices—many of which we haven't imagined yet—will explode, as will the quantity and diversity of the people around the world who use them."

Jeremy Keith, *Resilient Web Design*

👁 Responsive designs are systems, not things.

• Think in digital metaphors

Design software often presents rigid boxes to fill in; a few habits of mind can help us stay loose.

Say "screens," not "pages"
The words we use shape the possibilities we see. Software defaults like "artboards" or "canvases" can create mental models of static pages, as in a magazine. But in digital design each screen is a *window,* not a page. Each button is a *bubble,* not a brick. Notice your language, critique its connotations, and update your metaphors.

See components, not screens
It's easier to imagine (and create) responsive components than whole websites. Typography, copywriting, and even logos can adapt to their surroundings. Always keep an eye out for modular patterns within each screen. It often helps to return to extremely low fidelity and work with blocks, not individual symbols.

Spend time in code
When you see a beautiful site, resize your browser window back and forth like a real web designer and notice when and how the layout shifts. Prototype in interactive mediums so you feel a design's personality.

Show multiplicity, not singularity
Help collaborators remember the range of containers for a system. Mock up screen size variations side by side to convey the multiplicity of each design (and to help people spot the differences).

"Fluid grids, flexible images, and media queries are the three technical ingredients for responsive web design, but it also requires a different way of thinking."

Ethan Marcotte, "Responsive Web Design"

Which elements must always be fully visible? Which ones can hide until needed?

Consider 3D layers in space

How might the invisible become visible? What qualities might the new space have?

Print design has one layer; digital design has infinite layers. Pause before cramming every element into one rectangle, and think about using visibility and depth instead.

A pixel grid is a flat field to fill, but also a collection of optical illusions. Visual effects can trick the eye into perceiving a third dimension; I'm always amazed at how a simple gray gradient convinces my brain that a menu is floating above a background.

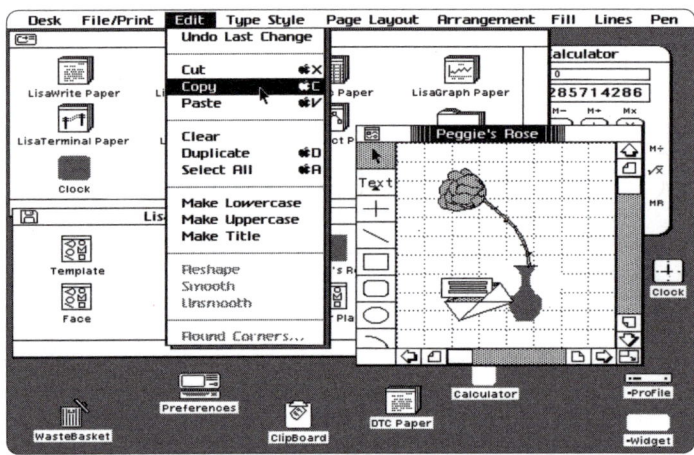

Apple's original Lisa desktop used overlapping menus and panels on a "desktop" metaphor. Modern systems still frequently use "window" and "folder" metaphors.

Artificial 3D gives us a suite of additional design options. Gestures allow us to navigate spatially, pulling or pushing additional elements into view. Layers can rearrange existing elements or overlap them. New components can have a fixed position and size, or the ability to move and resize. If a feature is hidden, consider some options for when and how it appears in space. Think about systems of elevation.

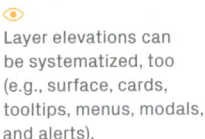

Layer elevations can be systematized, too (e.g., surface, cards, tooltips, menus, modals, and alerts).

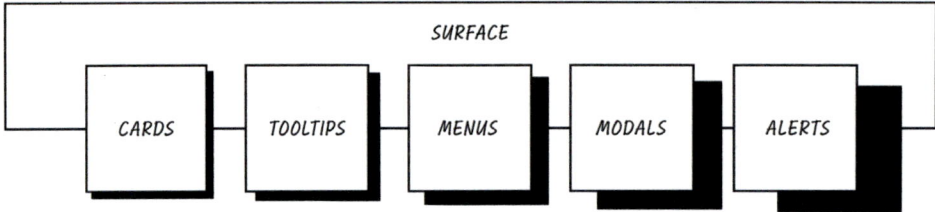

Remember 4D layers of time

There are many ways to place each element in space, but we can also use the variable of time. The most frequently used tools generally need visible real estate on the screen, but secondary features may hide in a panel that appears, a menu that drops down, or some other invisible container. Very important features may have both visible triggers and invisible access (like keyboard shortcuts).

Layout audits are a helpful way to analyze inspiration and sharpen your eye. Google Docs (left) hides a lot of functionality in menus; Scrivener (right) allows extra functionality to be always accessible or easily hidden.

Visibility preferences oscillate along with minimalism and usability preferences. Clear and familiar tabs used to be the default navigation pattern; then space-saving hamburger menus became popular; then obvious tabs became popular again because visible elements get more clicks. Return to each screen's priority list for direction.

- Create architectural principles and parameters

Once a layout is blocked out, explode it. Design structures must adapt to multiple screen sizes and proportions: screens may be small or large, vertical or horizontal, and widths do not stay proportional to heights.

Which widths are fixed? When do fluid elements change?

Typical responsive screen widths.

Each layout can be fixed-width or fully flexible, but steady underlying principles will increase consistency across the world of devices. Consider common ratios:

- *The rule of thirds:* A visual principle dating back to the 1700s, the rule of thirds says to place key elements one or two thirds of the way across and down your layouts. (Many photography apps now provide these guidelines automatically to encourage better compositions.)

- *The golden ratio:* A similar principle is the golden ratio, strongly associated with the Fibonacci sequence and found in nature as spirals. The ratio of the two parts is equal to the ratio of the sum to the larger part (i.e., $a/b = (a+b)/a$, or 1.618:1). It's more like fifths than thirds, with proportions roughly 3:2 (62%/38%).

- *Custom grids:* Any ratio can be pleasing if it suits the situation; the Parthenon uses a 4:9 ratio for its famous harmony. Web developers often default to a 12-column grid, but print designers often use odd numbers of columns for more interesting or usable structures. Look for a balance that suits the particular content. (This book needed a certain width for its gutters and roughly twice that for marginalia; those constraints plus the page size led to an 11-column layout grid.)

THINK IN 4D // FLEXIBILITY // 103

How do elements adapt to changing devices?

Decide how layout variations will affect each specific element. Certain content will not display or function well at all sizes.

- *Size:* Is that left-side column always 20 percent wide, no matter how big the screen gets, or does it have a maximum? Does that window require a minimum width to work? Are input areas the same size on all devices?
- *Position:* Does a nav bar stay on the left side on all devices, float to the top on narrow screens, or slide to the bottom of touch screens for easier thumb access?
- *Control:* Are qualities like width, height, position, or visibility adjustable by the user? What symbols indicate this capability?

• Offer alternate views or modes if needed

Which use cases need specific, standalone designs?

If you can't decide between two layouts, the answer might be "both." Alternate views can let people see and use the same content in two ways (for example, as a list view and a map view of locations). To prevent errors, make sure it's very clear which mode the user is in.

- *Views:* Would the information benefit from multiple arrangements to serve different scenarios? Do multiple architectural metaphors make sense (e.g., list, grid, column, or map views)?
- *Modes:* Is content always editable, or is it sometimes locked? Can people see preview modes before actions are committed? Are there different editing workflows to serve (retouching mode versus animation mode, for example)?

EXERCISE: Content blocking

Explore a variety of layout options quickly and easily.

 Visual designer

 Engineer

Colored box wireframes are fast ways to plan fluid templates, turning information hierarchy into visual hierarchy.

1. Start with a prioritized list of needed elements. Group similar things into larger buckets if possible (e.g., a toolbar, a sidebar, an article header).
2. Arrange the buckets according to audience priorities, interface metaphors, or web standards (e.g., search bars at the top right, navigation bars on the bottom on mobile).
3. Refine each bucket's size and behavior according to its expected content. Remember visible and invisible states; not everything has to appear all the time.

Prepare for live content

Responsive design means that containers are fluid; digital design means that the content is too. A headline might be one line or many; a bio might be one word or one paragraph; a user might submit all the optional info or none of it. Fully responsive systems prepare for a spectrum of content states.

"Designers working with static tools have had a tendency to only design best-case scenarios."

Brad Frost, *Atomic Design*

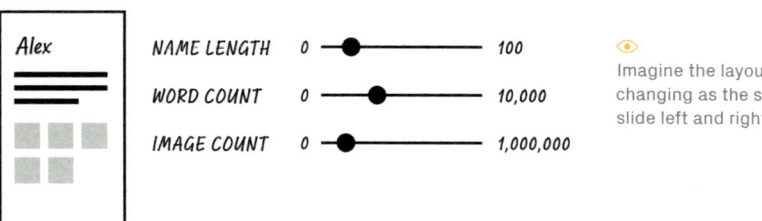

Imagine the layout changing as the sliders slide left and right.

Design for no content

Mockups might show a finished state, but it takes users some work or luck to get there. Consider emptiness: the "null" state in a database. Zero search results, 404 file not found pages, empty folders, and zero submissions are open opportunities for delightful moments. Evernote's null states give tips on how to do more with the app, while Sunrise's empty to-do list celebrates that accomplishment. Slack's reaction search shows a "crying" emoji if you get no results. Chrome has a dinosaur jumping game people can play when the internet is down.

What might visitors appreciate on "empty" screens? Does an empty element disappear, or show a null state?

Design for all the content

Mockups might present a simple list, but actual databases might yield hundreds or thousands of results. For each device, estimate the quantity of results the audience finds useful on each screen. Consider different ways to reveal more: pagination, infinite scroll, or other patterns. Set limits for user contributions if needed (maximum character or word counts, for example).

How does the design handle "too many" results?

Design for real people

Mockups might use top-notch photos that look great and impress everyone, but real designs look very different once people submit their own. We often design a "just right" scenario, but a strong template must handle the weirdness and rawness of real life. Real names vary greatly in length and in structure; real photos have a variety of styles. If designs depend on excellent user-generated content, you may want to help people with some starter content or image libraries to choose from.

How do designs look with real content?

• Design for translation

How do designs hold up in other languages?

Mockups might exist in your native language, but people might not. If a site is multilingual, text can vary greatly in length. German is famous for exploding carefully designed navigations. Right-to-left languages may flip a design's hierarchy. Even if your site is in a single language, headlines can vary greatly in length.

• Design for privacy

What might people want to keep hidden?

Certain content might not be appropriate for all viewers or contexts. Spoiler alerts or NSFW flags can help people avoid seeing things they don't want to see. Consider both positive and negative relationships between a creator and an audience—the viewer might be a controlling parent or an abusive ex. Take advantage of personal devices, but also design for shared, insecure, potentially embarrassing contexts.

EXERCISE: Null / full states

Plan for no content and all the content.

Visual designer
Engineer

Revisit each component and design states that accommodate changing content.

1. **Null state:** Nothing has been entered or found. Does the visitor need coaching? Could the design prevent this empty state?
2. **Partial state:** One, two, or several things have been entered or found. Do they need different treatments or progress indicators?
3. **Full state:** The container has reached its maximum capacity. Does this mean something is "done"?
4. **Overfull state:** There is more content than space allotted. Does it cut off, scroll, paginate, or trigger an error?

REMEMBER: FLEXIBILITY

Refine the hierarchies

 Priority lists

 The 80/20 rule

Build fluid containers

 Content blocking

 Expectation effect

Prepare for live content

 Null / full states

 Flexibility-usability tradeoff

Patterns
4D IMPRESSIONS

Impressions over time become an experience, and visitors can see the consistencies or discrepancies among many different screens and symbols. Smart systems thinking breaks ideas down into modular elements and recombines them in consistent ways to form cohesive experiences. Patterns may be graphic, typographic, functional, or structural; each pattern also has its own micro-timeline of states, transitions, and timing. Successful product design uses consistent patterns to increase familiarity and ease.

KEY QUESTIONS	EXERCISES
• **Repetition:** Which symbols can and should be reused?	Components
• **States:** How does each element change over time?	Transitions
• **Retention:** Does the experience bring people back?	Loops

COGNITIVE PRINCIPLES

- **Modularity**
The degree to which a system's components can be replaced, split apart, or recombined with others to provide flexibility and variety in use.

- **Consistency**
The level of aesthetic and functional similarity in the design and usage of components, both internally (within the system) and externally (within industry conventions).

- **Mere-exposure effect**
The tendency of people to develop a preference for things simply because they are familiar.

Reuse functional patterns

> "Each pattern describes [...] the core of the solution to [a] problem, in a way that you can use this solution a million times over, without ever doing it the same way twice."
>
> Christopher Alexander, *A Pattern Language*

It's easy to think of digital experiences as linear progressions like books or movies, but interactive design is exponentially more complex. Content appears in multiple places and contexts, and visitors follow a variety of paths, so digital designs need print-style navigation systems like pagination and indexes, plus uniquely interactive constructs like forms and transitions. The larger the project, the more important it is to find patterns and reuse them.

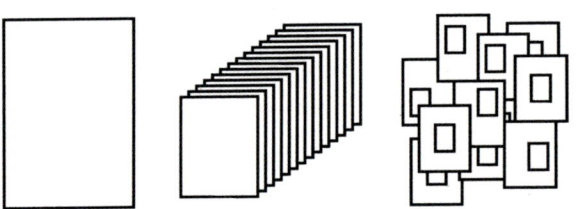

Posters, books, and sites each manifest increasing levels of complexity, and the need for patterns increases proportionally.

Design systems, not screens

> "Our first design system at GE [...] was purposely done to drive adoption of design standards by a team of 10 designers trying to get some 40,000 software developers globally to make consistent-looking software."
>
> Jeff Crossman, "GE's Predix Design System"

Design systems are collections of principles, styles, and components that standardize choices across many screens and contributors. They're Lego sets for building interfaces. Engineering teams like NASA have used them for decades, but newer design software and approaches empower visual designers too.

Creating and managing a design system is such a complex task that it has become its own career specialty, so designers often need to use or expand an existing system rather than building everything from scratch. Moreover, digital design has progressed past the time when we needed to invent the wheel, and people don't always care to learn a different interface model for each site they visit. So, designing systematically often means constantly zooming out to see if patterns already exist and then choosing ones with the right functional and communicative qualities for the project at hand.

If we do have (or want to create) a unique scenario, designing systematically means clearly defining the parameters for each new pattern, reusing relevant pieces of other patterns, and refining all the multidimensional details. If interaction models or visual styles change unnecessarily from screen to screen, visitors will be confused and codebases will be bloated.

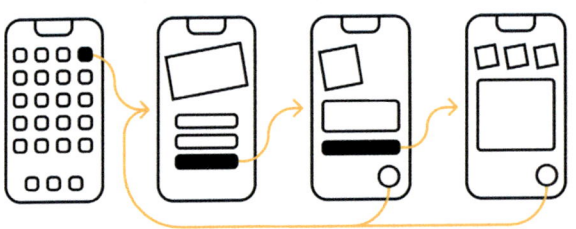

Patterns create consistency across time.

The core idea of a design system is modularity, but the exact layers and labels depend on the project, team, and tools. Brad Frost's popular book *Atomic Design* broke things down into pages, templates, organisms, molecules, and atoms; a system by GE called its layers applications, features, templates, components, basics, and principles. Conceptually, I think of a design system as consisting of five layers:

Root-level **principles** provide consistent rationales for initial and ongoing design choices (e.g., mental models, interaction metaphors, stylistic priorities).

Brand **palettes** specify 2D or 4D styles (e.g., color, typefaces, spacing, images, sounds, transition variables), ideally split into design *primitives* (the options in the palette, such as dark blue or Helvetica) and design *tokens* (the rules for application, e.g., links are dark blue).

Principles and palettes combine into simple interface **elements** that work in any context with any content (e.g., buttons, checkboxes, fields).

Larger **components** or modules standardize functionality and layout choices for specific contexts or content (e.g., lists, banners, pagination).

Architectural **templates** provide consistent structural containers for similar content (e.g., profiles, galleries, articles).

COMPARE Semantic levels in a design system

"The whole reason any of this even started and why we want to display these things in a uniform or unified way is all about the brand, because brand isn't just logos. It's how people use and experience your company's service or product."

Jina Anne, "What Are Design Tokens?"

Let's look at different types of patterns. A lot of systems lump components into a gigantic alphabetical list, but I think it's helpful to look separately at functional groups: graphic, typographic, input, action, container, and architecture patterns. The following spread has a collage of patterns for easy reference.

Once again, our field does not have standard terminology, so I've included alternate names in common use. (Yes, some of these patterns could go in multiple categories. Fight me.)

COMPARE Interface patterns, grouped functionally (next page)

TYPOGRAPHIC

H1 ## H2 ### H3 #### H4 ##### H5 ###### H6

Paragraph paragraph paragraph paragraph paragraph paragraph

`<code code code code>`

Page Header
Subheader

1. Ordered List
2. Ordered List
3. Ordered List

- Bulleted List
- Bulleted List
- Bulleted List

Definition List: means this
Definition List: means this
Definition List: means this

Tooltip / ⓘ

BADGE

ⓘ Alert / Notification

Snackbar / Toast

Chat / Messaging
Chat / Messaging

"Block quote quote quote quote"
Cite / Author

Label
[   ]
Hint

FIGURE CAPTION

GRAPHIC

Photo | Video 01:20 | Map | Pattern | Chart | Image List / Grid

Avatar | Avatar Group +3 | Logo | Stepper / Timeline | Progress Ring | Progress Bar | Spinner

Chip | Icon | Divider / Rule | Doodle | Progress Tracker > Step > Step

---

ACTION

☰ App Bar ▾ ⋯

Breadcrumb → Parent → Child → You are here

Menubar | File | Edit | View

Button Bar | Buttons | Button Group

← | 1 | 2 | Pagination | 4 | 5 | →

B *I* U ≡ ≡ ≡ 🔗 📎 🖼 🙂

Launchpad

Tabs | Tabs | Tabs | **Tabs**

Button | + Button | +

Tag ✕   Tag ✕

Toolbar / Utility Bar

Clickable Icon

Link

○ ○ ● ○ ○
Carousel Indicator

⏮ ▶ ⏭
Playback Controls

👤 Nav Drawer
📁 Nav Drawer
⭐ Nav Drawer

Nav Rail

▾ Disclosure Menu
  ▸ Child
  ▸ Child

📁 Directory Tree
  📁 Child
  📁 Ooh ooh

ARCHITECTURE

Big 3 (search see browse) | Feed (sorted stream) | Grid (visual browser) | 2-panel selector | 1-window drilldown

INPUT

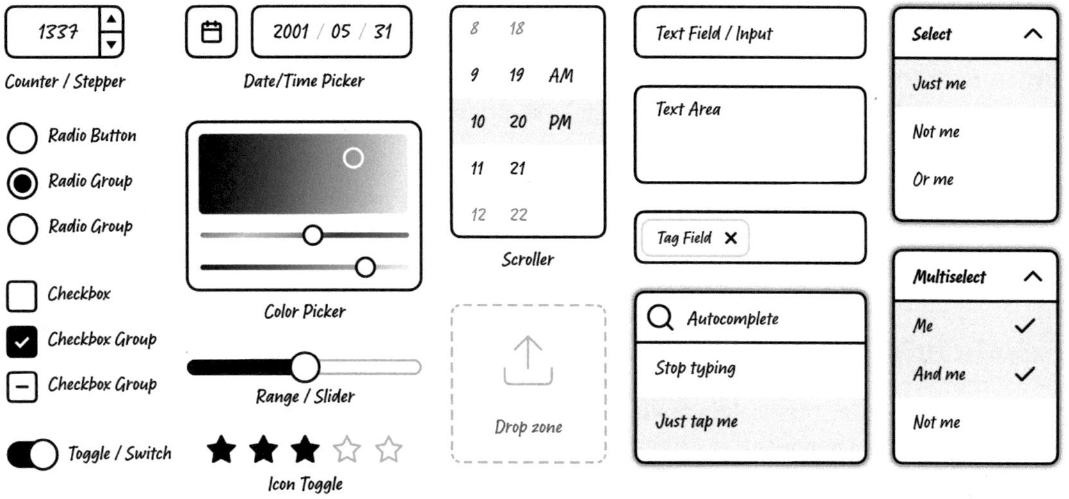

- Counter / Stepper: 1337
- Date/Time Picker: 2001 / 05 / 31
- Scroller: 8, 9 19 AM, 10 20 PM, 11 21, 12 22
- Text Field / Input
- Text Area
- Tag Field ✕
- Select: Just me, Not me, Or me
- Radio Button
- Radio Group (selected)
- Radio Group
- Color Picker
- Autocomplete / Stop typing / Just tap me
- Multiselect: Me ✓, And me ✓, Not me
- Checkbox
- Checkbox Group (checked)
- Checkbox Group (indeterminate)
- Range / Slider
- Drop zone
- Toggle / Switch
- Icon Toggle (★★★☆☆)

CONTAINER

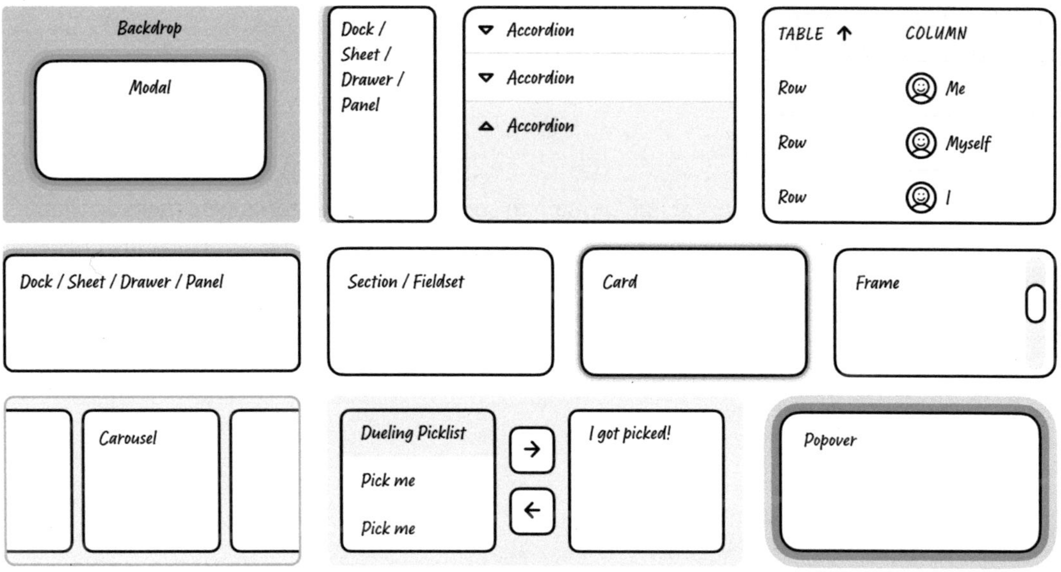

- Backdrop / Modal
- Dock / Sheet / Drawer / Panel
- Accordion / Accordion / Accordion
- Table ↑ / Column — Row: Me, Row: Myself, Row: I
- Dock / Sheet / Drawer / Panel
- Section / Fieldset
- Card
- Frame
- Carousel
- Dueling Picklist: Pick me, Pick me → I got picked!
- Popover

ARCHITECTURE

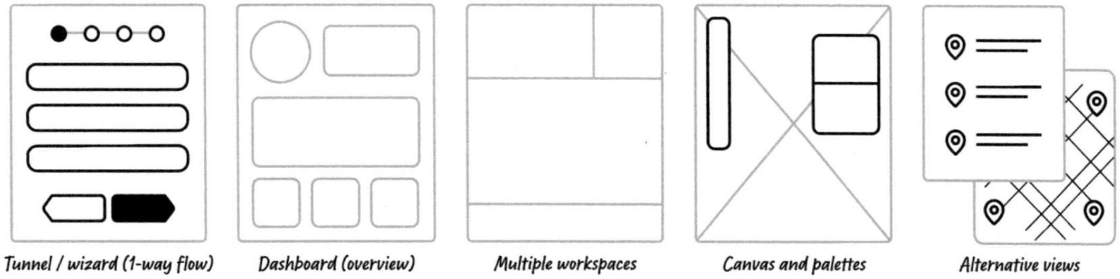

- Tunnel / wizard (1-way flow)
- Dashboard (overview)
- Multiple workspaces
- Canvas and palettes
- Alternative views

THINK IN 4D // PATTERNS // 111

- ## Create typographic patterns

Text patterns include both the standard elements found in HTML (or other languages) and larger structures for different verbal communication patterns. Designers should use a consistent system of type styles across all components. Understand semantics—what a text element is—and make sure its form follows its distinct function.

H1–H6 • Paragraph • Code • Page header • Subheader • List (ordered, bulleted, definition) • Tooltip • Badge • Alert/Notification • Snackbar/Toast • Chat/Messaging • Blockquote • Cite/Author • Label • Hint • Figure caption

- ## Create graphic patterns

Many people describe themselves as visual learners (validated statistics are hard to find, but in my experience it's a majority), so graphic patterns are often popular and usable choices. Make sure graphics are consistent aesthetically and functionally. If they're interactive, consider how the styling might differ to let people know what's clickable and what's not.

Photo • Video • Map • Pattern • Chart • Image list / Grid • Avatar • Facepile • Logo • Stepper • Progress (ring, bar, spinner, Tracker/Path) • Chip • Icon • Divider/Rule • Doodle

- ## Create action patterns

Usability principles say that users should remain in control; action patterns help them do that. They allow navigation or reformatting of the experience, and may capture information at the same time. Progressive disclosure is a frequent principle to consider: Should all options show up immediately, or could some pieces hide until needed?

App bar • Breadcrumb • Menubar • Buttonbar • Launchpad • Tabs (horizontal, vertical) • Button (default, icon, floating action) • Pagination • Tag/Chip/Pill • Toolbar / Utility bar • Clickable icon • Link • Carousel indicator • Playback controls • Navigation (rail, drawer) • Disclosure menu • Directory tree

- ## Create input patterns

Interactive systems need information, and input patterns gather it. Designers should know the existing components in the chosen programming language and familiar patterns for similar contexts. Input patterns should be consistent internally (with one another) and may be consistent externally (with other standards). Consider both usability and aesthetics.

Counter/Stepper • Radio button • Radio group • Checkbox • Checkbox group • Toggle/Switch • Date / Time picker • Color picker • Range/Slider • Icon toggle • Scroller • Drop zone • Text field / Input • Text area • Tag field • Autocomplete / Lookup menu • Dropdown/Select • Multiselect

- **Create container patterns**

    Containers help organize, emphasize, or hide content. Proximity is the underlying principle for containers: Which elements are similar and should be grouped? What style of grouping will communicate elements' meaning and functionality? Styles can be skeuomorphic or novel.

    Backdrop • Modal/Dialog • Dock/Sheet/Drawer/Panel (bottom, side) • Accordion • Table • Section/Fieldset • Card • Frame • Carousel • Dueling picklist • Popover/Popup

- **Create architecture patterns**

    Architecture patterns templatize entire sections or screens, both to convey the organization or functionality of the experience (the information architecture) and to help visitors remain oriented as they move through time. Jennifer Tidwell's encyclopedic *Designing Interfaces* has details for many different IA patterns; here are some of my favorites (slightly renamed or expanded).

    Big 3 (search, see, browse) • Feed (sorted stream) • Grid (visual browser) • Two-panel selector • One-window drilldown • Tunnel/Wizard (one-way flow) • Dashboard (overview) • Multiple workspaces • Canvas and palettes • Alternative views

Patterns evolve as our cultures and technologies do; keep developing your design vocabulary with additional examples as you spot them.

EXERCISE: Components

Reduce, reuse, and recycle design work.

1. Find a repeated pattern in your design, and figure out what type it is.
   I have a lot of screens with a group of buttons; that's an action pattern.
2. Look at some sites, apps, and pattern libraries that show that pattern in use.
   Skim this book or visit the resources list online.
3. Decide what format best serves the particular audience and use case.
   This feature is for snowboarders, who don't want to take off their gloves on the mountain, so they'll need extra-big touch targets and might like a voice input option.
4. Sketch some options at low fidelity.
   A dropdown menu to save space, a radio group to show all options at once, or a button bar to include icons.
5. Polish the details and variations at high fidelity.
   Find online tutorials to get up-to-date instructions for each software program.

Create consistent patterns for content or functionality.

 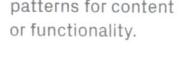 Visual designer

 Engineer

Fill the in-between states

Every digital design is animated, even if it seems static: each screen must load its elements over time. Interactions also don't have to jump to a new screen instantly; we can add transitions that improve usability, add differentiation, and make the experience come to life. 2D symbols benefit from a variety of 4D states.

Design the states between actions

States are the various forms an element takes over time. They're like user flows for each element, showing the effects of each micro-interaction and delivering additional feedback throughout an experience. States can be functional, conversational, or just delightful.

React to action

User interface states add clarity to large or small actions. Imagine a visitor seeing a button, moving their cursor over it, clicking it, and moving their cursor away. Imagine someone else tabbing through the interface using only a keyboard. If nothing happened, it'd be less clear what to expect. Confirmation states can show what the user did, or what the system did (the file is uploading; the credit card is processing). Consider partially-there and fully-there states.

How does interaction affect the element?

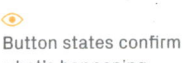

Button states confirm what's happening.

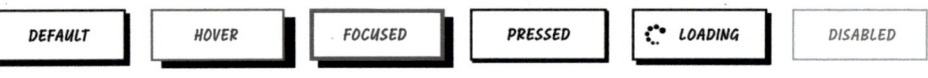

Coach better action

Input elements are conversations between a visitor and the system; the system can simply listen quietly, or can help people do better. Imagine someone typing good, mediocre, or garbage data. Think about ways a brand might respond at that moment. Feedback states can be visual or verbal, quiet or loud.

What guidance could improve input quality?

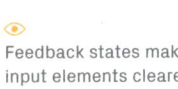

Feedback states make input elements clearer and more usable.

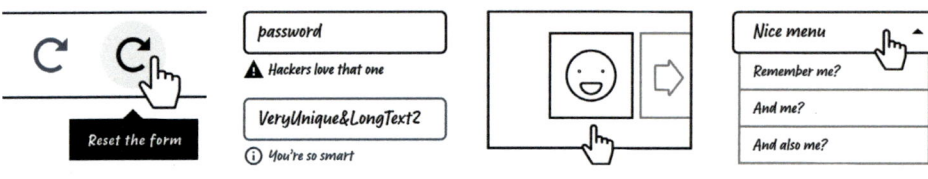

Make space

Digital designs are fluid in multiple dimensions; they're not paint-by-number books where we just fill flat surfaces. A collapsed or hidden state can eliminate irrelevant information until it's needed. Imagine accordion menus that show only a title until tapped, or keyboard keys that are just big enough to tap but then overlay an enlargement for clarity. Spatial states make interfaces skimmable, then readable.

What information could wait to show up?

Note: It's easy to forget the menu that's implied by a dropdown button or the content that's revealed by each accordion. If you're working through higher-fidelity screens or flows, comb through each design to make sure they include every secondary state. Overly clean and simple interfaces might be missing a lot of details.

Are the results of each action understood?

• Consider the transitions between states

Zooming in further, we can consider the moments in between one state and the next. Transitions turn static screens into connected experiences. Good transitions have purpose, consistency, and usability.

"Unlike evaluating algorithms, heuristics are harder to nail down. [H]ow quickly should a scrolling list glide to a stop after you've flicked it? [At Apple] we always made demos to evaluate the possibilities."

Ken Kocienda, *Creative Selection*

Have a purpose

Good transitions don't disrupt or distract from an experience—they improve it. The purpose of the animation should direct its design.

Grab attention	Soften a state change	Fill gaps in time	Create spatial relationships	Add personality or set a mood
pop in a headline	fade in a menu	spin a loading GIF	pan between tabs	animate an icon

COMPARE
Transition purposes

Be consistent

Good transitions are consistent with one another, with the brand strategy, and with the laws of physics. The iPhone's scrolling is not a linear slide; it gradually comes to a stop as though slowed by friction and gravity. Realistic animation is 4D skeuomorphism—it makes interfaces feel more familiar and usable.

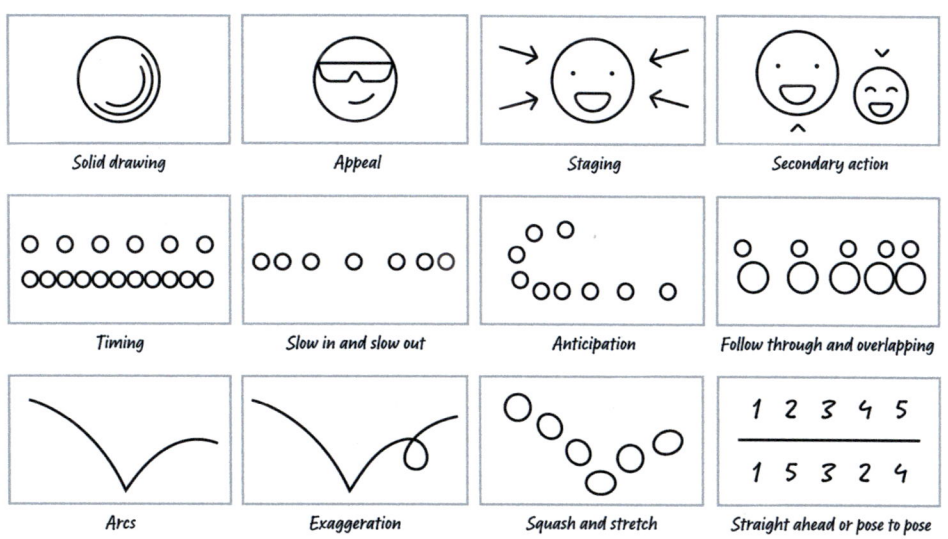

Disney's twelve basic principles of animation, introduced by Ollie Johnston and Frank Thomas in *The Illusion of Life: Disney Animation*, help animators make transitions realistic and compelling.

THINK IN 4D // PATTERNS // 115

Support usability

Good transitions reduce the cognitive load on users by, for example, providing spatial and temporal relationships to the content, a sense of where it came from and where it can go. Think about the cards flying off the screen in a dating app, or the pull-to-refresh effect at the top of a timeline. Transitions can also increase efficiency, condensing multiple taps or clicks into one.

> "Animation also aids in perceived performance. […] Customers were willing to wait almost twice as long for the custom loader."
>
> Sarah Drasner, "Animation in Design Systems"

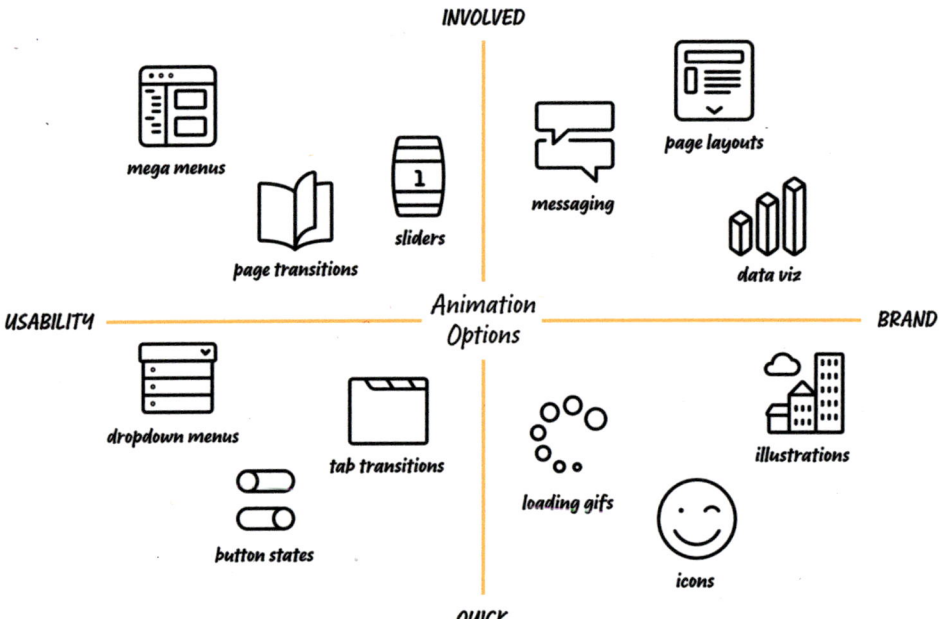

COMPARE
Animation options, inspired by Rachel Nabors's "Communicating Animation"

Be systematic with timing

Timing affects an audience's reactions; delays or surprises have psychological effects. Bad transitions can damage brand equity, usability, or conversion, while refined timing can do the opposite. Digital designers need to develop this polish just like a comedian needs to workshop their joke delivery: deciding the order for each story, refining the length of each beat or pause, and developing a signature style.

> "[A] hierarchy of easing […] can be especially useful for brands that use motion as a core method of conveying their design message."
>
> Val Head, "Including Animation In Your Design System"

Transition at the right time

Once we've drafted some content and functionality for an experience, we can outline its interactive personality. Images can gracefully slide in to lead the eye; a button can suddenly wiggle to grab attention. Consider tension, resolution, and other tricks of time-based artforms like film, music, and dance. Immediate reactions provide clear confirmation, but intentional delays can simplify first impressions or create anticipation. Drama helps people pay attention to something, remember it, and tell others.

Should the transition happen now or later?

Build a consistent space

Certain UX/UI patterns have transitions that shape perception. Drawers sliding in create a sense of space; layers fading in create a sense of depth. A "flick" has a different feeling and intention than a "scroll." Interactions that follow real-world physics will seem believable or even tactile, but interfaces can also contradict expectations to seem futuristic or magical. Whichever model you select, be consistent. (And use interactive prototypes to feel and validate the actual experience.)

Is this world realistic or fantastic, predictable or surprising?

Don't disrupt larger goals

Return to the visitor's goals, and make sure that transitions assist progress, not confuse or delay it. Jaunty pops of action may be fun to design, but gentle fades between scenes may be more usable. If transitions are too abrupt, people may not perceive or retain the details. If transitions are too slow, people can get frustrated and task completion can drop. Find the right balance for the audience and the task.

How fast or slow is too much?

EXERCISE: Interstitials

Transitions from screen to screen aren't always as simple as they look in our design software; significant rearrangements of pixels often create confusion and delays for the external visitors actually using the experience. Interstitial designs that smooth and connect the steps in a process can orient, soothe, or delight visitors.

1. Choose a key moment in an important flow: a peak experience where the service can meet people, or a difficult delay where you risk losing them.
2. Decide if the visitor's goals and emotional state at that moment would be better served by either top-notch usability or memorable branding (if you had to choose one).
3. Think about the flow and content of the screens: Do they imply a quick transition, or a more involved one?
4. Sketch practical or delightful interstitials that could fill the gap.

Design an in-between moment

 **Visual designer**

 **Engineer**

• Streamline repeated use

When a person completes a flow, the interaction doesn't necessarily end. One option might send the visitor farther down a path. Another option might keep them active where they are. In game design, this is called a *loop;* we move from lines to circles. Longer processes like researching a purchase often involve many loops of exploration and evaluation (Google calls this "the messy middle"), and the priorities for the experience design may change. We may foolproof a flow for first use, but what about for its five hundredth use?

Look for interactions that might be repeated, as well as for repeatable micro-interactions inside them. Return to the key usability principles of clarity, efficiency, proactiveness, and consistency as you design and evaluate each loop. Let's dig a little deeper into how.

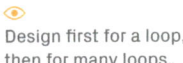

Design first for a loop, then for many loops.

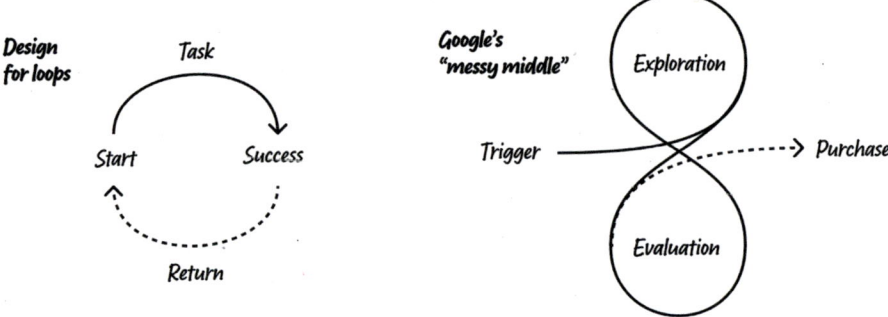

• Reconsider hierarchies

What is clutter for a returning visitor?

First, evaluate clarity. A returning visitor has a different set of priorities, and certain orientation elements will become noise, not signal. What's clear for a new visitor will often be clutter for an experienced one.

If I've never been to a site before, I might just want clear pricing, "how it works," and sign-up information. If I know all that, I'll be looking for the things I find most valuable on the site, whether that's functionality, friends, new content, or something else.

The principle of wayfinding is relevant here: How can each visitor (new or returning) get oriented, decide on a route, monitor their progress, and find their destination?

• Choose efficient patterns

How many steps does each loop require?

Next, analyze efficiency. Count the taps and time it takes to complete each task. One extra second may not stand out in a standalone flow, but if it's an extra click every time you check your email, it adds up.

Streamlining data entry can save people a lot of time; it can also increase input quality and improve success rates. A client I worked with had no autocomplete on their search field; as a result, searches on phones were mostly one-word entries because thumb-typing is no fun.

Simpler symbols are one good way to increase efficiency. A set of radio buttons may take more space than a dropdown menu, but it requires only one tap. Gestures like swipes can replace multiple taps, and have the extra perk of being both efficient and fun. Think about how each symbol affects a trip through time.

Memory is another way to support efficiency. "Save" features help people retain their drafts or preferences, rather than reentering details. "History" features let people pick up where they left off instead of redoing all their searches or clicks. Find ways to reuse previous work.

Bulk edits are an advanced feature for efficient designs. Savvy users often want ways to work with multiple items at once, whether that's moving, editing, labeling, or deleting. For any list of selectable elements, ask yourself if it would benefit from "select all" and "deselect all."

And on a grander scale, efficiency may inspire a whole new concept. When I worked on the design research and strategy for a car-buying site, we found that "shortlists" were key tools that people used as research goals and then as purchasing hubs. So we designed a digital version. Remember your ability (or responsibility) to be creative and make things up.

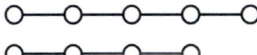 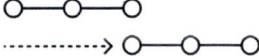 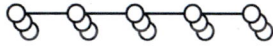

Efficient patterns shorten a task, continue the past, or function *en masse*.

- ## Provide smart defaults

What's better than efficient work? No work. Products that know their users well can eliminate a number of steps with smart default settings. Sliders don't have to start at zero; dropdowns don't have to start with a boring "select." Proactively filling elements with common values can feel like the welcome service of an attentive assistant.

How can I save visitors a step?

Be mindful of ease versus inclusivity. Find defaults that welcome all types of visitors, in both functionality and language. An input that forefronts one age bracket or location will save time if you're in that demographic, but also risks creating the perception that the community is predominantly composed of that selection.

Defaults also shape digital culture and expression—how many Google Docs have you written in 11pt Arial because that was the default? Inertia is a major cognitive obstacle; people may not care enough to fiddle with optional settings. Be sure that defaults are safe, and won't compromise any data or experiences if people leave things as they are.

• Build consistent signals

Which elements should be consistent? Which should be unique?

Consistency is clarity over time, and inconsistencies are extra obvious in loops. Double-check internal consistency in the experience: see if signs and symbols mean the same thing throughout all steps and states.

Then, zoom out. Flows are arbitrary segments within much larger experiences. Imagine a whole life cycle of flows stitched together, from awareness to onboarding to expertise. Look for external consistency with other experiences.

Finally, codify the wayfinding elements: any iconic visuals or distinct labels that will appear as links in other experiences. An uploading loop may be clearly indicated by a camera icon or photo album image, but not if a photo gallery feature is already using that signpost. Return visitors must navigate a sea of text and images to find their way back; make mappings and naming conventions clear and consistent.

Consistent signals can function across contexts.

EXERCISE: Loops

Streamline an experience for repeated use.

Researcher
Visual designer

Remember the bias to see new features as a new user would. Design for loops, not lines.

1. When and why might a visitor return? Where might they land? (It's not always the homepage.)
2. What elements are less relevant for experienced users? How might they be minimized without confusing new users?
3. What additional features might experts need? How might they be added without cluttering the interface for basic users?

REMEMBER: PATTERNS

Reuse functional patterns	Components	Modularity
Fill the in-between states	Interstitials	Consistency
Streamline repeated use	Loops	 Mere-exposure effect

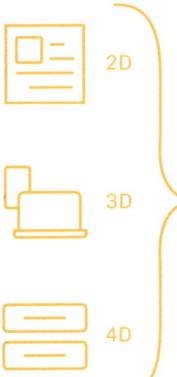

CREATE: Screens

Whether you're wireframing content and functionality or producing high-fidelity mockups, you'll find that 2D design is a collage exercise that benefits from 4D thinking throughout. Once you've set the high-level goals and steps for a user flow, zoom in to organize and optimize the design of each step.

1. **Boundaries:** Confirm the screen sizes and alignment grids for the site. For each rectangle, remember that it's a window, not a page—the layout can scroll or zoom!

2. **Content:** Think about the type of content that will satisfy the particular audience: do they want to look or read, skim or deep-dive? Paste all the content onto the screen like it's a pile of puzzle pieces. Don't worry about layout yet; just get it all on there.

   - *Images:* Consider ways to tell a story visually. Find photos, illustrations, videos, or icons that serve the mood and bandwidth of the visitors.
   - *Text:* Add valuable words for the target audience and for SEO bots.
   - *Functionality:* Find or create UX/UI patterns that communicate interactive possibilities.

3. **Position:** Arrange and rearrange your elements to tell a story. Work mobile-first to force prioritization, or desktop-first to stimulate free thinking. Create vertical and horizontal rhythms; consider dimensional effects like overlaps (if they're part of your design system).

4. **Emphasis:** Adjust the emphasis of various elements, using scale, contrast, or repetition to create a focal point for the page and lead the eye through other key elements. Revise boundaries, content, and positioning as needed. Make sure the visual hierarchy reinforces the information hierarchy.

   - *Scale:* Make key text or images large enough to be skimmable, readable, and compelling. Make secondary elements smaller to match their relative importance.
   - *Contrast:* Make key elements stand out with color, weight, or styling changes.
   - *Repetition:* Use design patterns consistently, and reiterate key messages.

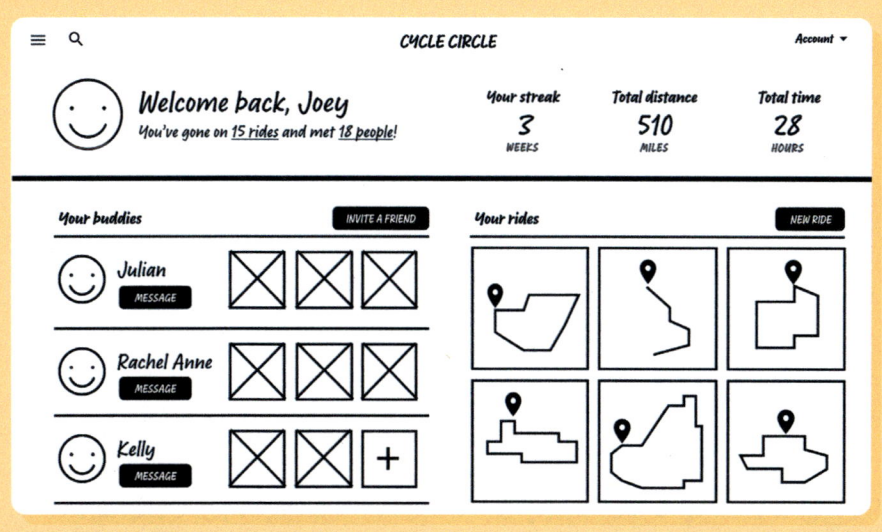

Arrange and balance elements for digital display.

How many steps does it take to book a flight?

It's more nuanced than we might imagine: the process includes searching, comparing, selecting, purchasing, and confirmation phases, each with a number of branches or optional paths, each involving a number of steps for legal, business, branding, or customer service reasons.

How many steps *should* it take to book a flight?

It depends on our design principles: simplicity versus density, guidance versus freedom. Usability is a core concern, but so is safety—some paths need maximum ease; others need more friction. We're not just designing information, we're designing behavior.

Interaction designs blend symbols and actions into usable flows; product designers can choose popular or innovative styles. Familiar symbols can increase comprehension and reduce information overload; creative solutions can simplify unique workflows or add new patterns to our shared vocabulary.

In this phase we'll work with symbols, usability, and paths. This section is functional, focused on defining and refining the elements in a product experience. The chapters in this section are more conceptual; they prompt deeper thinking about the aesthetics and ethics of interaction design.

PRACTICE

2D symbols: Define consistent design principles, pick elements with the right functionality, and reduce cognitive load. Map symbols to their effects consistently, choosing aesthetics and functionality that increase clarity and prevent garbage input.

3D usability: Select appropriate input formats, prevent wasted effort, and give good feedback on action. Make key elements very visible and undo extremely easy, but always test actual performance versus stated preferences.

4D paths: Choreograph enjoyable steps toward a goal, inspire and assist progression, and take the time to predict and prevent exploitation. Disclose information step by step as needed, helping people overcome inertia and avoid any unpleasant consequences.

Flows: Sketch the steps and content in one experience, and evaluate the usability of various options. Refine the order and formatting of the functionality.

Symbols
2D INTERACTIONS

Digital design languages have evolved over decades, reflecting technological and cultural trends, as well as the evolving principles of particular platforms. Many symbols have specific functional connotations; designers need to select elements with the right constraints for each interaction. Symbols can take standard or innovative forms, using icons, shapes, or text to reduce cognitive load and increase interactive enjoyment. Successful product design chooses or creates symbols that effectively communicate possibilities.

KEY QUESTIONS	EXERCISES
• **Semantics:** What is the purpose of each element?	Design principles
• **Rendering:** How can pixels communicate functionality?	UI styling
• **Simplicity:** Can we reduce cognitive load?	Iconography

COGNITIVE PRINCIPLES

- **Mapping**
The conceptual relationship between the capabilities of a system and the symbols or objects providing control of it should be intuitive and consistent.

- **Aesthetic-usability effect**
People perceive aesthetically pleasing interfaces as more intuitive or usable, and also have more tolerance for minor issues.

- **Garbage in, garbage out**
The output of a system is only as good as the input it receives; quality interactions need helpful features, constraints, previews, and feedback.

• Define design principles

Crafting symbols to represent functionality is the core task of user interface design. I consider UI a subset of UX with a visual focus, but there's no hard line between the two (except when written UX/UI). Some of the thinking occurs simultaneously, and all of it should come from shared design principles. Let's look at some ways that user interfaces can reflect philosophies and not just personal preferences.

👁
Work toward functional UI, effective usability, and emotional UX (based on Craig Kistler's "New to UX? A Quick Overview").

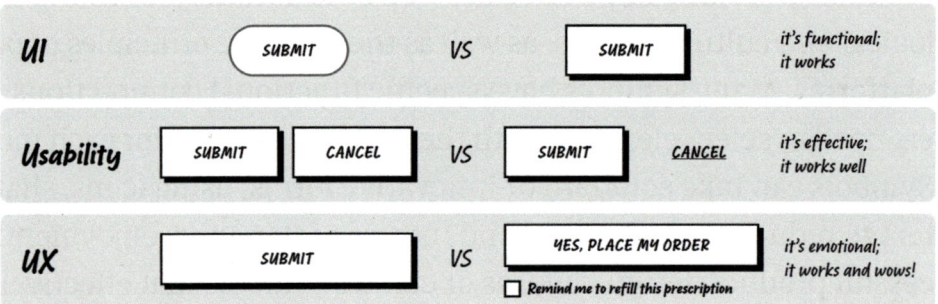

• Understand UI trends

To think more deeply about UI, think more deeply about the medium. In digital design there's really no such thing as a button; there's only a grid of pixels behind sensors and glass. We color pixels to create realistic or imaginative symbols that communicate information or enable interaction. "Buttons" are an illusion; what other illusions might we use or invent? Our choices sit within the history and evolution of technology, psychology, and aesthetics.

👁
Where we started: the MS-DOS interface in 1981.

```
C:\> Enter
```

Let's look at the events and ideas that led to four major UI trends: skeuomorphism, flat design, material design, and brutalism.

Skeuomorphic design

Skeuomorphic design mimics 3D objects to convey interaction methods in 2D. It translates our experience using physical devices into a digital arena.

When digital design was new, people had no references. Computer interfaces were text-only DOS prompts requiring particular keywords. Skeuomorphic GUIs from Xerox PARC and then Apple gave people a familiar model for this mind-blowing leap in technology: "desktops" with folders, clipboards, and trash cans.

> "[A] minimal spirit is rarely a lovable spirit."
>
> Stephen A. Mouzon, "How Steve Jobs Hit What Walter Gropius Missed"

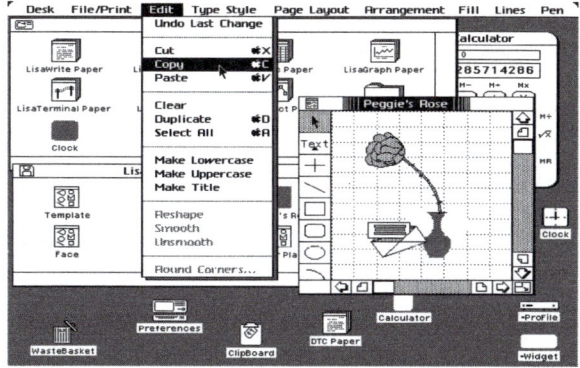

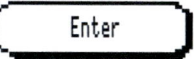
The "desktop" interface on Apple's Lisa and Macintosh computers was 1984's visual explosion.

As skeuomorphism evolved, its realism increased but its intention was the same. The original iOS Podcasts app (inspired by Braun's TG 60 tape recorder) had reels that rotated to show it was playing, a tortoise/hare switch for playback speed, and "screws" to hold the UI in place. If you knew how to use an old tape player, or even just play with switches and buttons, you knew how to use that interface.

Steve Jobs apparently loved skeuomorphism (he was the one who insisted on the address book's "leather" cover), and Apple still has a lot of it. When it's done well, it makes for beautiful, clear, unique, memorable digital art—like a classic car, according to designer Neven Mrgan. *Trompe l'oeil* depth effects also bring usability benefits; buttons that seem to stick out and depress add clarity to interactions (as well as a satisfying punch; it's like popping bubble wrap).

Apple's Podcasts app replicated a classic tape player; Web 2.0 styles became increasingly shiny.

Obviously, it takes a lot of time and craftsmanship to polish all these shapes and shadows. Web 2.0 skeuomorphism used shiny gradients and shadows in nearly every element, but as responsive design became the norm, it became difficult or impossible to create flexible and scalable designs in such a hi-fi style. Moreover, skeuomorphism limits interface metaphors to the device being imitated. As people grew more savvy, they were ready for UI design that was less literal.

Note: if people say the skeuomorphism trend is over, they're usually talking about pseudo-3D UI styling. The use of real-world models for interface design is unending.

"Less is more."

Mies van der Rohe

Flat design

In 2010 Microsoft launched their Windows Phone OS, and its flat interface was a stark departure from popular design at the time. Maybe we just couldn't take any more drop shadows. Or, as the world got increasingly busy, we wanted our interfaces to be a bit simpler; trends are often a reaction against an existing pattern.

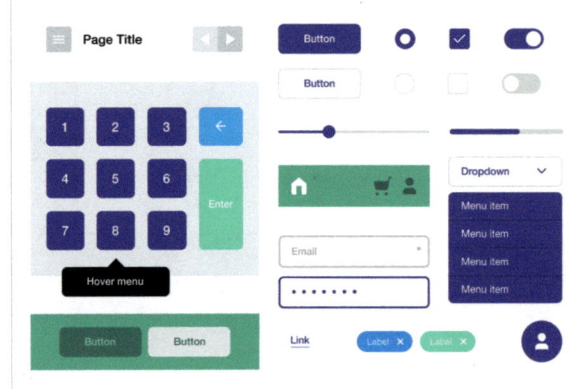

Flat design (like Microsoft's Windows 8 interface or its many later implementations) removes all fake depth effects and often uses bright colors to convey interactivity.

Flat design removes the illusion of 3D from UI, using only 2D symbols to convey 4D possibilities. No shadows, no metaphors—just color and shapes and imagery and typography. (And animation, which often helps bring things to life.)

Flatness reduces the quantity of visual information to process. It saves space by omitting drop shadows and borders. It's much faster to create and easier to maintain. And it allows you to make entirely new metaphors for interaction.

But flat design loses some usability. It can reduce comprehension, especially for less technically minded users. When Apple changed its calendar app from dimensional to flat styling, people complained that it was no longer clear what was tappable. Even Apple couldn't bring themselves to go all the way, keeping the skeuomorphic look on keyboards and switches.

The popularity of flat design was possible because people had become more sophisticated computer users. Links didn't always have to look like buttons: certain icons, positions, or words were now assumed to be clickable. MS-DOS or Terminal windows, those bare-bones layouts that prompted the creation of graphic user interfaces (GUIs), became a design inspiration. We had come full circle.

Flat design was overwhelmingly popular—until it became too popular.

Material design

After a few years of flat design being the chic, *de facto* style, everything started to look the same. It got boring.

Google launched Material Design in 2014, bringing back drop shadows and the z-axis in a big way. They used the metaphor of paper to communicate clear interaction cues—the project code name was "Quantum Paper." I think of Material as flat design on 3D elements, like graphic design on layers of paper. Buttons didn't have any internal shading, but did have huge drop shadows to make them pop off backgrounds. They were flat elements cut out and stacked in a virtual third dimension.

"More and more, more is more."

Rem Koolhaas, *Junkspace*

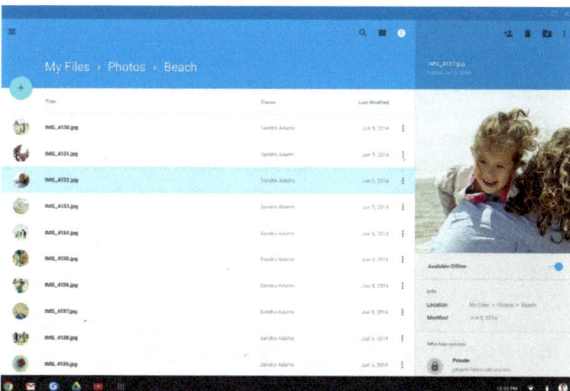

Material Design's first version was like flat design on artificial layers, often communicating interactivity through color and motion.

Material also dug deep into 4D design, including audio signals and motion effects. It was perhaps the first design system to provide such detailed guidelines on transitions, effects, and timing. It was flexible and practical, but more fun and tactile than cerebral flatness.

Richer, more complex UI trends also reflected the evolution of frontend libraries. Technical tools and teams could manage much more complicated design systems, and so visual languages became more polished and cohesive. Google also provided a suite of great tools to support Material's usage, from icon libraries to color palette generators. It was easier to use it than not to use it. (Note: Material is Google's internal design system, so it continues to evolve for their use, but they launched it publicly to serve the entire world of web and app creators.)

Material and its offshoots brought a professional level of polish to a much wider range of sites. But some people didn't want to wear suits.

> "Always remember that you are absolutely unique. Just like everyone else."
>
> Margaret Mead

Brutalist design

As design systems continued to grow in complexity and polish, the pendulum swung away from these cheerful, expensive, corporate executions and toward more direct, raw, idiosyncratic styles. The trend was to reject the trends.

Brutalist design, named after the visually austere postwar style of architecture (which was *not* named for its appearance but for its primary material of raw concrete, or *béton brut)*, uses "undesigned" interfaces to avoid the slick commercialism of flat or skeuomorphic design. Designers tend to ignore classic typography and layout principles, as well as usability and even accessibility guidelines. Pascal Deville, who coined the term in 2014 and created the Brutalist Websites directory, also identified three subgroups: Purist, Minimalist, and Artist / Anti-ist.

Purist	Minimalist	Artist / Anti-ist
Bare-bones styling, using the system defaults of the web (black text and blue underlined links, like plain HTML), shows that you're not spending money trying to persuade or manipulate the audience. Craigslist and Drudge Report are the classic examples.	Efficient, performance-focused principles can lead to radical design choices. Removing layers of styling gives a more direct or serious tone; the simplicity conveys honesty. Many fashion brands started to lean this way, letting their images shine.	Conceptual or countercultural leanings, often expressed through playful styling and typography that ignores classic design principles, create an innovative or ironic tone. *Bloomberg Businessweek* had a long run of delightfully ridiculous designs.

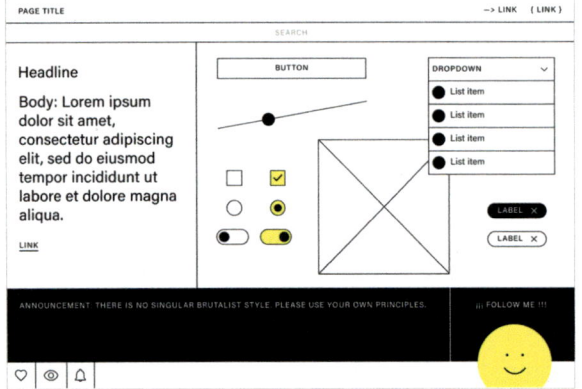

Brutalist design (like HAWRAF design studio's playful site) ignores traditional design guidelines and has no singular aesthetic across sites. Experiences may communicate interactivity with HTML defaults, minimalist logic, or expressive inventions.

I think of Brutalism as "ugly" design, rejecting classical principles of "beauty" in favor of eye-catching non-corporate expression. Like postwar Dadaism, it reacts to and reflects modern life with bluntness or absurdity. The web continues to expand, and the diversity of styles within it does too.

What's next?
All these approaches show the pendulum of style: action and reaction, novel and then normal. If you want to try to guess what's next, look to the sources of trends: technology and culture.

• Consider technology trends

UI design merges tech and aesthetics; when the former changes, the latter does too. Keep up with technology developments and you'll be ahead of design trends.

New design software
When Photoshop was the primary design tool, we saw grungy or shiny styles that were natural to Photoshop. When Sketch became the primary interaction design tool, we saw simple geometric styles that were easy to make in Sketch. Each new application has styles that are easier or more natural, so they become a default.

What can new design tools do?

New coding technologies
The Masonry library made it easy for any site to build a Pinterest-style layout, so many did. The Bootstrap framework streamlined design and development, leading to a lot of Bootstrappy sites. Machine learning made large-scale data processing more accessible, so images and content became more dynamic. Each new programming capacity popularizes more advanced techniques.

What can new coding tools do?

New device hardware
When the iPhone launched and made it easy to reach the web on your phone, responsive layouts became widespread. As touchscreens rolled out, bigger buttons became a default. As bandwidth speeds increased exponentially, web video went from impossible to expected. Every technological evolution creates new usability patterns.

What can new devices do?

New typographic tools
Once Typekit made it easier to use non-system fonts online, web typography exploded. And when variable fonts made it possible for a single file to contain all of a typeface's styles, dynamic identity and layout designs emerged. Each new typographic capability moves the treatment of text forward.

What can new type technology do?

Your tools shape your designs. Know and push technical boundaries.

• Be aware of cultural trends

In the remix era, trends are more micro than macro. The internet removes gatekeepers; "good style" does not ripple down from an entrenched circle of editors but out from each community's chosen icons and dialects.

What formats fit modern networks?

What styles serve modern mindsets?

Which previous eras had similar principles?

What is unpopular and therefore fresh?

Networks

Each new tool supports certain forms of expression, or creates new ones. Pinterest made communication more visual, Instagram more polished, TikTok more real, Clubhouse more verbal—all had their moment of influence.

Psychology

Design serves deeper needs than task completion. Dark Georgian houses suited a buttoned-up culture; modern glass houses reveal an exhibitionist transparency. Maximalism is a form of entertainment; minimalism is a balm for overwhelm.

Nostalgia

Fashion trends supposedly loop in three-decade cycles. Look back 30 years for retro inspiration (or 15 years for maximum uncoolness); look even further for classic parallels. In uncertain times, people may lean even harder on the past for a feeling of safety.

Counterculture

Truly unusual styles are repulsive at first; they're so unfamiliar they often register as "bad." But bolder audiences are ready to leave behind the present and move into the unknown. The ugliest possible color combination may lead to something new; countercultural styles create an antidote for the baseness of popularity.

Trends and aesthetics are subjective; to find the right vernacular, understand the culture that connects people.

• Define design influences and principles

> "Understanding not only the what, but the why, behind the design of a system is critical to creating an exceptional user experience."
>
> Marco Suarez, *Design Systems Handbook*

All these visual styles or trends have underlying design principles that distinguish them from one another. Designers may choose to prioritize tested usability principles, the audience's aesthetic preferences, or their own personal taste. (Are underlines on text links good because of increased usability or bad because of decreased legibility? Do drop shadows add clarity or clutter?) Strong brands require clear principles that guide many decisions across many screens.

Inspiring design principles might go beyond simple visual guidelines, expressing philosophical beliefs about the role of technology in people's lives. For example, the Calm Tech movement's principles include ideas that technology "should require the smallest possible amount of attention," "should inform and create calm," and "should make use of the periphery." These principles stand out in a culture that often prioritizes the opposite, support the pursuit of ideals amid distracting times, and gather practitioners with similar beliefs.

Design principles can feel very abstract—the best way to understand their craft is to compare the principles defining large design systems or movements and analyze their effects. Principles may be very broad and conceptual, outlining metaphors and personality; or very detailed and practical, providing use cases and rationales. Structures depend on the brand and team.

For example:

Google's Material principles inspire designers with tactile references like print design and prompts to remember transitions in time:

- Material is the metaphor
- Bold, graphic, intentional
- Motion provides meaning

Shopify's Polaris principles guide designers with detailed contextual rationales for states, sounds, icons, space, typography, and color:

- Communication is key
- Colors have meaning
- Colors follow accessibility guidelines

Imagine a contrasting interface with design principles that say:

- Flatness is the metaphor
- The tone is quiet
- Imagery provides meaning

Imagine a contrasting interface with color principles that say:

- Personality is key
- Colors create emotion
- Colors follow brand guidelines

Principles provide stable values for interactive personalities. Let's create some.

EXERCISE: Design principles

Companies do design principles very differently—descriptions or examples, general inspiration or specific do's and don'ts—but here are some ideas I've found most helpful in product strategy and experience design. Use any or all of these instructions and example principles as thought starters. Notice what type of interfaces each principle helps you imagine.

1. **Highlight user research insights.** Spell out any of the audience's consistent needs or preferences, in their own words whenever possible.
   Seamless Service: we combine piecemeal processes into simple one-stop shops.

2. **List any metaphors for interactions.** What type of space, material, or life is a consistent model?
   Electric Energy: we create bursts of excitement, instant connection, and sharp clarity.

3. **Reference the cultural inspirations.** What are the social, environmental, or technological references that inform the visual and experiential vocabulary?
   Art World Elegance: we remove all nonessentials and let each piece shine.

4. **Incorporate any practical constraints.** For example, accessibility guidelines have huge effects on color palettes and typography; a design principle to prioritize access will help people think about it early and often.
   Always Accessible: we ensure equal opportunities and AA standards for every visitor.

5. **Broaden principles that are too specific to be useful across an entire platform.** Resilient principles leave room for contextual variations; they're not specifications, but inspirations.
   Videos, not text. → Show, don't tell, with as much richness as possible.

6. **Focus principles that are too general to be ownable.** Universal design or accessibility principles should inform all brands, but won't inspire a unique personality.
   Understandable. → Deconstruct, diagram, demystify.

Define interface metaphors, styles, or practical constraints.

Strategist

Visual designer

Writer

• Refine functional details

Design principles need usable expressions: specific UI symbols. Each interface element can have styling that's standard or surprising, minimalist or maximalist; each stylistic choice also has functional impacts. In theory, we could represent every single action with a button, but this would risk creating inefficient, inelegant, or frankly incorrect interface patterns. Advancing designers increase their vocabulary of input types, know each one's limits, and polish its presentation. Let's talk details.

• Start with element semantics

What "is" the input, functionally?

"You do need to know some art history. [...] The conventions you decide to ignore and the conventions you decide to repeat are as important, if not more so, than what you invent."

Carol Bove, *AKADEMIE X: Lessons in Art + Life*

Semantics is the study of meaning. In a design context, it's the association between styling and function. On a deeper level, it's the relationship between the UI and the underlying technology. All design drafts must turn into code eventually; savvy designers prepare for that transition early on. We think about how each element will be built, not just how it looks.

Semantic designs map well to code, and to viewers' mental models for what an element "is." For example, most people understand underlined blue text as "a link." Surrounded by a rounded rectangle, the text is now "a button," and people might not expect to leave the current page when clicking. Set in a line with other links, the text becomes "a tab," so people would expect only the content below the bar to change. Standard HTML elements are another design vocabulary to learn and use.

COMPARE
HTML input elements

Links	Buttons	Pickers	Fields
Technical connections between ideas, screens, or functions	Standard selectors that constrain input to very specific structures	Scenario-specific selectors that increase clarity or reduce error	Text collectors that allow people to speak in their own words or in set formats
<a href="/home">Take me home!</a>	<input type="button">	<input type="color">	<input type="text">
	<input type="checkbox">	<input type="date">	<input type="url">
	<input type="radio">	<input type="time">	<input type="email">
	<input type="submit">	<input type="week">	<input type="password">
	<input type="reset">	<input type="month">	<input type="search">
	<input type="file">	<input type="tel">	<textarea>
	<input type="image">	<input type="number">	
	<select>	<input type="range">	

• Acknowledge and communicate constraints

What limits does the input need?

Smart UI symbols also provide appropriate input boundaries, clearly communicating what's needed and what's not allowed.

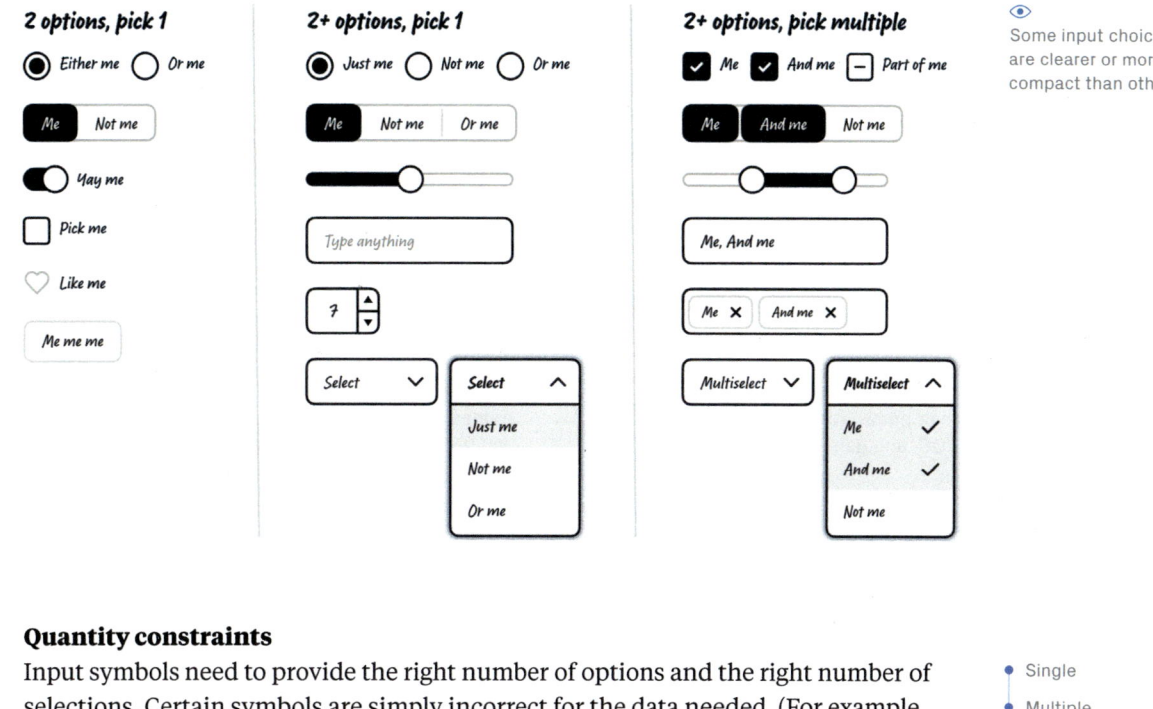

Quantity constraints

Input symbols need to provide the right number of options and the right number of selections. Certain symbols are simply incorrect for the data needed. (For example, if a list allows only one selection, it needs radio buttons, not checkboxes.) Include and clearly communicate any input limits to prevent errors and save people time.

- Single
- Multiple

Space and time constraints

Effective UI symbols fit the particular audience's screen, time frame, and needs. Dropdown menus take up less space, but require an extra tap. Radio buttons make all options one-click, but require more room. Sliders are more minimal and fun to use (especially on touchscreens), but harder to control precisely. Create the best first impression possible, then disclose more on request.

- More visible
- More compact

Format constraints

Input symbols can be visual, verbal, or numerical; they can be rigid sliders or loose drop zones. Open fields allow people to speak freely and let the system sort things out; this enables more individual precision. But open fields can be much more work: it's not the prewritten text and single click of a button, but dozens of taps on a keyboard or multiple seconds of dictating (that some recipient must also parse later). Use open formats when you need to hear from an audience in their own words, if and when you have the bandwidth to process them; use structured formats when speed is a priority.

- Structured
- Freeform

Device constraints

Responsive or multiplatform experiences should consider equivalent behaviors on each device. Zooming might happen through pinching, sliders, or plus/minus buttons. File uploading might use camera access, drag-and-drop, or click-to-select. Choose UI symbols that can either serve the chosen device, or adapt to many platforms.

- Clickable
- Touchable

- ## Accommodate cultural variations

What does natural language sound like for this audience?

A third refinement to UI symbols is cultural: accommodating an audience's standards, not just yours. Things like names and forms of address vary greatly in length and format, and often affect interface or database design. Icelanders might not expect to be greeted with a salutation; Brazilians might have three or four family names. (See the W3C's "Personal names around the world" guidelines for some examples.)

COMPARE
Input selection scenarios

Scenario	Potential Elements	Selection & Rationale
A clinic visitor must use an iPad at a kiosk in the lobby to enter their name, address, DOB, and gender.	Input fields Calendar pickers Dropdown menus Radio buttons Image upload Voice input	The device has a camera and the user should have their ID handy, so I'll use the **image upload** pattern and ask people to photograph their driver's license to input all the info in one step. As a fallback, they can also type their name and address in text fields, enter their birth date in a three-part date field, and select their gender from a dropdown.
An insurance form needs to know the relationship of two people listed as insured.	Input field Autocomplete Dropdown menu Radio buttons Checkboxes	The full list of relationships is very long, so I'll split it into Family, Professional, and Legal relationships, since they're quite different. A relationship might be more than one type, so I'll display those top categories as **checkboxes**, and then reveal a secondary **dropdown menu** once one is checked.

- ## Imagine unique approaches (if justified)

Could unique UI differentiate the product, or drag it down?

Semantics, constraints, and culture might also call for a brand-new UI symbol. Special forms like color, time, or date pickers can increase clarity and reduce error. And who's to say we've come up with all the good design patterns already? "Swipe right" is now a standard because Tinder popularized it; there are always new ways to push the industry forward. Scenario-specific design is a crucible for creativity.

Unique interactions can also define a product, especially if they reinforce its brand distinctions. Password managers should polish features that emphasize security (like a multitiered password strength model); fashion companies should innovate on luxurious or bleeding-edge experiences (like facial recognition). Unique experiences are more memorable and buzzworthy—as long as users actually use them.

However, custom design patterns do require custom principles, designs, code, and documentation. This means a larger initial outlay and continued investments. It may be smarter to use existing standards like Apple's Human Interface Guidelines or Google's Material Design; they're familiar for visitors, well-documented for designers and engineers, and cost-effective for businesses.

Note: Working within existing design systems can be a master class in itself; they're generally full of excellent examples and explanations (I worked on a Material project for two years straight and learned a lot the entire time). It can also lead to great portfolio pieces demonstrating practical professional skills.

- # Return to design principles

  Once we've settled all these functional needs for an interface element, we can refine its final form. A radio button doesn't have to be a dot in a circle; the list could be a grid of images where the viewer taps to select one, or a "cover flow" pattern where they flip through a 3D pile of thumbnails. Newer interface patterns like toggles (on/off switches) are technically checkboxes, they're just styled skeuomorphically to convey a familiar model. As mentioned earlier, interface design is where the lines between UX and UI or visual design get really fuzzy.

  To create cohesive interactive brands, not isolated elements, use consistent design principles and systems for all interface choices. Talk with developers about existing or possible elements, and visual designers about brand or layout considerations; product design is a collaborative effort.

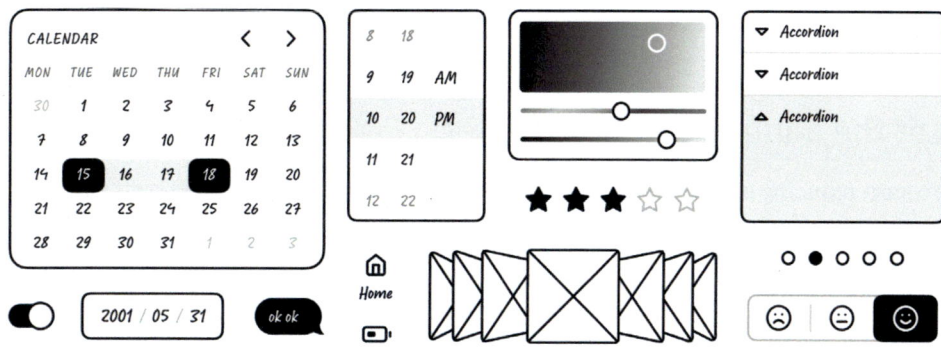

Interface elements can use skeuomorphic metaphors, web/app standards, or symbolic logic.

EXERCISE: UI styling

Turn design principles into smart and appealing symbols supporting interaction.

1. Define the symbol's semantic type, based on content and functionality.
2. List any input constraints (such as quantity, space, time, format, or device technology).
3. Research needed cultural variations.
4. Decide if this symbol is an opportunity to differentiate, or a place to follow standards.
5. Use defined design principles to make stylistic choices.

Create effective and consistent interface patterns.

 Visual designer

• Reduce cognitive load

"A designer knows he has achieved perfection not when there is nothing left to add, but when there is nothing left to take away."

Antoine de Saint-Exupéry

Our final consideration for symbol selection is internal: its cognitive impact. In psychology, cognitive load is the amount of working memory used for a process. There are three types, and we can try to accommodate or reduce each one.

Intrinsic load	Germane load	Extraneous load
The inherent difficulty of the task or topic	The mental schemas needed for the task or topic	The design of the interface and its fit to the task
e.g. addition vs. calculus	e.g. maps or workflows	e.g. visual or verbal

Poorly designed interfaces don't represent ideas appropriately, match the simplicity or complexity of a task, or help people manage information. Simple and intuitive interfaces build clear models and symbols while removing visual and mental clutter.

• Let the audience define clutter

To start reducing clutter, first realize that it's subjective. Two interface terms that can help us see clutter more clearly are affordances and signifiers. *Affordances* are the actions available; *signifiers* are the symbols seen. The relationship between the two is not always direct.

Why do older people tend to hate Snapchat? Its signifiers are all icons, and its affordances often invisible (requiring gestures). Swipe where? To do what? Younger audiences, even toddlers, will paw through touchscreens intuitively, but mature audiences have other standards and are frequently less exploratory with interfaces.

Why is Facebook popular when it's so ugly? It's littered with signifiers, especially text and web-standard symbols, which tend to be obvious rather than clean. It even doubles up icons and captions for extra clarity.

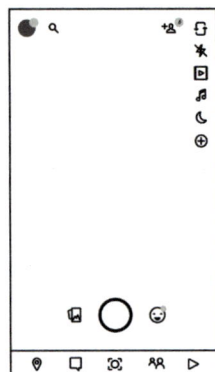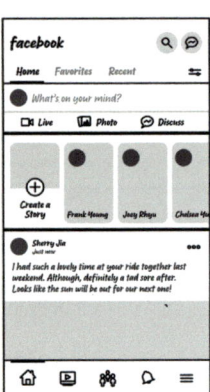

👁 Snapchat and Facebook have very different principles regarding signifiers.

One interface is not universally better than another; each interaction model appeals to a specific audience. "Usable" means different things to different users. Adding signifiers makes an interaction model more obvious; removing them makes an interface simpler. Visual clutter is not clutter if the audience needs it.

For each affordance, weigh visible and invisible signifiers.

- ## Choose the clearest symbol possible

    To reduce extraneous cognitive load (any mismatch between an interface design and a task), choose appropriate interface patterns (see the Patterns chapter and the preceding section in this chapter). Then, reduce the amount of information viewers must process. At the smallest symbolic level, once we've decided that signifiers are necessary, this means choosing clear icons.

    Condensing text into icons, using familiar or intuitive visuals for common features, can help users master interfaces more quickly and enjoyably. Viewers can skim for visual signposts instead of reading each and every line of text.

    Unfortunately, visitors don't get to pick the symbols in every interface, so they may not understand your clever creations. Icons that fail to translate across cultures or skill levels increase cognitive load instead of reducing it. The now-standard "hamburger" icon took years to become common practice.

    The classic example of unusable signifiers is a "Norman door," where you don't know whether to push or pull it. Pushing or pulling to open is the affordance; door hardware is the signifier. A handle or knob communicates "pull me," but many architects use them on pushable doors, too. Clearer signifiers like flat panels visually communicate the thing you need to do well in advance of running into it.

    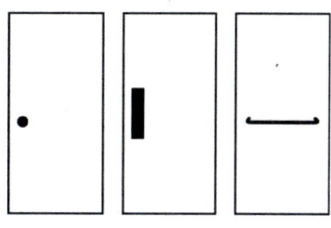

    👁 What do you do with the third door?

    Symbols don't have to be graphics; the clearest symbol for an action may be a word (menu icons often perform worse in usability testing than the linked word "menu"). Language is its own set of signifiers, and words have particular usage patterns in digital design, so consider all their connotations. A "register" button may imply a longer process than a "submit" button; a menu of verbs may spur more action than a menu of nouns. (See the Words chapter for more ideas.)

    For each affordance, explore a variety of signifiers for both visual appeal and comprehension. If "a member can add an image," does the signifier have to be a "plus" button? Could it be a camera button, a drag-and-drop target, a search field, or an "add image" link? Consider standard patterns and differentiating ideas; consider both text and icons.

    👁 Icons may be obvious to you, but may not necessarily be clear to a different audience.

- **Be consistent with symbolic choices**

  To reduce *germane cognitive load* (the lift required to learn the interaction model for the experience), again make sure the chosen model is appropriate for the task, and then ensure consistency among symbols. Once people understand a symbol's meaning, they can reuse that knowledge across the whole system. A "hamburger menu" icon makes a side panel slide out; a "dropdown" icon makes a small layer appear. When symbols are consistent, people don't have to stop and think about their meanings each time.

  Consistency should be both visual and conceptual. Symbols need steady styling, but also cohesive design principles (e.g., icons all represent motion, or humanity, or physical technology). Don't just copy and paste icons you find around the web—they will clash.

  Icons should match one another stylistically and conceptually.

  Consistency of symbols also includes colors. Print design often uses color expressively, but product design uses color functionally. Red is a standard error color, blue text signifies a link, and gray communicates disabled states. Brand palettes that use these colors might be sending mixed messages, and might need some modernization.

  Highly usable products are consistent internally (across all experiences) and externally (with larger platform or web standards)—see the Usability chapter for more details. Android, iOS, and other platforms have their own icon sets and UI libraries; to reduce cognitive load, be consistent with those familiar symbols.

- **Consider some hints**

  Intrinsic cognitive load (the difficulty of a subject) can't be reduced, but we can design interfaces that coach people through challenging tasks. Each interaction is like a conversation; well-crafted prompts will generate better responses, and sometimes a person needs to be told exactly what to do. Hints aren't clutter if they're helpful.

  ### Label spaces well

  What are you asking?

  Accessibility guidelines require labels on fields, but many other elements also benefit from a bit of framing text. Try phrases or questions for more conversational and less robotic experiences.

  ### Indicate essential action

  What should I do now?

  Busy visitors may not want to complete every step; highlight the most important ones visually. Let people know which inputs are required (red asterisks are standard), so they don't get errors and have to go back.

Communicate any constraints

Icons in fields and hints underneath them help clarify the expected input format and reduce errors. Spelling out any requirements reduces errors and reentry.

What do you want from me?

Provide good examples

Blank pages or fields can be less than inspiring. Example content can show people what "good" looks like and give them an easy model to follow.

Can you give me an example?

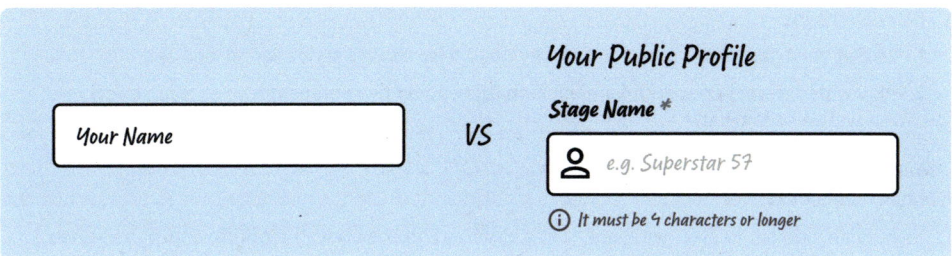

👁 Prevent errors; show people any requirements and what "good" looks like.

- ## Consider multiple layers of meaning

Finally, circle back and consider multiple ways of experiencing the product. People have different capabilities and preferences (see the Inclusivity chapter), and will experience different types and amounts of cognitive load.

What's the fallback?

Color vision deficiency and other differences in perception may throw off overly simple systems. For example: red/yellow/green is a common system for error/warning/success messages or symbols, but red-green is the most common form of colorblindness. Screen readers will not see any of the icons you've carefully chosen unless they also have alt text or captions.

Accessible symbols layer multiple signifiers. Consider icons on top of message containers, patterns on bar chart colors, text labels on color pickers, or shape variations on top of icon states.

Reduce cognitive load with symbols that serve multiple forms of cognition at once.

Create visual signifiers for the available affordances.

 Visual designer

 Engineer

EXERCISE: Iconography

As with art direction, icon selection processes vary depending on the phase and fidelity of the designs. Choose icons that add clarity, not confusion (or choose not to use them). Talk with engineers about modern technology options and ways to render icons cleanly.

Low fidelity (sketches)
Focus on the idea

1. Revisit your design principles to identify good themes and styles for an icon set.
2. Play with different concepts for each icon (they could be representational or abstract, innovative or familiar).

Medium fidelity (wireframes)
Focus on the utility

1. Find an icon set to start with, one that's standard on the chosen platform and/or designed for legibility at the expected size (e.g., 16px squares).
2. Fill any holes in the set with icons drawn with the same fills and stroke width; they should all look like they were drawn by the same artist.

High fidelity (mockups)
Focus on the execution

1. Decide on the final display sizes for each icon on each screen size.
2. Determine whether the idea for each icon will work at all sizes or require adaptations (e.g., an XS version with less detail; an XL version with more personality).
3. Optimize each icon for legibility at its final display size; make sure it has enough detail to communicate the idea and not confuse it.

REMEMBER: SYMBOLS

Define design principles

Revise functional details

Reduce cognitive load

 Design principles

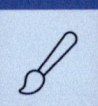 UI styling

 Iconography

 Mapping

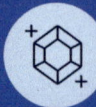 Aesthetic-usability effect

 Garbage in, garbage out

Usability
3D INTERACTIONS

Interactions happen on a variety of three-dimensional devices, each with special features or kludgy constraints. Usable designs help people complete tasks using a spectrum of input devices, from mushy fingers to quiet breaths. Clear, consistent, contextually appropriate forms of information and interactivity prevent frustration and lost time. Empathetic, multisensory feedback communicates the effects of action and encourages additional engagement. Successful product design helps people complete their tasks efficiently and enjoyably.

KEY QUESTIONS	EXERCISES
• **Inputs:** What interaction methods are most natural?	Touch target test
• **Ease:** How does the design perform in the field?	Task completion test
• **Feedback:** What happens in response to each action?	Flowchart

COGNITIVE PRINCIPLES

- **Visibility**
  Usability increases when a system's capabilities, outputs, and status are clearly visible.

- **Forgiveness**
  Designs should prevent errors, minimize their effects, and make recovery easy (expect problems, not perfection).

- **Performance versus preference**
  The most usable designs are often not the ones people say they prefer. The only accurate way to assess usability is to observe interactions with the design.

For each input, what format is most accurate? Accessible? Enjoyable? On-brand?

"Design is not just what it looks like and feels like. Design is how it works."

Steve Jobs

• Select easy input formats

A visitor comes to your interior design app. They have an idea for their living room in mind; how will you get it out of them?

The most obvious input formats are visual/verbal standards like fields, buttons, and menus. But the most natural form of communication might be gestural, vocal, or photographic. And the most efficient input method might be invisible—sensing a visitor's environment, proximity, movement pattern, or heart rate.

2D design programs make it easy to forget we have options and constraints in other dimensions. Looking at a design is very different from physically using it. Devices have friction and gravity; ease of use depends on the context. Dig into the moment: Are people painting or pasting, dancing or debugging? Zoom out from your eyeballs and consider your thumbs, your breath, or your pulse.

Accessible designs also provide multiple ways to accomplish a task (read the Inclusivity chapter for more details). Maybe someone is in a quiet library where they can't speak, or on a shared computer where they can't connect their account. Responsive designs have to work for both fingers and mice—and styluses and trackballs and screen readers and keyboards and more.

Let's broaden our ideas for input options.

• Type

Maybe keyboards?

Keyboard inputs were the original human-computer interface, and are still easiest in certain scenarios (think about all the times you've opted to search rather than slog through a navigation menu). Keyboards also provide speedy shortcuts for advanced users: it's much faster to hit *Z* on a keyboard than to grab your mouse, slide it over, make sure your cursor is within a 20px square, and then click. Keyboard-only input is a required accessibility test: non-visual users might be tabbing through designs and hearing rather than seeing them. Start each design with keyboards in mind.

• Click

Maybe mice, pens, or trackballs?

Cursors and clicks were the next evolution in computer interactions, and UI standards like links, buttons, and pickers provide the ease of familiarity. But too many clicks can become a chore; one-click selection options (from tags to stickers to GIFs) can make inputs simpler or more fun. And it's not just mice that click; pens, trackballs, or trackpads might require some accommodations to make designs truly easy and usable.

• Tap

Touchscreens blend visual and tactile input, allowing unique interactions. In fact, they're so special that it's worth spending some extra sentences on the particulars of their usability.

Maybe fingers?

We've been promised the Minority Report vision of touchscreens for decades: giant walls of information, somehow super simple to use with magical sweeping gestures. The reality is not so glamorous. And very bad for our necks.

Touchscreen design must accommodate fat fingers on smooth surfaces in a variety of environments; experiences are error-prone. People might be in a shaky bus where it's hard to drag and drop, or have shaky hands that make it hard to hit a small checkbox. Surfaces are often tiny, and half of the equation is a mushy human fingertip (or even worse, a thumbpad)—the input device tends to cover up the target. Easy-to-use elements must often be larger than expected or have creative assistive features.

iOS enlarges each key so that it's still visible when tapped; NoKey's curved keyboard is more usable for thumbs.

Usability on touchscreens also varies depending on the device and how someone holds it. Phones are often held with one hand, so touch targets in the bottom or bottom-left part of the screen are easiest to reach (if a user is right-handed). Tablets tend to be held with both hands, so areas on the sides and top are more usable. On a desktop or wall-mounted display, things in the top and middle are easiest to see and click. Give thought to how and where each containing device will be touched.

These are the most usable areas on each kind of device, according to *Tapworthy* by Josh Clark.

THINK IN 4D // USABILITY // 145

- ## Gesture

Maybe hands?

Gestures move taps into the fourth dimension. Additional fingers, variations in time, or clever usage of space can make an interface feel multidimensional: pinch to zoom out, drag to pan, pull down to refresh. Gestures must be learned—but once they're learned, they live in muscle memory. One swipe can replace multiple taps (and be much more fun).

Luke Wroblewski's *Touch Gesture Reference Guide* presents a variety of options (CC BY-NC-SA 3.0).

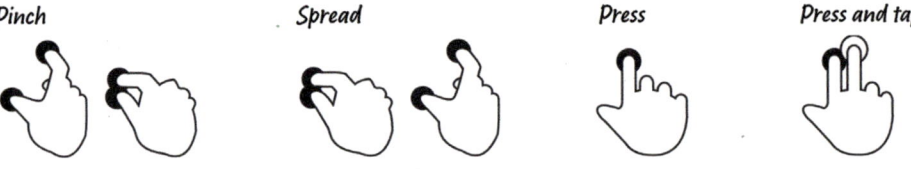

- ## Move

Maybe motion?

Fingers and cursors on screens aren't the only movements happening to devices; many kinds of motion can affect a mobile device. Picking up the phone, walking with it, running with it, putting it face down or face up—all of these actions can be interpreted as input. Cameras can pick up physical gestures like exercise, dancing, or hand movements, and lack of motion is also an input, depending on how you measure it. Consider usable movements.

- ## Speak

Maybe voices?

Interface design can be invisible: voice user interfaces (VUIs) strip design down to hardware, language, and logic. A flowchart may be the only deliverable. VUIs offer both convenience (like hands-free interactions while users drive, cook, or relax) and accessibility (like letting older or low-sighted users speak rather than struggle with a confusing app). Easy voice inputs must allow for different accents, phrasings, and contexts; usability principles like feedback and forgiveness are extra important.

In voice interfaces, the logic is the design.

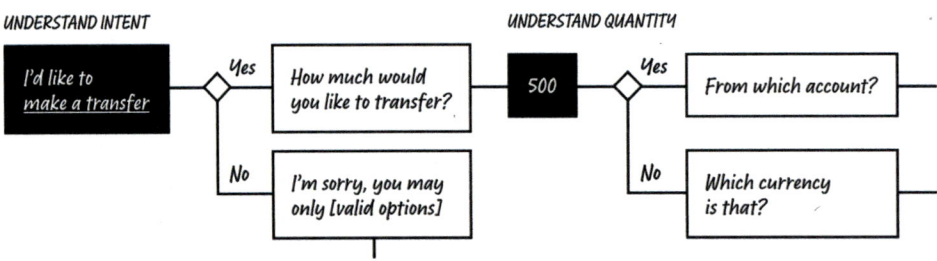

"Be adaptable: Let users speak in their own words. Be personal: Individualize your entire interaction. Be available: Collapse your menus; make all options top-level. Be relatable: Talk with them, not at them."

Amazon, *Alexa Design Guide*

- **Sense**

    Hardware and software can provide intimate details about a person's location, direction, altitude, motion, proximity, or environment (see the Personalization chapter for more ideas). Sensors can grab physical details like heart rate, temperature, or fingerprints, validating an identity or logging its changes. Easy inputs are streamlined. Think of all the internal or external sensations that could provide instant insights.

    Maybe conditions?

    > "The Nest auto-detects when you've been away for a while and turns off the heat or AC. [...] When we don't show up in the room [...] it is still user input!"
    >
    > Claire Rowland, Elizabeth Goodman, Martin Charlier, Ann Light, and Alfred Lui, *Designing Connected Products*

- **Connect**

    Data entry is not super fun; an easier route could let people link accounts or devices where it already exists. Photo albums, contact lists, wallets, and many other data sources are a few clicks away. Be sure to ease people's minds with information on how connected data is stored and what it will be used for.

    Maybe uploads?

- **Think**

    Brain-computer interfaces (BCIs) like Synchron already allow people to post their thoughts using only their minds. What might people use in the future?

    Maybe thoughts?

EXERCISE: Touch target test

Fitts' law says that the smaller a target is, the longer it takes to reach accurately. Usable touchable elements often need to be much larger than we expect. Interface guidelines often set 44 or 48px as a minimum size, but an MIT Touch Lab study said the average index finger is 45–57px wide (¾") and the average thumb is 72px wide (1")!

Make interactive areas big enough for cursors, fingers, and thumbs.

 Visual designer
 Researcher
 Engineer

1. Check each touchable item in a design, and see if it's large enough to accurately use with fingerpads (57px) or thumbpads (72px). Pro tip: include the white space around the element in the touch target as an extra safe area.
2. Watch for touch target issues in a task completion test: do people have to try more than once to hit the target? Do they need to be able to see what their finger or thumb is on?

44   48   57   fingerpad   fingertip   72   thumbpad   thumbtip

• Communicate constraints

Once you've zoomed in to choose usable inputs for each action, zoom out to analyze the usability of the entire flow. Usability is a huge field of study, with new studies and patterns emerging constantly, but four core principles remain constant: clarity, efficiency, consistency, and proactiveness.

• Be clear

> "It doesn't matter how many times I have to click, as long as each click is a mindless, unambiguous choice."
>
> Steve Krug, *Don't Make Me Think*

Clarity is the foundation of usability. Interfaces should clearly communicate past, present, and future (what's done, what's up, and what's next). This can be a lot of information; expect several iterations to make sure processes, symbols, and language are clear. Consider both conceptual and visual clarity.

☐ **Create conceptual clarity** by matching the audience's mental model, communicating the system's status, and providing examples of desired behaviors. Do naming conventions make sense to users? Do forms include info on how to enter good input or fix errors?

☐ **Create visual clarity** by reducing clutter and providing obvious next steps. Can you shorten word counts, shrink secondary elements, or delay optional information? Can you emphasize the primary call to action?

Communicate past, present, and future.

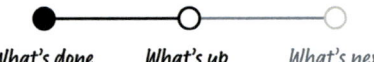

What's done   **What's up**   **What's next**

• Be efficient

Efficiency is a second usability essential. It's a core measure in task completion tests: How much time does a process ask of its participant? When tasks are efficient, they feel easier and more fun.

☐ **Choose input elements with fewer steps,** and provide shortcuts to help people jump around if they don't need to plod through every step. Measure task time, including loading time, data entry, and pauses; see if alternate UI designs can reduce the steps and time things take.

☐ **Make errors easy to fix.** Elements like input sliders may promise one simple swipe, but usability tests often show people struggling to select a certain number and spending a lot of time in the back-and-forth. Analyze backward flows as well as forward ones.

☐ **Streamline repeat usage.** Small optimizations like a "Save & add another" button instead of just "Save" can halve the work in bulk editing. Histories can let people pick up where they left off. Autocomplete on search can reduce both data entry time and cognitive load. Let computers supplement and support human memory.

Volume ─────────────────────────────
○ 1 ○ 2 ○ 3 ○ 4 ○ 5 ○ 6 ● 7 ○ 8 ○ 9 ○ 10 ○ 11 ○ 12 ○ 13 ○ 14 ○ 15 ○ 16
○ 17 ○ 18 ○ 19 ○ 20 ○ 21 ○ 22 ○ 23 ○ 24 ○ 25 ○ 26 ○ 27 ○ 28 ○ 29 ○ 30
○ 31 ○ 32 ○ 33 ○ 34 ○ 35 ○ 36 ○ 37 ○ 38 ○ 39 ○ 40 ○ 41 ○ 42 ○ 43 ○ 44
○ 45 ○ 46 ○ 47 ○ 48 ○ 49 ○ 50

👁 Please use efficient patterns.

• Be consistent

Consistency, both internal and external, is a third core usability critique.

☐ **Maintain internal consistency** across all screens and moments to reduce the cognitive load for users, saving them time and effort. Navigation items should have the same order from screen to screen; functions should use the same labels. Any inconsistency should be intentional, providing a better user experience for a specific scenario.

☐ **Increase external consistency** with other experiences and standards to bring that existing knowledge to this new place. When people say something feels usable or intuitive, they often mean it feels familiar. People expect to find the search bar or shopping cart link in the top right corner of a screen. You don't have to put them there, but you should have a reason for putting them elsewhere.

"A good way to describe consistency is 'using the same solution for the same problem.' [...] But you also need to check for differences in devices, user characteristics, or business goals that might introduce new constraints and make it a new problem."

Kathryn Whitenton, "When Is It OK to Be Inconsistent in User Interface Design?"

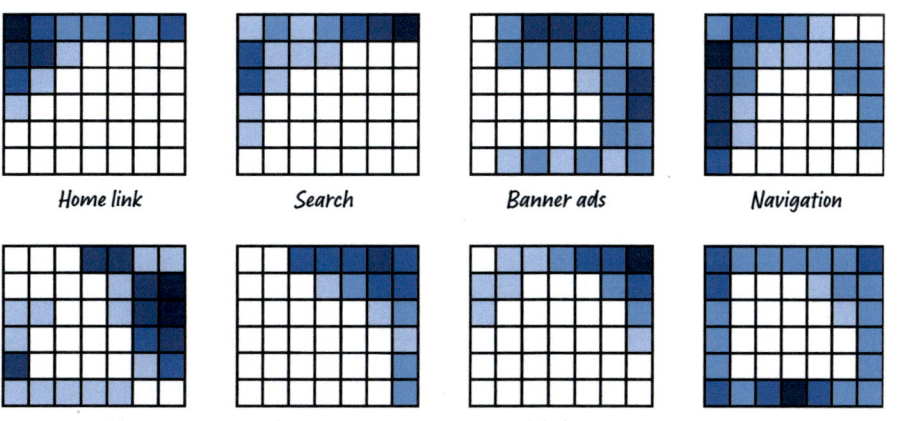

Home link   Search   Banner ads   Navigation

External links   Shopping cart   Help link   About us

👁 People expect to find web elements like search and help in familiar places (based on "Preliminary Examination of Global Expectations of Users' Mental Models for E-Commerce Web Layouts" by Michael Bernard and Ashwin Sheshadri).

THINK IN 4D // USABILITY // 149

• Be proactive

> "Painful effects which are likely to occur should be anticipated and avoided."
>
> *The Yoga Sutras of Patañjali,* translated by T.K.V. Desikachar

Proactiveness is the final pillar of usability: taking the extra steps to shape more productive behavior. Error prevention is a key principle in both usability and accessibility standards.

- ☐ Create appropriate boundaries, matching the audience's skill level and the task's complexity. Bicycles have training wheels for novices; highways have guardrails for cars. Structured input field types like date pickers or range sliders ensure people enter valid data from the start, while custom specifications like minimum or maximum lengths on text fields prevent errors and wasted time. The riskier the action, the more design constraints it needs.

- ☐ Design forgiving elements. Consider extra padding on targets, sliders that quickly snap to allowed values, and search results that understand what you meant to type. Expecting perfection from people just creates problems.

- ☐ Require confirmation on serious actions. Repetition increases attention and security: the redundancy of reentering a new password is annoying, but it prevents the serious error of getting locked out of your account. The weightiest actions need confirmation of intent. Review can happen before or after tapping the killer button: the "arm/fire" pattern of shopping carts (review your order, and then click purchase) or the "are you sure" pattern of deleting an account (click delete, and then click confirm).

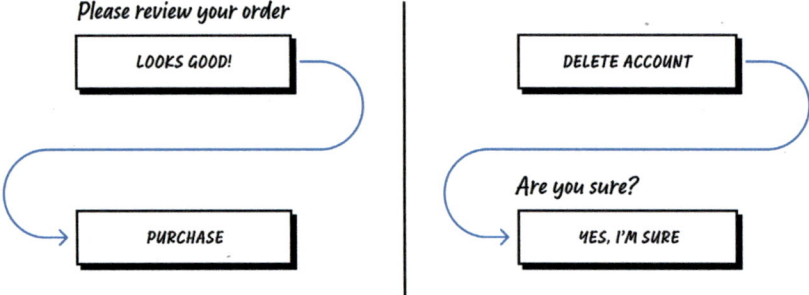

"Arm/fire" and "Are you sure" patterns prevent serious errors.

• Be patient

One small caveat on usability: if an interface is truly innovative, it will take some time for people to learn. Usability tests reflect and reinforce common standards; if you're taking a risk on a new pattern, it may test worse at first. Get deep enough with studies to understand when people are struggling, and when they're just learning.

> "It is almost impossible to carry out experiments on expert use of radical new interfaces for the simple reason that no one will ever spend enough time on a research prototype to become truly skilled."
>
> Colin Ware, *Information Visualization*

EXERCISE: Task completion test

Task completion tests are the most fundamental usability evaluation: Can a person achieve their goal? Designers may partner with researchers to work with target audiences, but it's also valuable to understand and practice proper research methods yourself. Even low-fidelity testing can reveal many useful insights.

Evaluate the efficiency, effectiveness, and enjoyment of a proposed experience.

Researcher

1. **Give context**
   Say how and why visitors may have arrived at the screen you're about to show. It can be something generic to set a context or mood, or something specific to focus and drive them.
   "Imagine your friend sent you a link to this site and you're checking it out."

2. **Get first impressions**
   Show the first screen and get the participant's analysis of its focal point, the site's purpose, and the strongest call to action before you explain any details.
   "What's the first thing you notice? What do you think this is for? What would you do first?"

3. **Assign a task**
   Ask the participant to attempt a task. Phrase it as a scenario, not a tutorial. Make your instructions as neutral as possible and let them proceed without guidance so you get to see their unexpected mindsets and methods. Don't lead the witness!
   "Imagine you want to register for this event. Please show me what you would do next."

4. **Observe issues**
   Quietly note anything that confuses, escapes, distracts, or hinders people. Notice how long the task actually takes, from loading time to learning time to data entry. Don't give them any hints (unless they've gotten totally off track)!
   "What are you trying to do? What do you think that thing does? What are you looking for? Where would you expect to find it?"

5. **Get final impressions**
   Once the task is complete, ask for overall takeaways. Hear how people will remember it or describe it in their own words, to see if your flow is solid or still leaky.
   "How does this compare to your existing process? What else would you like it to do?"

6. **Iterate**
   The point of testing is iteration and improvement. If you want quantitative insights, then keep the prototype as consistent as possible among users so you can accurately compare the data across all sessions. But if you're just trying to remove as many issues as possible, and a user test reveals an obvious design flaw, go ahead and fix it before the next session.

Give good feedback

What feedback is clearest, most efficient, or most enjoyable?

Congratulations, you've helped or convinced someone to do something! Now what?

On the system side, some logic happens. On the user side, many changes may occur. Clicking a button may imply a simple UI change or an immersive new experience. But clear feedback needs to do three things: confirm, evaluate, and prompt.

What happened?

- **Confirm the action.** Let someone know the system is working. Their input was received; the Wi-Fi was steady. Confirmations may range in scale from minimal (a color change) to maximal (lots of new content loading). These can also be educational moments, if visitors are hungry for information.

How was it?

- **Evaluate the action.** Give people more understanding and context. The password was strong enough; the image was too large. This feedback can be positive, negative, or neutral; serious or celebratory. (The Words chapter has more details on shaping copywriting for particular brands and moments.) People might need benchmarks or other comparisons to fully understand evaluations.

What's next?

- **Prompt additional action.** Help people fix errors, discover additional options, or move on to new spaces: *Please log in to do that; read this article to learn more.* Be strategic: revisit the goals for the visitor and for the business. Provide feedback that aids progress toward both types of goals.

These three feedback requirements help product designers and content strategists decide *what* gets communicated (the content). The other part of the experience is *how* it's conveyed (the format). Feedback can be visual, auditory, tactile, or multimodal. Let's explore the options.

Visual feedback

When I touch a screen, I expect it to react. But how? Pixels can rearrange in infinite ways: standard patterns or surprising new choreography.

The clearest response is often text, including iconic messages. Typically these are styled to reiterate their meaning (success, failure, warning, or tip) and placed near the related element (put error messages underneath a field, not at the bottom of a form).

For additional feedback layers, adjust the UI. Styling is a high-fidelity focus, but we can start plotting styles in planning stages too. Buttons get pressed and disabled states to show activity; tabs get "selected" styles to show location; typos get jagged blood-red underlines to reinforce ancient spelling hegemonies.

Pixels can also play with space. If the input was a navigational action, the feedback may benefit from a spatial approach. Movement like panning or zooming can let people know they're going up, down, or sideways in the information architecture.

Visual feedback can include verbal, visual, or spatial clues.

- ## Auditory feedback

  Sounds can provide foreground information (like a verbal response from a home assistant), but also background emotion or auditory symbols of meaning. Quick taps or dings can reinforce visual metaphors; longer melodic phrases can convey a whole mood. Material Design calls these signals "earcons," and has a lovely set of guidelines and examples ranging from loud to quiet (hero, notification, system, or ambient sounds) and realistic to imaginative (skeuomorphic or abstract sounds).

"The best way to understand and experience the power of sound design is by trying sounds out, auditioning sound with visuals to hear what it adds to the design, and using the guiding principles provided."

Conor O'Sullivan, "Designing Sound and Silence"

- ## Tactile feedback

  Phones, watches, and other enabled hardware can give a physical response. Quick vibrations from a smart watch are like a hard-to-ignore tap on the shoulder; shaking in a video game controller makes the game feel more lifelike.

  Invisible but important layers of usability feedback include our sense of touch. *Haptics*, a field of communication that includes both tactile and proprioceptive feedback, can enhance usability in both silent and non-silent situations. When a car's steering wheel vibrates to tell you you're nearing the edge of the lane, you can react without even thinking. When pixels behind glass combine with physical sensations, the digital metaphor feels more real. Apple and Android's design systems both provide thorough guidelines for haptics in digital design. There are default vibration patterns for standard UI like switches and pickers or events like selection and notification, plus customizable controls for design-specific scenarios.

"Earcons" and haptics can reinforce or replace visuals and increase usability.

The core usability principles of clarity, efficiency, consistency, and proactiveness apply to haptics, too. Do the rhythm, sharpness, and intensity of the signal correlate with existing communication patterns (the nudge of a friend's shoulder, the grip of a bouncer's hand, or the buzz of an electric fence)? Does the signal's duration occupy an appropriate amount of time in the recipient's attention span? Consider the context of the vibration, the sensitivity of the user, and the total volume of all feedback signals combined.

Diagram the logic behind an experience.

Subject expert
Engineer

Workflow diagram: Show how a user completes a process, and how different forks or ending points happen.

Data flow diagram: Show where a design's data comes from, and where it goes.

Swimlane diagram (see exercise in the Relationships chapter): Show who is involved in a flow, and when each person is involved.

EXERCISE: Flowcharts

Flowcharts diagram all the paths, logic, and results in a system, not just a single flow. They're a choose-your-own-adventure book visualized. Flowcharts help teams catch all the details of all scenarios, not just the ones that were mocked up in UI. What happens if someone gets stuck? When is data saved or deleted? And for non-visual designs, the logic *is* the design.

1. Find a symbol library, or use the ones below that come from classic engineering diagrams. Use software that includes magnetic arrows for easy connections.
2. Choose a starting point: either the very first screen of the flow (to consider all requirements), or the first screen relevant to the flow (to create a simpler diagram).
3. Step through each action and plot each condition. When and how will people get feedback?
4. Look for unconsidered questions or dead ends. What happens if people aren't logged in? If the Wi-Fi is down? If data already exists in the system? If it doesn't?

Circle start / end	**Diamond** condition	**Arrow** connection	**Box** step	**Wavy Box** document	**Cylinder** database
Says "Hey, Siri" *Opens app*	*Logged in?* *Paid?*	*If yes* *If no*	*Calculate* *Print*	*PDF* *Image*	*Saved* *Deleted*

REMEMBER: USABILITY

Select easy input formats

Communicate constraints

Give good feedback

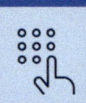 Touch target test

 Task completion test

 Flowcharts

 Visibility

 Forgiveness

 Performance versus preference

Paths
4D INTERACTIONS

The path to complete a task can take many shapes, but people get tired if there are too many steps, confused if steps fall in an unexpected order, or overwhelmed if the steps are too complicated. Timely incentives that connect to deeper motivations (including visual, chemical, practical, psychological, or social rewards and penalties) can provide the energy to continue; ethical systems use noncoercive tactics and responsible guardrails. Successful product design choreographs delightful steps through time, encouraging advancement while preventing harm.

KEY QUESTIONS	EXERCISES
• **Content:** What information or functionality do people need?	See/do lists
• **Progression:** Why would someone take a next step?	Incentives
• **Ethics:** What are the boundaries of good behavior?	Ethics check

COGNITIVE PRINCIPLES

- **Inertia**
People are reluctant to change, and tend to leave things as they are (due to status quos, sunk costs, confirmation bias, or cognitive dissonance).

- **Progressive disclosure**
To reduce cognitive load, display only key information and options at first; then reveal more details as requested.

- **Loss aversion**
People perceive the pain of losing something as much stronger than the pleasure of gaining something, so they avoid negative consequences much more strongly than they pursue positive ones.

Choreograph the steps

"UX before design is boring, design before UX is a disaster."

Design firm
Anton & Irene

Digital designs are arrangements of interactions, not things. We design verbs, not nouns; shopping, not a store. Each screen has steps leading up to and away from it. We choreograph approaches and departures that suit the particular skills of the participants.

Each step has a certain amount of content and functionality, but it's up to us to define the elements and arrange them in time. We can start to get clarity by dividing each moment into smaller and smaller moments, as if we're seeing the events in slow motion, so we can rearrange and recombine them. We can increase our clarity by working backward from the most important moment: reaching the goal. But let's dig deeper into the nature of goals, and how they affect designs.

Understand higher-level goals

Typical design initiatives focus on tasks a visitor is attempting to finish, trying to make each one as easy and pleasant as possible. These are the most tactical goals.

Basic: a person wants to complete a task.

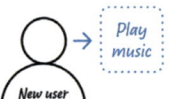  

However, tasks don't exist in isolation; people have underlying motivations that shape their particular needs for a path. Engineering stories often frame this as "a user can *X* in order to *Y*." Someone who's trying to play music in order to see what an app does will have different preferences from someone who's trying to play music to host a party. These goals are more strategic, with some vision.

Bigger: a person is doing the task to achieve a goal.

 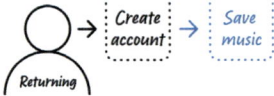 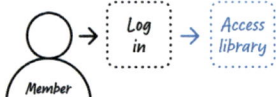

Sophisticated designs consider a visitor's deepest goals. Trying a service is just a step; we could say the *real* goal is to be inspired creatively, prepared at work, or connected to a community. These goals are very intimate psychological drives that might inspire very different images, animations, or functionality in a design.

Best: a person wants to *be* something.

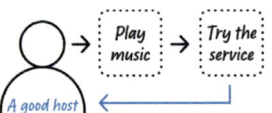  

The Powers Motivational Hierarchy calls these deep motivations "be" goals (personal values), which spur "do" goals (practical achievements) broken down into "motor control" goals (executional steps). "Be" goals are larger, more lasting desires; they can inspire more emotional designs and deeper relationships.

Powers Motivational Hierarchy

- **"Be" goals** (principals): Be a good partner → Ideal self
- **"Do" goals** (programs): Make dinner
- **Motor control goals** (sequences): Chop onions

The Powers Motivational Hierarchy (from Charles S. Carver and Michael F. Scheier, *On the Self-Regulation of Behavior*) models the relationship between what we do and why we do it.

"Be goals are the most stable; Do and Motor control goals are transitory. Be goals are states of self-perception."

Alan Klement, "Know the Two—Very—Different Interpretations of Jobs to Be Done"

For example, designing for an achievement ("designer wants to attend an event") helps us create a practical flow. Breaking it down into detailed tasks ("designer gets the address") makes sure we have all the necessary content and functionality. But thinking about *why* the person wants to attend the event ("designer wants to learn skills for their job," "designer wants to see cutting-edge work," or "designer wants to build relationships with people in the industry") tells us how to shape the best experience.

Start each flow at the end: the practical "do" goal and the aspirational "be" goal.

• Arrange the phases of action

Moving from high-level goals into a sequence of events requires some trial and rearrangement, as well as an understanding of the audience's mental model for the task.

Start with the framing context. Paths don't begin at the first screen someone sees, but on the threads that got them there. People encounter an idea or workflow and carry that expectation with them elsewhere (the *anchoring effect*). A referral from work or from social media can come with very different explanations and expectations. Understand the context for the visit.

What anchors do visitors carry?

Threads to the experience come with expectations.

What's the best first impression?

What do visitors want to accomplish first? Think about a given context and where it would send someone. It's often not the homepage (searches usually take people to product or article pages), and it's a key moment to nail. First impressions tend to have an outsize impact on decisions (the anchoring effect again), and the way we phrase or style information affects both initial reactions and subsequent choices (the *framing effect*).

👁 *Initial impressions frame the rest of the experience.*

What would they see, then do, then see, then do...

What happens next? It depends on the visitor's goals, habits, and understanding of the process. The mental models visitors carry around with them become anchors that designs need to address. If a business offers sales support before a visitor has completed their research, the offer may be confusing or uninteresting.

Paths should also serve the visitor's emotional state. Resolving fraud on your account has a different tone than depositing money—one may need to be as direct as possible; the other may have opportunities for secondary experiences.

Remember that you have the license to make things up. Product design is not just the arrangement of things on a screen; it's often deciding what things should even exist.

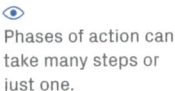 *Phases of action can take many steps or just one.*

• Get specific with content

What's not needed by basic users? By repeat users?

As the path emerges, the specific details on each screen will need to be resolved. Three principles can help us decide what to keep when.

Progressive disclosure
A first experience with a product is like a first date: you don't want to overwhelm someone with too much information too soon. Progressive disclosure has been a usability principle since the 1980s. Functionality appears step by step; secondary content hides until it's needed. This increases comprehension, decreases cognitive load, and reduces input errors. Designs also look simpler and cleaner because less stuff appears on each screen.

Progressive disclosure patterns include tooltips, popup modals, navigation drawers, dropdown menus, accordion panels, content snippets, carousels, tabs, settings, lazy loading, and new pages.

One-click access

The opposite of progressive disclosure is one-click access. Having more elements visible on a screen prevents the extra taps needed to open menus or load additional content and speeds up the overall process. Workflows to manage complex scenarios or large data quantities often require denser displays of information.

Tiered control

The principle of control says that available features should match users' expertise: beginners prefer visual simplicity and structured guidance, whereas experts want advanced controls and efficient shortcuts. You could hide expert features in an accordion or menu, or hide orientation text in a tooltip or modal. One design will not fit all.

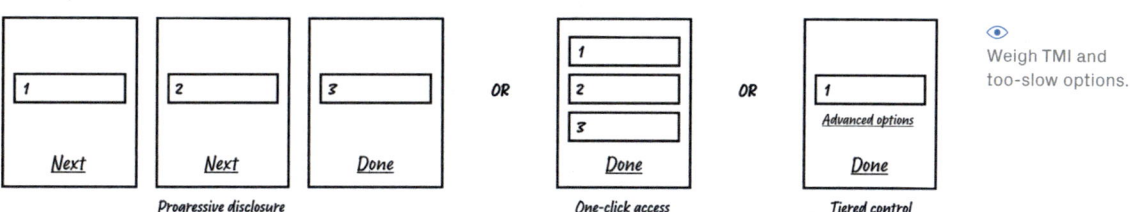

Weigh TMI and too-slow options.

Keep questioning your assumptions for each step. Think like an engineer, and split elements into pieces—the smaller the chunks, the easier they are to rearrange in space and time. Think like an editor, and make sure each element is essential—the simpler the layout, the smoother the flow.

• Think multidirectionally

Ideal flows proceed in one forward direction; real flows can involve a lot of back-and-forth. As you finalize the content and functionality for each step, think about alternate directions or nested flows. Accessibility guidelines say all inputs should be reversible and all errors correctable.

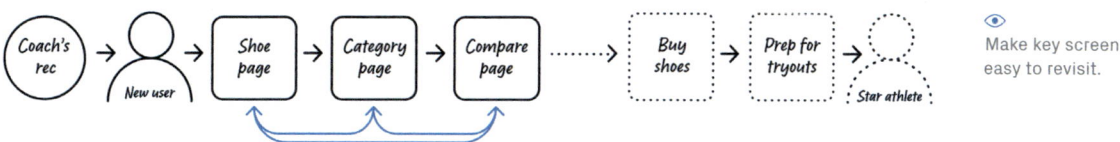

Make key screens easy to revisit.

Undo

Imagine a struggling visitor who messes up each and every step; they need flows that go backward. "Back" buttons and command-Z are traditional, keyboard-friendly patterns for simple errors; swiping, shaking, two-finger taps, or more creative gestures can be enjoyable options for particular contexts.

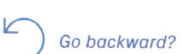

Go backward?

 *Do it again?*

Redo
Sometimes you need to undo an undo. Smart systems will save appropriate data and make it simple to restore. Redo is also a huge time-saver for repeated actions like applying consistent styling; think about whether actions may be repeated.

 *Start over?*

Reset
Single steps backward can take a long time; flamethrower functions like "clear all filters" or "restore defaults" quickly provide a clean slate.

 *Something else?*

Rethink
Complex flows have many microinteractions. If I made a typo 20 characters ago, I could backspace 20 times; or carefully tap between two characters and delete one; or double-tap to select the word and then choose delete from a menu; or click a "fix typos" button; or something else entirely. Create nested flows to define all the steps.

Draft the content and functionality needed for a flow.

🐬 Subject expert

EXERCISE: See/do lists

Design with words: list the content and functionality a particular visitor needs at each step.

1. Pick a particular type of visitor and identify their immediate <u>task</u> to be done, their larger <u>"do" goal</u>, and their ultimate <u>"be" goal</u>.
   A teenager wants to <u>buy shoes</u> in order to <u>prepare for tryouts</u> and <u>be a star athlete</u>.

2. Select an expected landing page, and list what that visitor would first want to see and do.
   The teenager lands on a shoe page, sees <u>sneaker photos</u>, and <u>zooms in on details</u>.

3. Repeat; list what that visitor would see and do next. Proceed until they reach their goal.
   The teenager then sees <u>reviews</u> and <u>filters for the worst ones</u>.

👁 Ryan Singer's UI shorthand is a simple way to start designing flows (see the Prototyping chapter for more details).

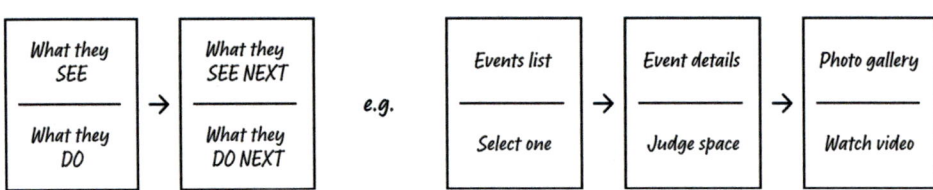

• Inspire and assist action

The simplest flows consist of two parts: cause and effect, action and reaction. But it takes energy to move forward; people often need help to achieve that first step. Advanced design thinking moves beyond the logical and practical to the emotional and psychological; simple nudges can have huge effects.

"Fun is the maximum amount of choreography for the minimum amount of effort."

Kelli Anderson, designer

The next section will provide ethical guidelines to prevent exploitation, but let's start with the positive, noncoercive ways to inspire action. Behavioral scientists have developed many, many different models for remembering the most effective influences on behavior. My favorite is the simplest—making things easy, attractive, social, and timely (EAST)—with some product-specific principles added to each part.

EAST

• Make action easy

Inertia has a huge influence on interactions. It takes time and mental energy to change behavior; visitors often bounce if things take too long or look too hard. People tend to do what they've already done before, or choose the simplest option. Use these tips to make things easier.

Remove the biggest barrier
One smart approach to UX design is to find the biggest obstacle in a process and focus on reducing that. Barriers to entry can be technical, practical, or psychological.

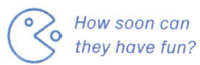
What's stopping them?

Provide instant accomplishments
One of my favorite game-design principles is "low time-to-fun." Games tend to drop people right into the action, coaching and rewarding them for each small step, instead of forcing long onboarding tutorials. Direct feedback is a usability principle and instant gratification is a psychological one. Give people a quick win.

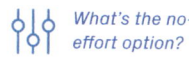
How soon can they have fun?

Design the defaults
People tend to go with the flow of presets. The font a text editor provides is often the one we use; the place we've saved our photos is the one we keep on using. Build in default settings that support user and business priorities.

What's the no-effort option?

Ask for a commitment
The principle of *precommitment* states that people will follow through more often on things they've actively committed to, in order to maintain their self-image. Insurance companies that had users sign "my answers are accurate" at the beginning of a form instead of the end received more accurate answers. Having people declare their goal helps them achieve it.

What do they hope to achieve?

Prime later steps
Repeated messages prime behavior and influence later action. You can increase the success of later steps by introducing clues about them earlier.

What's ahead?

"Gamification is a design process that optimizes for human motivation in a system, as opposed to pure efficiency."

Yu-kai Chou,
The Octalysis Framework

• Make action attractive

Congratulations, you've designed a logical, functional, easy interaction! It's also super boring, sorry. It feels like work, no thanks. Do you have any games?

Gamification is the overused phrase but valuable practice of making experiences fun using elements of game design. It's not about "gaming the system" or manipulating the audience; it's about serving deeper human drives for connection, feedback, and achievement. We could slap on some badges, points, and leaderboards and call it a day, but gamification is more meaningful when it considers characters, goals, action, and resolution to add both productivity and entertainment to an experience.

Action is more attractive if you make functionality fun. Know visitors' motivations and design rewards they'll enjoy.

What eye or ear candy would be fun?

Interactive rewards
Feedback messages provide useful confirmation that an input was received; added eye candy can make them even more fun and memorable. Animation, humor, and color are great interaction design elements that can encourage positive actions with reciprocal or delightful reactions.

How might experiences increase anticipation, surprise, or recall?

Chemical rewards
Dopamine (a neurotransmitter in the brain's reward system) is known to reinforce rewarding behaviors versus punishing ones, but its release is nuanced. Levels don't increase when rewards are regular! Only when they're anticipated, remembered, or greater than expected. Give viewers a boost by promising rewards, displaying past ones, or overdelivering on them. Rewards must also suit the audience's temperament; game design expert Jane McGonigal notes that "extroverts tend to produce more dopamine in response to social rewards—smiling faces, laughter, conversation, and touch, for example. Introverts, in turn, are […] highly sensitive to *mental* activity, such as problem solving and puzzling and solo exploration."

How might companies reciprocate investment or loyalty?

Practical rewards
For serious endeavors, the principles of respect and reciprocity come into play. When customers trust you with their time or money, the gains should be parallel. Airlines reward frequent fliers with travel add-ons such as special lounges or partnerships. Banks may give out lollipops for branch visits, but large financial investments are rewarded in kind (with reduced fees or increased earnings, for example).

How might a visitor's status or self-image improve with use?

Psychological rewards
Ego and identity are powerful principles. Badging systems reflect human needs for respect and affirmation, and help other people make comparisons. There are many ways they can be structured and expressed: decorative graphics, categorical labels, participation awards, seals of trust, or arbitrary points. Some people see action as a personal challenge; others are more motivated by community reactions.

Avoidance rewards

Loss aversion is one of the most powerful cognitive biases in human behavior: studies show it's up to nine times as powerful as positive rewards. (On the flip side, if an experience delivers unpleasant news or results, designers have to think hard about how to keep people engaged.) Fees and penalties may seem patronizing or obnoxious, but they work; people spend disproportionate energy trying to avoid negative events, and feel great satisfaction when they do. I've interviewed many people who made big financial decisions in order to avoid insignificant bank fees.

How might risks or losses drive action?

• Make action social

Social proof and *the law of large numbers* are textbook principles used by startups to push growth, and "crossing the chasm" from early adopters to the mass market requires role-model users. But we can be more sophisticated than just showing popular influencers and impressive stats; principles of community-building can create personal and interpersonal experiences.

> "Without question, when people are uncertain, they are more likely to use others' actions to decide how they themselves should act."
>
> Robert Cialdini, *Influence*

Show popularity or authority

It takes a lot of work to make an informed decision; it's often simpler and faster for people to follow the herd or a trusted authority. Large-scale sites can display statistics, using the law of large numbers to validate their authority. Smaller-scale sites can show celebrities or friends to generate similar confidence. Consider role models, stats, or stories that might inspire people.

Whom do people trust?

Support self-representation

Avatars and other visual representations of users fundamentally change the psychology of an experience, moving the player from audience to participant or even protagonist. As digital identities become more important, expressive tools become more valuable. Make the experience theirs, not yours.

How do visitors like to see themselves?

Build teams, not individuals

The more socially connected someone is to a product, the more likely they are to stick with it. Help people bring and see their friends (or colleagues)—whoever input or influence might be most appreciated or enjoyed. Support lateral connections and communication to build real community.

Whom else do people like to involve?

As with dopamine rewards, social rewards vary by personality. According to Gretchen Rubin, author of *Better Than Before,* some people need and crave outer accountability while others rebel against it. Think about where a particular audience falls on the spectrum.

- ## Make action timely

"Just as no building lacks an architecture, so no choice lacks a context."

Richard Thaler, *Nudge*

Timeliness is relative, but people often need a little bit of nervous-system invigoration to actually get things done.

It should go without saying that messages should be honest; far too many sites create false pressure by communicating alerts like "14 other people are looking at this property," but actually using random number generators in their code.

How many chances are available?

Reveal any scarcity
If things are less available, people tend to choose them more or value them more (the *scarcity bias*). Limited windows (games available only once a day, for instance) force people to want the thing more often. If something is genuinely limited in quantity, let people know.

When will it be too late?

Communicate any urgency
Many people need deadlines in order to get things done sooner (or at all). Appropriate time limits can help people, not stress them out. They can also add some drama and excitement to the experience.

What's their context?

Make it personally relevant
Return to any journey maps and make sure the experience is sensitive to the underlying feelings, thoughts, and needs of the audience at that particular moment.

EXERCISE: Incentives

Brainstorm ways that game-design elements could satisfy logical or psychological drives.

Researcher
Strategist

What behavior do you want to encourage? Digital experiences and rewards can affect people's actions both on-site and off.

1. Choose a flow: who is acting and why (a target audience trying to do something in order to be something larger).
2. Identify the biggest barriers to completing the flow (physical, logistical, or psychological).
3. Sketch audience-appropriate ways that each next step could be easy, attractive, social, or timely.

• Prevent exploitation

Nudges help us move people forward. Let's also think about when we should hold back.

The *fundamental attribution error* reminds us that free will is not as strong as we may think; choices are strongly shaped by outside influences. Product designers must decide what level of persuasion is effective and also ethical.

Onboarding flows that ask you to commit right off the bat, exclusive limited-time offers, and opt-out subscription patterns all use known psychological tendencies to create the results they want. Many startups now employ behavioral scientists to help shape their product strategy. And the audiences aren't always ready for it.

Stephen Wendel, former head of behavioral science at Morningstar, noted that "the last decade has shown us the tremendous power of applied behavioral science to do good: from saving people time to saving their lives. It's also shown us the downsides. To be frank, there's some shady shit going on in our field, and unless we call it out and fix it, we should expect regulation if not outright vilification." (Read Samuel Salzer's *Behavioral Design in 2020 and Beyond* report for more notes from specialists.)

"In many areas, ordinary consumers are novices, interacting in a world inhabited by experienced professionals trying to sell them things."

Richard Thaler, *Nudge*

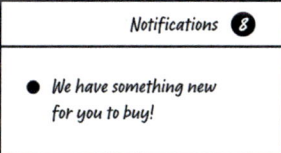
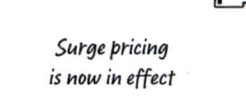

• Recognize and avoid manipulative patterns

Business pressures or thoughtless designs can push people down a path that doesn't serve them. *Antipatterns* (also known as "dark" patterns or deceptive patterns) are confusing or misleading interface elements that hide or contradict a person's desired action—"subscribe" actions hidden as tiny checkboxes within long forms, or "cancel account" links that change position and styling at each step. Beware of goals that prioritize only revenue or growth.

To create long-term relationships and ethical products, confirm that each part of the interaction is clear and supportive. Protect the people you serve, and beware of veering into these manipulative areas of behavioral design.

"Addiction is finding a quick and dirty solution to the symptom of the problem, which prevents or distracts one from the harder and longer-term task of solving the real problem."

Donella Meadows, *Thinking in Systems: A Primer*

Is it confusing?

Confusion

It's manipulative to style designs in a way that contradicts their function (restyling "never mind" buttons as primary ones, for example; or de-emphasizing a "cancel account" button when it's the visitor's intent; or hiding important terms in fine print). Prevent the unfortunate or intentional misuse of a design system; make clarity a principle.

Is it difficult?

Obstruction

It's manipulative to block users from intended actions because they would reduce a company's revenue. Preventing error is a usability principle; requiring a phone call to cancel an account is shady. It should be as easy to opt out of services as it is to opt in to them. Prioritize visitors' goals as highly as the business' goals.

Is it devious?

Coercion

It's manipulative to bias action options with psychologically damaging or passive-aggressive text, for example, with unsubscribe buttons on fashion newsletters that say things like "No, I hate looking good." Maintain empathetic design standards.

Is it hard to quit?

Addiction

It's manipulative to overuse chemical rewards in unsupportive ways. The brain's reward system is as hackable as any other; notifications and other dopamine bursts create loops that often outweigh our better judgement. Consider the high-frequency, long-term impacts of each flow and make habitual participation benefit the user as much as the company.

Is it shady?

Exploitation

It's manipulative to take people's information and use it in ways that don't serve them. Some car-share services triple prices when users' phone batteries are low, figuring they're desperate enough to agree. Balance revenue metrics with happiness metrics.

Is it exclusive?

Discrimination

It's manipulative to provide unequal services to less-advantaged individuals. We're building a digital world, and we must slow down to think deeply about whom we might be including or excluding. Redlining (denying loans to people based on where they live) had noxious societal impacts for decades; bandwidth and technology gates can create similar inequities. Make equal access a vital principle.

• Create friction and guardrails

"Software engineers are really more like social engineers."

Jonathan Harris, "Different Ways of Looking"

Internally, we have to guard against businesses incentivized to behave badly; externally, we have to prepare for visitors ready to do the same. Avoiding manipulative designs isn't enough; each design must look past its idealized VIPs to consider the inevitable troublemakers. Product design often focuses on making action fast and easy, but what if that action is destructive or abusive?

Penalties aren't fun concepts, but they keep people safe. Negative incentives recreate some of the natural healthy barriers between people and their impulses. Again, loss aversion is one of the most impactful cognitive biases, so simple obstacles to or penalties for harmful behavior can have significant impacts at scale.

Friction is another key strategy for safety; inertia can overpower a lot of impulses. Misinformation is a particular issue in the digital age; creation flows have become too easy. Analog types of information have more fact-checking and decay, and products that replicate these barriers can fight the increasing ease and realism of fake news.

Pauses are another simple technique to reduce antisocial behavior. Trolling feeds on the excitement of negative replies; sophisticated systems reduce the availability of those perverse rewards. Stanford neurobiology professor Andrew Huberman coaches us to "understand 'reward prediction error' and you will never reply to a negative comment again. Negative comments open a dopamine anticipation loop (in the commenter). Respond and the circuit closes; they get rewarded. Don't respond and their dopamine will eventually drop below baseline." Make sure a design won't reward bad behavior.

Take a subversive eye to features and imagine their abuse. Molly Clare Wilson named some "personas non grata" that are great to test with: naif, truther, prankster, opportunist, surveillance, fraudster, stalker, abuser, swarm, and terrorist. See how a design holds up against each one.

Naif Truther Prankster Opportunist Big Brother (Surveillance) Fraudster Stalker Abuser Mob (Swarm) Terrorist

Molly Clare Wilson's "personas non grata" help us imagine the destructive participants in a system.

• Design caring systems

Product designs have increasingly large impacts on culture (online and offline). In my opinion, creating a social product creates the responsibility of governing that microsociety. Experiences need clear codes of conduct and mechanisms for enforcement. Designs need ethical frameworks for behavior change.

Richard Thaler, an economist who won a Nobel Prize for his work on decision-making, says ethical nudges have three components. They must be easy and cheap to avoid. They should be transparent and never misleading. And they should attempt to improve the welfare of those involved.

Real compassion and care for our audiences is the foundation of ethics. As designer and artist John Maeda says, "It is often impossible to separate ethics from emotions. Our emotions express how we care. Literally." Emotional connection is a professional skill, not a business distraction.

"We need to design choice environments that convert the initial emotional high and focused attention to long-term habits and norms that we will follow without emotional triggers."

Christina Gravert, "Why Triggering Emotions Won't Lead to Lasting Behavior Change"

When we design caring systems, we can have a real impact on the world at small and large scales. In *Reality Is Broken,* game designer and researcher Jane McGonigal writes: "Young people who spend more time playing games in which they're required to help each other are significantly more likely to help friends, family, neighbors, and even strangers in their real lives."

Don't make ethics an abstract subject; pause to ask questions and care about the answers.

EXERCISE: Ethics check

Consider the large-scale or long-term effects of a design.

 Strategist
 Subject expert

Writer L.M. Sacasas shared "41 questions we should ask of the technologies and tools that shape our lives"—here are five to start with.

1. What possibilities for action does this technology present? Is it good that these actions are now possible?
2. What habits will the use of this technology instill?
3. What feelings does the use of this technology generate in me toward others?
4. What are the potential harms to myself, others, or the world that might result from my use of this technology?
5. Upon what systems, technical or human, does my use of this technology depend? Are these systems just?

REMEMBER: PATHS

Choreograph the steps	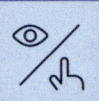 See/do lists	Inertia
Inspire and assist action	Incentives	 Progressive disclosure
Prevent exploitation	Ethics check	 Loss aversion

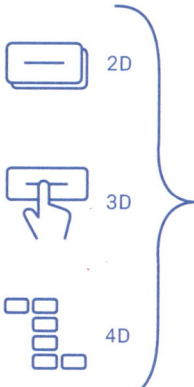

CREATE: Flows

Once you have a valuable concept for an experience, the next step is to figure out its content and flow. Choose an appropriate fidelity level for the questions at hand (shorthand, sketches, or wireframes), and have background research nearby for inspiration. Use the target audience's goals, moods, and typical habits to shape each step.

1. **Context:** Where are people coming from? Visitors coming from a Google ad may have different expectations than those coming from a friend's recommendation. In users' minds, pre-site steps are part of the flow. Sketch or list what they did to arrive.

2. **Landing:** Where do people land? Stakeholders often fixate on the home page, but visitors usually land on an article, product page, or profile. Sketch or list what they see as their very first impression: images, text, or functionality that orients them to this new experience.

3. **Activation:** What should visitors do first? A landing screen's biggest priority is to make sure people don't bounce; designers must find compelling ways to engage visitors' limited attention. Sketch or list the first call to action.

4. **Progress:** What's next? Consider all the subtasks needed to reach a larger goal (e.g., registering, getting the address, and showing up for an event). Arrange and rearrange the steps until they match or create an intuitive mental model. Sketch or list what people see and do on each screen.

5. **Success:** How does it feel? Pause at any completion moment; it's an opportunity to connect emotionally. Think about how you could celebrate the traveler's achievement. Sketch or list the signals of success.

6. **Send-off:** Where to? After visitors complete their goal, think about where else you could send them. People with the energy to complete one flow often have the energy or time to do a bit more. Sketch or list transitions to other flows.

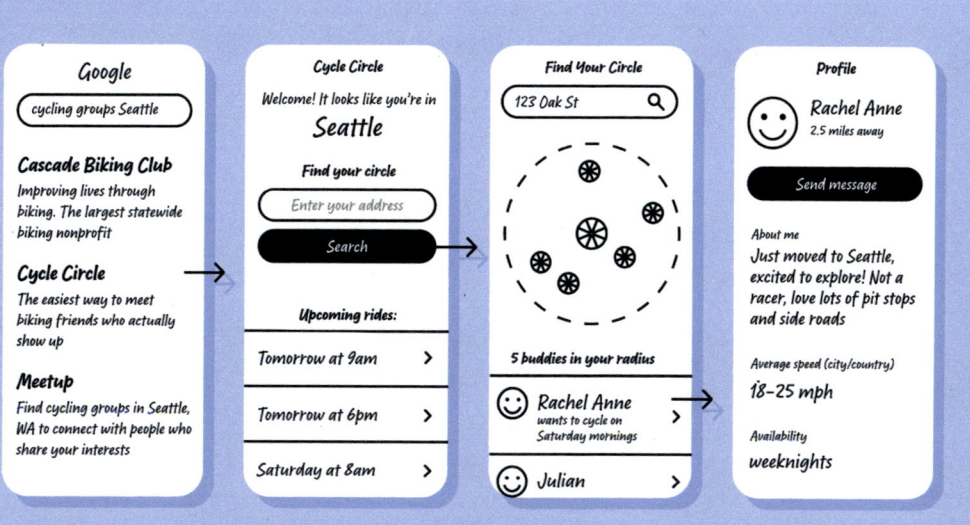

Sketch the starting point, steps, and send-offs for a scenario.

CRITIQUE: Content

Content is the primary thing to figure out in flows: what people see, and what they can do with it. Before we can analyze the usability of an element, it has to exist. Content could be text, images, or functionality; it could appear in large chunks or tiny pieces. Flows are back-and-forth conversations with an audience; see if the right ideas are happening at the right time.

Evaluate the words, images, functionality, and organization of a flow.

☑ Format
— What content types are most welcome (text, images, audio)?
— Do symbols and text clearly communicate the functionality, including constraints?
— Are patterns consistent from screen to screen?

☑ Order
— Are the steps and elements arranged in the right order?
— Does content need to be broken down into multiple parts, or combined into fewer screens?
— Is any repetition needed?

☑ Quantity
— What content and functionality are essential?
— Is the quantity enough to inform visitors but not overwhelm them?
— Are any other features needed for the task?

☑ Feedback
— After each input, what outputs are needed (state changes, errors, confirmations, or tips)?
— Do people need guidance?
— Are there ways to skip ahead or go back?

"Design dissolves in behavior."
Naoto Fukasawa

REMEMBER: INTERACTIONS

To summarize: product experiences are dynamic, not static. Every design should inspire ethical action; every step sits within larger contexts and goals. We need to think about 2D symbols, 3D usability, and 4D paths to create useful, enjoyable flows.

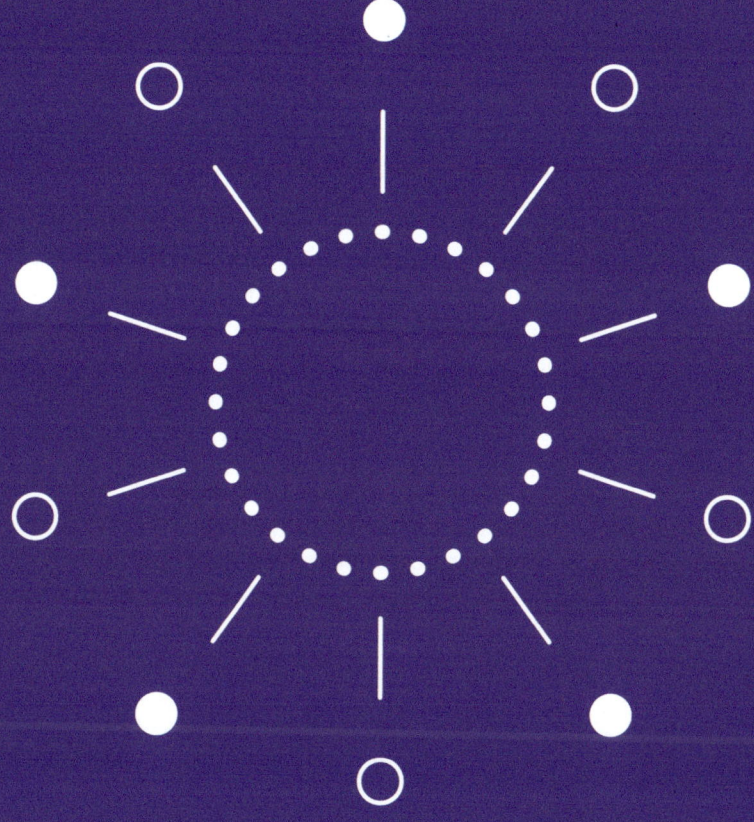

Memories

Memories are the aggregated internal impacts of an experience. They reflect the value of a product and create prompts for future visits; they're also fodder for word-of-mouth sharing. Simple, visual, emotional, and personal experiences tend to last longer in the mind. Strong memories are unique and meaningful. Designers should create valuable, differentiated, sticky experiences.

Without opening your phone: What are your three most frequently used apps or sites, and why?

Mine are currently Weather Underground, because it has the best graph of weather; Notion, because I've set it up as my personal dashboard for work and life; and TikTok, because I get so much good information and entertainment from the people there. But when I look at my phone's statistics, I see that Chrome, Spotify, and Gmail are actually the top three. Why don't I remember those?

When I visit TikTok, it's because I'm bored or want a momentary boost and the feed is very personalized to my tastes. When I go to Notion, it's because the whole setup is customized to match how I think about particular tasks. When I use Weather Underground, it's because their visualizations best present the information I want. It's those particular moments, personalized treatments, and compelling images that stick in my mind.

The value of an intangible, dynamic, often ephemeral product experience lies in the strength of the psychological imprint it creates. Most apps are downloaded and never used; many websites are forgotten and never revisited. Successful designs must be memorable. Deeper connections move past functional pragmatism into emotional highs and lows.

In this phase we'll consider images, personalization, and moments. This section is strategic, focused on creating memorable concepts for a product experience. The chapters in this section are divergent: they provide an array of considerations to inspire a wide range of ideas, not just the most obvious ones.

PRACTICE

2D images: Find the right feeling for an experience, show the value visually, and represent things appropriately. Recognize the long-term memorability of pictures, the simplicity of icons over some words, and the way photo alteration affects perception.

3D personalization: Choose the right platform; respectfully connect to the audience's devices, data, or community; and increase human connection. Make designs personal to increase their value and relevance; include peer references too.

4D moments: Map the context for the visit, identify moments that matter, and create unique value. Differentiate the experience for memorability, especially the peak and last moments, but allow for contextual or environmental surprises.

Concepts: Sketch a variety of valuable moments. Evaluate the resonance of each idea, and narrow the strongest features into memorable concepts.

Images
2D MEMORIES

Images synthesize a host of data points into a singular whole, helping both understanding and long-term memory. Emotional photos and videos can set a mood or tell a very specific story. Explanatory diagrams and illustrations can add new layers of connection or metaphor. Eye-catching icons and avatars can act as signposts for skimming. Solid layouts consider the impact of images, including locations, subjects, formats, scales, and styles. Successful product design uses memorable images to inspire visual and emotional experiences.

KEY QUESTIONS	EXERCISES
• **Atmosphere:** What feelings does the experience generate?	World-building
• **Visual storytelling:** What visuals best communicate the value?	Visual storytelling
• **Representation:** Which depictions are appropriate?	Art direction

COGNITIVE PRINCIPLES

- **Picture superiority effect**
  Images are more likely to be remembered than words (as long as they are distinctive and easy to label).

- **Iconic representation**
  The use of representational, example, symbolic, or learned images as interface elements can simplify controls and improve recall.

- **Face-ism ratio**
  The ratio of face to body in an image affects our perception of the person; we read headshots with a focus on intelligence and personality, body shots with a focus on sensuality and ornamentality.

• Find the right feeling

Visual designs, even wireframes and sketches, all have underlying moods: energetic or peaceful, silly or serious. Being intentional about an emotional direction will help inspire and guide not only image selection, but also many subsequent choices like layout, content, functionality, visual design, and copywriting. Mood-setting is a valuable exercise in early stages, and working with images helps us be more imaginative and not overly intellectual in our process.

Explore different spaces in the world, and imagine how they might translate into images and interfaces. Notice the more nuanced feelings. If you think of the experience as a café, is it busy or quiet, warm or cool, minimalist or maximalist? If you think of the experience as a conversation, is it intimate or public, focused or meandering, snappy or relaxed?

Is the experience like a good party, with lots of fun friends and surprising events?

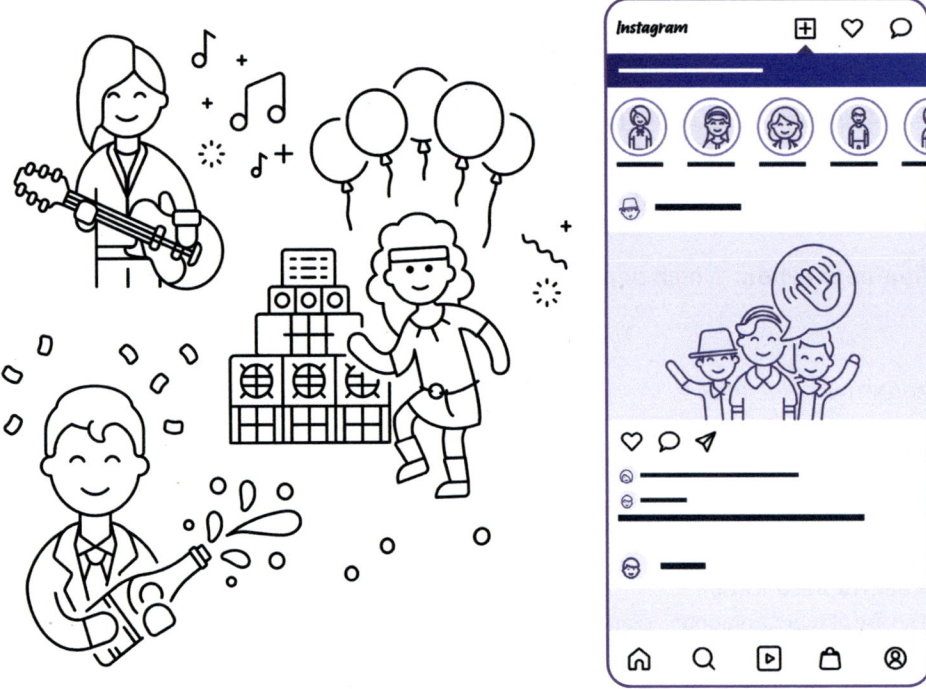

Instagram and other social apps often try to create a party-like experience, appealing to your visual senses and your emotions with lots of lifestyle images and bright colors.

Is the experience a quiet space for personal inquiry, removing all nonessentials?

👁 Google's search page was a revelation when it launched, providing a breath of fresh air amid all the clutter of the time. The experience prioritized focus (the user's goal) over immediate revenue metrics (typical business goals).

Is the experience a moment of awe, a showcase of technical virtuosity, or eye candy?

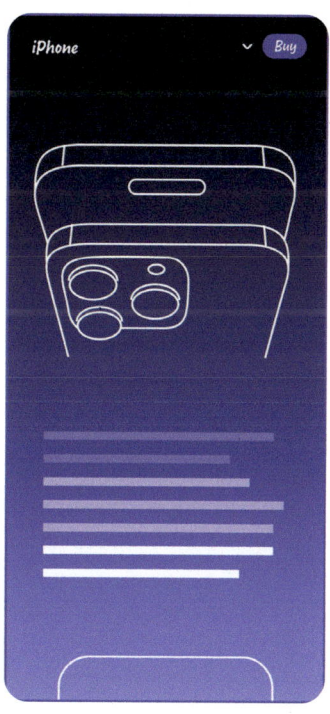

👁 Apple's marketing pages use sparkling close-up images of their technology and dramatic animations over rich gradients to convey the marvel of their new creations. Think about how different the experience is from a big-box retailer's site. How does it make you feel?

Is the experience like an unbroken stream of consciousness, like Kerouac typing On the Road on one long scroll of paper?

👁 iA Writer's interface stays clearly in the moment, hiding all words preceding the current sentence and the previous one (which has already faded). The editing area stays centered on the screen like a simple, classic typewriter.

I was surprised, as always, by how easy the act of leaving was, and how good it felt. **The world was suddenly rich with possibility.**

The collection (or lack) of images in an experience creates a vibe. Colors, symbols, and patterns produce a field of sensory impressions; faces, objects, and places introduce characters and culture. They trigger memories of similar things we've experienced, and the emotions those experiences carried.

> "World-building is just an exercise that you do to prepare for writing. [...] You use it to provide flavor and environment and effect."
>
> N.K. Jemisin

Product experiences can deliver familiar visuals or fantastic hints of a world to come. Award-winning science fiction and fantasy writer N.K. Jemisin teaches workshops on world-building as a preparation for writing, imagining new geographies, laws of physics, climates, architectures, people, genders, professions, technology, magic, resources, economies, religions, and power structures. Slight variations in just one or two of these variables can create dramatic new feelings. Imagine a new future that this product experience inhabits or creates.

Note: Thinking visually may feel extremely natural to you, or it may feel very difficult. Some portions of the population think visually/spatially; others think mostly verbally. If images don't come to mind easily, stick with stories.

EXERCISE: World-building

Design attempts to build some kind of new future, whether that's a tiny step forward from the present or a fantastic leap into sci-fi dreams. World-building exercises prompt us to imagine an alternate reality, and its landmarks, as a preparation for designing new experiences.

1. Jot down some feelings you're trying to deliver with a product experience—e.g., success, comfort, insight, reflection.
2. Think about experiences or environments you've had or seen that delivered some of those feelings. What elements do you remember—the space, the sounds, the colors, the people?
3. Imagine a world where everyone uses this product. What could it look and feel like? How would it differ from the world today?
4. Pull these ideas together in a format that suits you, whether that's visuals or visual language, on foamcore boards or in software. Consider:
   - **Landmarks.** What colors, textures, and symbols exist in this world? Is it technical or earthy? Minimalist or maximalist?
   - **Inhabitants.** Imagine the people (or other brands) in this product's universe.
   - **Activity.** What do people do in this world? Why and when do they interact with the product? What sounds or motions do they make?
   - **Language.** Grab or write poems, headlines, mantras, or manifestos that capture the design's spirit or vision.
   - **Feeling.** How do all of these elements make people feel?

Collect images, phrases, and ideas that convey the desired emotional experience.

- Strategist
- Visual designer
- Writer

• Show the value

"We don't think in words. The temptation to equate thinking with language is because words are more palpable than thoughts."

Alan Fletcher,
The Art of Looking Sideways

Visual storytelling is a core skill in communication design. Words can clearly outline specific benefits, but they are limited constructs for larger multisensory experiences. Humans existed for tens of thousands of years before language developed, and most are still highly visual creatures. People shouldn't have to read every word on a page to get the point. Always look for ways to be more visual.

Great images reinforce the product's value proposition, which could be practical, emotional, interactive, and/or differentiated. (See the Moments chapter for more inspiration.) Show, don't just tell, the value of the experience; seeing is believing.

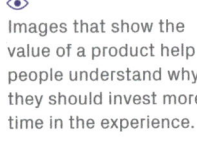
Images that show the value of a product help people understand why they should invest more time in the experience.

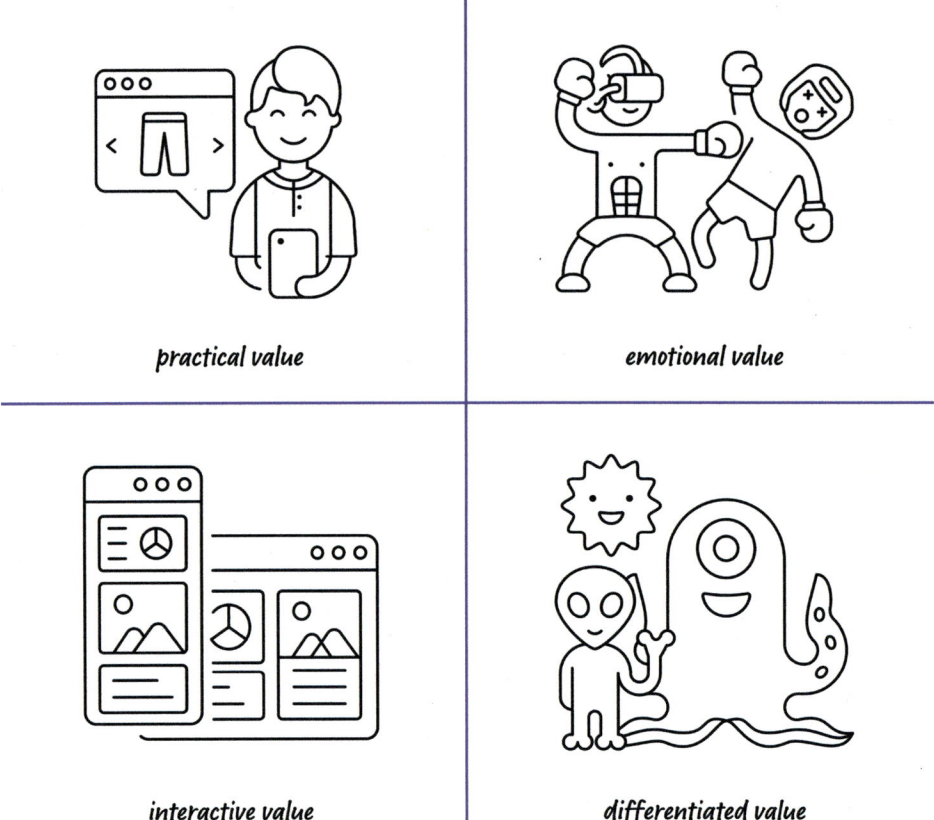

practical value — *emotional value*

interactive value — *differentiated value*

The scope and scale of images will vary greatly across different types of experiences. Marketing pages often take an editorial approach, using large and dramatic images like a magazine; signup flows are usually much more functional, focusing on interactive elements. But for any type of visual storytelling, think in terms of a leading hero (a key idea or action) and a supporting cast.

- Capture the big idea

   If there were only one image on the screen, what would it be? A full-width introductory section at the top of a screen is often called a *hero,* and this is also how we can think about our primary image for the experience: an aspirational vision.

   The right image can grab a slot in short attention spans or create a strong memory. GEICO's gecko is a fun and name-evoking image; Twitter's cute "fail whale" became an affectionate reference among users; Apple's humanized "Mac vs. PC" ads were retained far better than a comparison chart. Imagine ways to show benefits like wealth, connection, or ease as photos or demos. Try graphs instead of paragraphs.

   Aim for a memorable image. Ad-industry lore says that unusual images are most memorable, but studies seem to be mixed on that. Faces and intimate interiors do especially well on tests of recall, while landscapes and peaceful scenes do not. Also, make sure that a chosen hero image is received well by its intended audience.

"Design is a powerful weapon. Make pictures, not arguments, to win the war."

Leah Buley,
The User Experience Team of One

What image could convey the big idea?

◉ Metaphors set a mental model.

◉ Lifestyle images convey use cases and benefits.

◉ Product demos highlight utility or craftsmanship.

◉ Data visualizations relay quantitative benefits.

- Communicate the action potential

   For a moment in the middle of a complicated software workflow, hero images may be less relevant. A memorable visual could be the interface model itself: the image of a dashboard, a gallery, or a feed. The most valuable visual might also be a decorative element that adds emphasis to the primary action: eye-catching illustrations or photography in close proximity, for example.

What images would communicate a top-priority action?

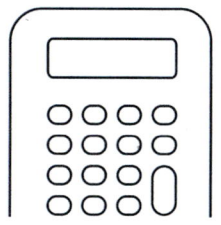

◉ UI elements represent possible interactions.

◉ Graphics can lead the eye to key elements.

- **Add supporting visuals**

What images would communicate secondary actions and emotional benefits?

On complex projects, it can be tempting to overexplain ideas with multiple headings and long paragraphs. Avoid the beginner's tendency to fill every screen with text and buttons; digital design is often skimmed, not read. Technical users may pore over every detail, but many will skip secondary text. Test layouts with image-focused viewers (like art school graduates or non-native speakers of the language) to see if people can get the gist of the experience from the visual elements.

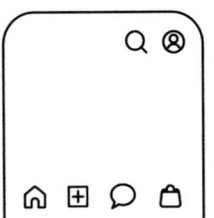

👁 Icons add familiar prompts and signposts.

👁 Backgrounds can reinforce the desired mood.

👁 User photos add friendliness and social interest.

👁 Lifestyle images provide context and/or a sense of place.

EXERCISE: Visual storytelling

Show, don't tell, the point of the page.

 Visual designer
 Subject expert

Imagine visitors who hate to read, who skim or skip all the carefully crafted text on a screen. Great images will make sure they still get the big idea and enjoy the experience. Good visual storytelling adds impact for everyone; images hit different than text or audio. Practice showing, not telling.

1. **Hero image:** Find or create a strong image that communicates the value of the experience. Consider metaphors, lifestyle images, product demos, or data visualizations.
2. **Action images:** Visually communicate what it is the visitor can or should do. Think about UI elements that convey the potential for action, or graphics that emphasize it.
3. **Supporting images:** Add more personality or clarity at important moments. Consider icons, backgrounds, user photos, or lifestyle images.

• Represent appropriately

Once you've selected a hero image and any supporting scenery, think carefully about the rendering. If the hero is a shiny new product, should the image be a close-up on the craftsmanship or a bird's-eye view of the integrated system? If the experience uses lifestyle scenes to help people see the product's impact on their lives, should you use imaginative illustrations or dramatic videos?

Art direction is an entire profession, but, like content strategy and branding, it's hard to separate from product design. Designers may direct or create final images themselves, or they may work with specialized collaborators. For initial concepts, just think about a style that fits; it can be created or farmed out later. Be bold to start, and then use practical project constraints to help narrow the options.

Let's look at some nuances of depicting products, data, and people.

• Represent products simply

A product screenshot is the easiest way to show an audience what they're going to get, and to make a digital experience feel more tangible. But product screenshots are often too complex to understand on the first impression, too informative for competitors doing their own research, and too dated in a matter of months. If you have to use screenshots, zoom in on key details and simplify, simplify, simplify. Play with the lens of focus; product shots can show a single design detail or the entire system's connections.

What part of the product is most compelling?

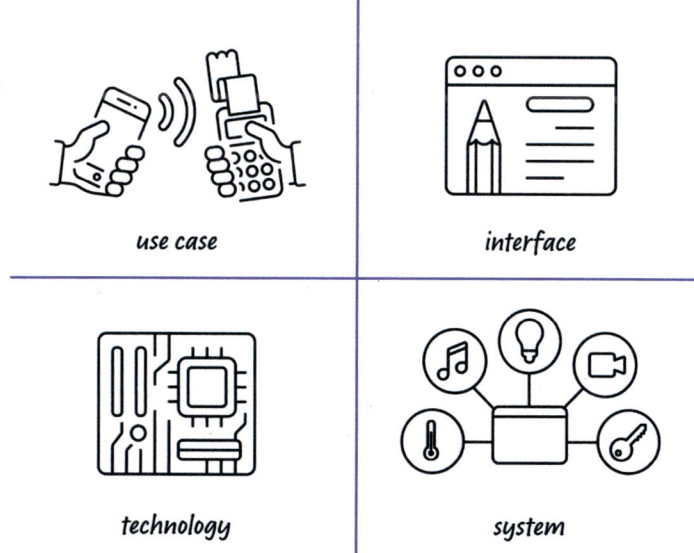

use case

interface

technology

system

• **Represent people respectfully**

How do subjects themselves wish to be seen?

Lifestyle images (showing when, where, and how an audience lives) can be the clearest, warmest way to tell a story about a product. Photos with people catch most eyes; humans are social creatures. Images of people in action can motivate similar action.

But, if we're working with images of people, we need to give serious consideration to appropriate representation. Images convey information and emotion, but also bias.

In a project called "Decoy," Canon told six different photographers six different stories about one man (an actor in real life). The portraits turned out very different (bright or shady, intimate or distant) depending on the photographer's understanding of the subject (lifesaver or convict, alcoholic or millionaire). Photo staging, cropping, and lighting communicate ideas too.

Canon's "Decoy" project showed how a photographer's ideas about a person affect how they capture the subject.

In a project that challenged the gritty, grimy ways we tend to portray topics like homelessness, photographer Rosie Holtom created positive, elegant portraits of unhoused people posed and dressed as they themselves wished to be seen.

Images are mirrors, and people want flattering reflections. Images are windows, and visual storytelling is not just what we look at but how. Respect the subjects.

• **Represent data usefully**

How might numbers feel more tangible?

Visual opportunities also arise with data. Facts and figures may be the fastest way to communicate information, but a big data table is TMI for many moments, and a random statistic is hard to put into context. Charts, graphs, and visual representations are often clearer and more valuable; as one financial services customer said about their savings account dashboard: "I just want to see the line going up and up."

Find useful, relatable representations for data. An intimidating number can transform into a compelling story.

- *Calculate:* Do the math for people. Help them understand what a promised benefit means for their wallet, their blood pressure, their waiting time.
- *Visualize:* Show the scale of the thing. Turn digital representations into real-world equivalents. Consider simple icons, clear photos, or dramatic animations.
- *Convert:* Communicate the impact of the number. A chunk of money could mean a roof over someone's head, a feeling of safety, a quantity of lunches.
- *Compare:* Provide benchmarks for the statistic. It may be helpful to know that it's higher or lower than average, a goal, a similar user's stat, a danger zone.
- *Contextualize:* Put the number into a timeline. Let people see it as part of a trend over time, not just an isolated moment. Sometimes it's not the data point that's relevant, but the change.

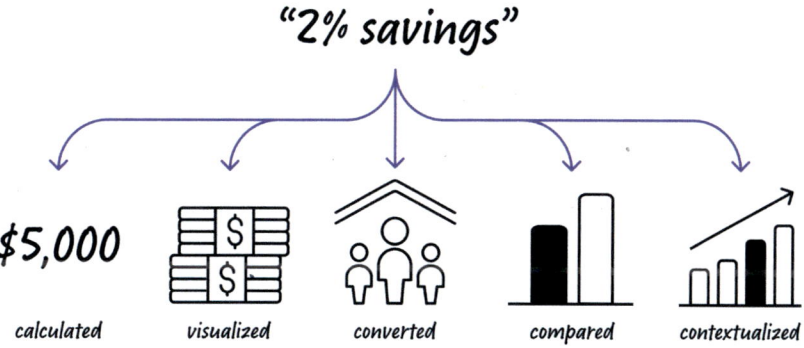

Numbers hit harder if they take the right form.

- **Balance bandwidth consciously**

   Lastly, consider the technical environments that deliver all these images. Bandwidth and load time are major constraints in emerging markets, but important worldwide. According to Google, the probability of visitors bouncing increases 32 percent as page-load time goes from one second to three seconds. Focus on the most essential experience you must deliver; consider cutting back on nonessentials. Keep talking to engineers for tips and tools to improve performance.

   "There's no point designing a nice, shiny, beautiful UI if it's going to take 20 seconds to end up on a user's device. They'll have left before they even got to see it."
   Harry Roberts, CSS Wizardry, via Lara Hogan, *Designing for Performance*

How might you deliver excellent experiences in low-bandwidth scenarios?

Select the subjects, formats, and styling of visual content.

 Visual designer

🗨 Strategist

EXERCISE: Art direction

Art direction is an entire career (selecting and directing illustrators, videographers, and others), but all designers have to play the role a bit when they make space for images in a layout. If you're deep in the weeds of app design you'll mostly be selecting icons, but if you're working on large screens or things like marketing pages, images are huge in size and impact. Larger brands will have detailed guidelines to follow; smaller brands might require some improvisation. Make the right decisions for each level of fidelity.

Low fidelity (sketches)
Make space for the art and think about its subject. Representations can be simple diagrams or stick figures; the idea is the focus.

- Who or what are the subjects (people, environments, interfaces)?
- Where are the subjects in the layout (foreground, background, inline)?

Medium fidelity (wireframes)
Refine the technical specs for the art. Use placeholder images rather than gray boxes to see how particular formats will affect the layout's perception.

- What format (photos, illustrations, videos, animations)?
- What size on each device (phone, tablet, laptop, desktop)?

High fidelity (mockups)
Find or create and polish actual images to get insights on design details. The quality of the images will affect the idea's perceived quality, so allot ample time to deliver at this stage.

- What style (dynamic, moody, friendly, geometric, typographic)?
- What cropping (close detail, panoramic environment)?
- What color (warm, cool, monochrome, rainbow)?
- What pacing (fast cuts, slow motion)?

REMEMBER: IMAGES

Find the right feeling

Show the value

Represent appropriately

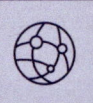 World-building

 Visual storytelling

 Art direction

 Picture superiority effect

 Iconic representation

 Face-ism ratio

Personalization
3D MEMORIES

Each product experience occurs on a certain piece of hardware used by a unique human being at a particular physical location. Memorable experiences intelligently serve those personal contexts and preferences using hardware, software, social, or environmental data to fill moments with more relevance, connection, and value. Human connections are especially powerful, allowing products to deliver the person-to-person inspiration, conversation, or collaboration people crave. Successful product design is high signal, low noise.

KEY QUESTIONS	EXERCISES
• **Profiles:** What data can increase relevance and meaning?	Data boundaries
• **Locations:** Where should the product meet people?	AEIOU research
• **Collaborators:** Who else would naturally be involved?	Swimlane diagram

COGNITIVE PRINCIPLES

- **Endowment effect**
People value items they own more strongly than equivalent items they do not own.

- **Signal-to-noise ratio**
The proportion of relevant versus irrelevant content in a design (assessed via general visual analysis as well as individual preferences) creates a measure of value.

- **Availability bias**
More recent or easily recalled events seem more prominent or important to people.

• Use relevant, ethical data

Irrelevant experiences are like digital junk mail, filling your mind and minutes with unwanted clutter. If you don't have a car, mapping apps that lead with driving directions repeatedly waste your time. Real estate newsletters that don't know your tastes are spam, instead of a competitive advantage. Categories like baby products can be irrelevant, outdated, or even heart-wrenching for certain people.

Personalization creates more meaningful, memorable experiences by reducing noise and increasing signal. Imagine a fitness app that leads with classes featuring the tone of music and guidance you prefer. Imagine a friend with food allergies who can browse custom menus where every dish is safe to eat. Personalized design saves people time and feels more magical. The challenge is to make it cool and not creepy.

Some people see privacy concerns as Victorian; others see personal data as precious. A thesis student I advised designed a social network for Chinese parents; when asked about privacy, she said: "Oh, Chinese people don't care about privacy, that's very American." On the flip side are the European standards that led to GDPR and other regulations. Personalization needs to reflect a particular audience's feelings about their data and its use.

Relevant product experiences intelligently maximize device capabilities, passive personalization, and active customization.

• Understand device capabilities

Where could data come from?

To design sophisticated interfaces, know what's happening behind the screen (especially mobile screens). Device hardware and software provides many details about its owner. Consider the full range of data available on a chosen platform.

 Location sensors use satellites and GPS to determine position.

 Proximity sensors say when the phone is close to an object or beacon.

 Magnetometers indicate north, supporting digital compasses.

 Moisture sensors alert users if the device contacts water.

 Barometers log air pressure and altitude data (e.g., steps climbed).

 Ambient light sensors detect the intensity of natural or artificial light.

 Motion sensors detect phone orientation and acceleration.

 Biometric sensors can detect faces, fingerprints, irises, heart rates, or blood oxygen.

 Gyroscopes track device rotation or twist.

- # Consider passive personalization

Passive data collection is the easiest method of data collection; many people who want a personalized experience don't want to do "work" to get it. This method can also yield more accurate personalization than complex preference-setting forms—self-reported preferences often differ from actual behavior. (How honest are you about every single thing you've clicked on?)

What data could create a memorable moment?

Anonymous web experiences can feel like you're sitting neglected in a restaurant, wishing the server would notice you need help; great service politely watches customers to see if they need anything. And digital experiences can watch multiple sources of action simultaneously, both on-site and off-site.

- *On-site data* logs taps and timing to create services that intelligently welcome people back or ingeniously serve them (like tools that note when visitors are clicking back and forth between products and reactively pop a service chat to try to help them decide).

- *Off-site (third-party) data* incorporates the tracks people have made elsewhere on the internet to deductively understand larger goals (like when you search flights to Orlando and subsequently see ads for Disneyworld).

Narrow or widen the lens of personalization sources appropriately.

Early in my career, research participants were usually irritated by sites that knew their preferences or browsing history. Now, they're much more accustomed to it, and often expect or desire it—as long as it saves them time and remains relevant. Personal data can provide delightful connections, or it can stalk you with things you looked at once and have no way to forget. Data has a limited window of relevance; remember to forget.

- # Consider active customization

Personalization makes the default experience one that's drawn from our own data; *customization* refines the experience based on intentional input from the visitor. It takes more work, but provides the most clear and obvious input model. Audiences, not algorithms, remain in control.

How might the audience be most comfortable sharing the data you need?

Active customization can feel safer and more respectful, even if passive personalization is possible (and faster). For example: location data could reveal an address, infer that it's "your home" or "your office" based on your routines, and list all the other product users who visit that place. It might be more polite to ask people to manually share that info, rather than grabbing it or assuming the connections are wanted.

👁 Sometimes it's more helpful to reveal less.

Looks like you're in...

Also remember that there are legal and ethical guidelines on data collection, storage, and deletion. GDPR has launched thousands of cookie-acknowledgement windows; HIPAA requires serious safeguards for medical information. Return to the Paths chapter for more ethical considerations: benevolence, transparency, and easy opt-out are essential.

Customization inputs can be structured or unstructured, for ease on the system's side or the visitor's.

- *Structured inputs* allow or force users to input their personal information in particular formats. (For example, Sephora asks a variety of specific questions about your skin so they can provide product recommendations and filter makeup reviews based on people with similar complexions.) This is more time-consuming for visitors, but it's extra efficient for businesses because people are adding data in the exact format engineers need it.

- *Unstructured inputs* can let users submit data in a format that's most comfortable for them: text, images, audio, video, or something custom. (Stitch Fix, for instance, has people submit Pinterest boards of their style inspirations). Unstructured data often increases participation and delivers more meaningful insights, but it does take longer to parse.

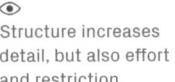 Structure increases detail, but also effort and restriction.

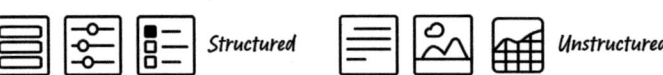

If you choose to develop more personalized experiences, remember that identities can be fluid. People may have different personas for different areas of their life; they may have static preferences, or they may be transitioning into new ones. Respect, connect, and protect diverse and dynamic perspectives.

EXERCISE: Data boundaries

Digital technology needs to respect and protect community members—especially the more vulnerable ones. Take the perspective of each person in each context: those sharing data and those seeing it; those who are centered and those who are marginalized. Consider these examples:

Outline data sources, potential features, possible risks, and needed controls.

 Researcher
 Subject expert
Engineer

Data source	Feature	Cool or creepy? Why?
Time zone	Personal greeting: "Good morning!"	?
	Personal greeting: "Sweet dreams, Sasha!"	?
Geolocation	See other pet owners in NYC	?
	See other pet owners in your neighborhood	?
	See other pet owners in your apartment building	?
Contact list	Link your contacts to see who's on the platform	?
	See what products your friends have viewed	?
	Message a contact about a product they bought	?
Browsing history	A special offer since you came here from Target	?
	A special offer since you look at comics a lot	?
	A special offer since you're clicking back and forth	?

Define your own data strategy, including ethical boundaries.

1. Brainstorm **personalized features** that might make your experience more enjoyable, efficient, or memorable. How might you create a special moment or routine?
2. List the **data sources** you have available to support this feature, both active and passive.
3. Analyze the **rewards** of each feature. Are they worth the effort of collecting and storing personal data?
4. List the **risks** of each feature. What issues could arise for the most vulnerable community members?
5. Define the **needed consent and controls**. How will you let people opt in or opt out?

Feature	Data source	Rewards	Risks	Control needed
Show neighborhood on profile	Geolocate user's regular location	Create a community vibe	Stalkers, discrimination	User can opt out of showing location
?	?	?	?	?

• Have a real-life presence

> "The fate of a memory is mostly determined by how much it means to us. [...] Memories that contribute meaningfully to our personal autobiography prevail in our minds."
>
> Hilde and Ylva Østby, *Adventures in Memory*

Product design often focuses on screens, but the full experience also includes physical and social elements. Memorable services exist in multiple dimensions, and better pictures of visitors' environments will help you design experiences that serve, prompt, or constrain action appropriately. Personalization might accommodate people's specific locations, bandwidths, or routines.

In the field of service design, the multidimensional connection points for a brand are known as touchpoints. Researchers Alisha Stein and B. Ramaseshan identified seven types of touchpoints for retailers, from digital to environmental to social.

- *Customer interactions* include word-of-mouth reputation, product reviews, and planned or unplanned interactions with other customers.
- *Store atmosphere* includes the site's layout, displays, amenities, design, ambience, and attractiveness.
- *Employee interactions* include greetings, continued attention, and personalized service.
- *Technology* includes the system's convenience, ease of use, and self-service capabilities.
- *Product interactions* include direct and indirect experiences of product quality or variety.
- *Process* includes navigation, waiting time, and customer service.
- *Communications* include promotional messages, informative messages, and ads.

A product experience includes real-world touchpoints, not just on-screen ones.

Customer interactions | Store atmosphere | Employee interactions | Technology | Product interactions | Process | Communications

Which touchpoints have the largest impact on this audience?

Strong service design links many different touchpoints. Products don't stand alone; they are part of larger brand experiences, and so we should think about the cohesiveness of the relationship across all timelines and dimensions.

The preceding section talked about personalizing the digital aspects of service; let's dig into the related real-world layers.

- **Meet people in-store**

    A 2021 McKinsey study said that the most important digital personalization for first-time customers was "making it easy for me to navigate in-store and online." Continuity and support navigating across dimensions helps both shoppers and businesses. Flows may go from screen to screen, screen to space, or space to screen; the first step may be digital or physical. Target's app lets shoppers map any in-store item, then see their own relative position once they're there; Polestar dealership kiosks let people input the preferences they've decided on in-store and send them to their phones to continue online.

    It's worth considering employees as users too. A long history of browsing a site may be relevant to staff trying to help the same shopper in person; a fruitful conversation with a knowledgeable employee could show up and inform later explorations online. Consider real-world inputs and outputs.

Could the product experience personalize the in-store experience, or vice versa?

- **Have a place at home**

    Home life is a second sphere for integrated experiences. Spatial memory is strong, and creating clear associations between a digital thing and a physical place can reinforce its recall. Lifestyle images (in product designs or marketing materials) and creative features can suggest the place and time where the product "lives" in someone's home. For example, the iPad's initial marketing showed happy customers using it to read the *New York Times* while relaxing on the couch, or to play games while snuggling in bed. Mental compartmentalization—associating certain ideas with certain places or times—is common, and can reinforce (or prevent) the urge to use particular apps.

    Homes are also full of unique habits and devices that could add to memorability. Physicality is major; one study of theater performers showed that their retention of a script was extremely high even months after the performance, and that reenacting the movements in a role further increased their recall (compared to purely verbal reports). Consider motion-capture devices, and how they might expand experiences.

How might physical experiences trigger product recall?

- **Show up to parties**

    A third type of 3D personalization is artificial: having a convenient presence in someone's digital world. Every app would benefit from a place on people's home screens; thoughtful icon design and valuable features may help make that happen. Websites can automatically earn a place in a browser's Frequently Visited section, but they could also get a dedicated and visible spot if the design provides a useful bookmark, bookmarklet, or browser extension. Don't be an island.

What other sites and apps could the product inhabit?

Meeting an audience where they already are often requires some customizations of expression to fit the tone and format of another place. Social media efforts are a prime example: formerly utilitarian brands now do aspirational Instagram portraits or goofy TikTok videos. Creative appearances on like-minded properties can be fun and expansive. Video games have marketing teams that sell virtual ad space to other companies (see the billboards in driving games); crossover cameos in other products can create surprising synchronicity. Be social, and get remembered.

• Follow up in good time

When could other highs and lows prompt additional digital experiences?

A final type of real-world presence is a proactive follow-up. Customers don't cease to exist after they finish shopping; they often love sharing unboxing or usage stories for products they like. Good timing is vital; I worked with one client who made sure to send "Why did you choose this item?" prompts immediately after purchase, when people were still high from their acquisition and most likely to give a positive response. Delivery day might be a great time to ask for photos or videos of the item in use; days or weeks later might be the best time to gather usage reviews or preempt customer service complaints. User journeys can extend beyond research and purchasing phases into usage and loyalty arenas.

People appreciate help finishing what they've started. Personal milestones can be a nice way to reinforce relationships, from the obvious birthday greetings to the more intimate celebrations of accomplishments with the service. I've heard from many financial services customers who wished their bank cared more about the amount of money they'd managed to save (and entrust to the bank). Identify and track significant behaviors—both actions and a lack of them. Find opportunities to reconnect.

Observe the target audience in its natural environment.

 Researcher

EXERCISE: AEIOU research

AEIOU is a popular framework for ethnographic research that provides five helpful categories in which to arrange observations (but encourages you to make them your own).

1. Observe the audience in action (through interviews, videos, or real-world shadowing), and note:
    - **Activities:** What goals, modes, or processes are people going through?
    - **Environments:** What are the different settings, and how do they affect behavior?
    - **Interactions:** What steps are regularly or occasionally involved in the activities?
    - **Objects:** What tools or resources do people use?
    - **Users:** What are the roles, preferences, and prejudices of the people involved?
2. Summarize the consistent patterns you notice across a number of people.
3. Sketch ways you might serve those needs, habits, and preferences appropriately.

• Build human connections

The final key element of personalization is people. Great personalization reflects not only an individual's tastes, but also their relationships. Staring at a screen can look like a solitary activity, but we're often using it to connect with other people. The top-down dynamic between a product and its users pales in comparison to the horizontal connections among the whole community.

The most popular, useful, or sticky apps let people bring their friends or make new ones; an isolated tool is often forgotten. Human connections, whether practical or aspirational, make products more meaningful and powerful. Online relationships can be even more frequent and important than offline ones.

Networks may be simple mirrors of someone's real-life relationships, or novel ways to form new communities. The first social networking apps brought the web of human connections into an always-accessible online map. The next phases allowed people to go beyond maps of their real-life connections and meet new people based on shared interests. Later networks grew to support multifaceted or changing identities.

However, not every product needs to be a full social network. Experiences may just need a few friends, collaborators, advisors, bosses, or family members. Bring in the connections that provide the deepest value for a particular audience.

"Since people aren't natural-born hermits, in fact we're all really communication junkies […] any kind of a user interface design must include person-to-person collaboration through the medium of the machine."

Alan Kay, "Doing with Images Makes Symbols"

• Add warmth

Adding friendly faces to an interface is a simple way to increase its emotional attraction—people tend to pay attention to images of people. Imagine a college fund dashboard that's a plain list of numbers, and then another version with a photo of the toddler it's supporting. Bringing friends to a party makes people more comfortable there, and likely to stay longer. Photos can trigger personal memories, future aspirations, or just some imagined warmth in a 2D space. Consider adding headshots, profiles, lifestyle images, or videos revealing the humans behind the screens.

"Every time you think your project is about a 'thing,' it's not—it's about people."

Adriana Valdez Young, "To Practice Inclusion, We Need to Let Go of Designer-Centered Design"

What friendly faces or materials would be welcome?

👁 User photos let people see who else is there, or who benefits from the service.

👁 Profiles increase intimacy and allow navigation via curation of photos, videos, or other materials.

- ## Add validation

Who is a trusted source on this subject?

Social validation is another key source of personal relevance. Seeing a significant number of people already using a product gives a potential user the confidence to try it; seeing certain friends already there adds insights on the product's character. In user research, I frequently hear the need for benchmarks and peer references; people crave inspiration and information from "people like me" (and the conformity bias shows we're more likely to do things that others do).

   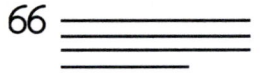

◉ Stats, ratings, reviews, and testimonials provide quantitative or qualitative validation from others.

◉ Activity from peers or friends provides more specific insights and relevant inspiration.

- ## Add inspiration

Who inspires this audience the most?

Inspiring figures are a third element of social personalization. In marketing, "crossing the chasm" from early adopters to the mass market requires shifting the story from features and benefits to trusted role models. Relationships can be social or *parasocial* (one-sided connections to public figures); influencers and algorithms now supplement or replace families and communities as go-to sources.

◉ Following people, brands, or groups lets individuals curate their perfect feed.

◉ Reactions (e.g., like, dislike, bookmark, tag) let viewers become voters who vet and shape an experience.

- ## Add emotion

What relationships help deliver the desired feelings?

Important but less visible parts of social connections are shared values or emotions. The design of products affects the tone of conversations and relationships within them; we should try to understand what people are feeling (or wanting to feel) and how it affects what they want to see or do with others. Nuanced products address the motivations and contexts for interaction with others, and build on them.

◉ People may want partnership in work or learning experiences.

◉ People may need compassion: a friendly ear or helping hand.

◉ People may want solidarity as part of a larger movement or fight.

• Add conversation

A fifth level of personalization is conversation: enabling light chats or serious discussions with the right people. You may see a product as an app for photo sharing, dog walking, or food delivery, but these tasks are just specific types of communication and relationships. Many mature apps add messaging as their community grows (whether text, audio, photo, or video), and chat can become the most emotional and sticky feature in an app.

What forms and topics of conversation would be valuable?

◉ Public posts and replies create broad connections.

◉ Private messaging connects self-selected groups.

◉ Muting/blocking hides or prevents undesirable interactions.

• Add collaboration

Finally, consider product-specific ways people would like to involve others; even to-do apps have collaborative use cases. Parents may act on behalf of a child; workers may need approvals or delegations; friends may need help. As you create ideas for an experience, list or map all the other people involved. Personalization may mean incorporating not only the right data, but also the right people. And the more collaborative the experience is, the more retention and referral prompts you build.

Who else might be involved in the moment?

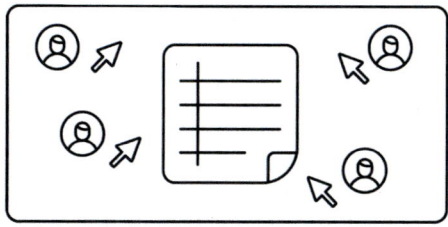

◉ People often like to share material or tasks with others (in common or innovative patterns).

◉ People may appreciate ways to reuse or build on existing work (annotate, sprout, duet).

Map the different collaborations or hand-offs in an experience.

 Researcher

 Engineer

EXERCISE: Swimlane diagram

1. Choose a primary user. In a horizontal row, list each step they take toward a goal.
2. Add another row each time they interact with another person or system. Draw arrows to indicate the collaborations or handoffs.
3. Think about how the process could be easier, safer, or more fun.

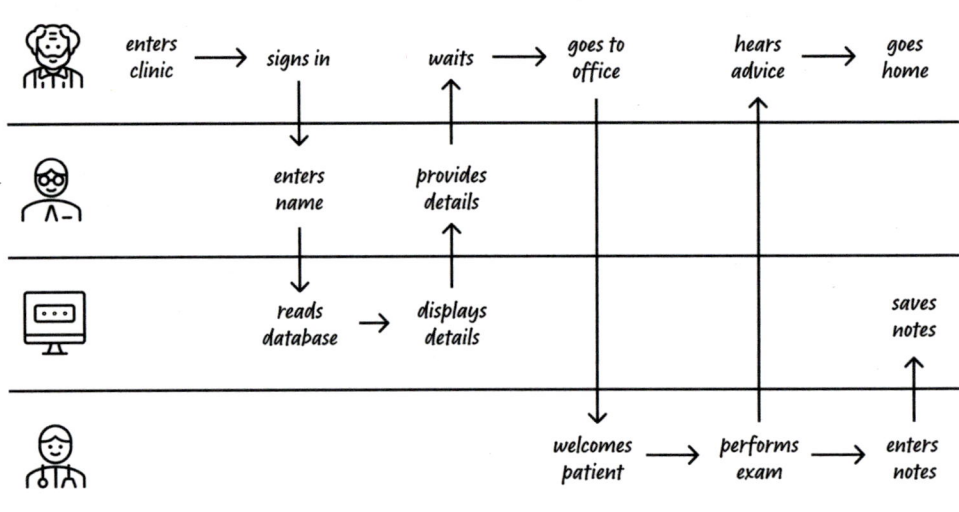

REMEMBER: PERSONALIZATION

Find relevant, ethical data

Have a real-life presence

Build human connection

 Data boundaries

 AEIOU research

 Swimlane diagram

 Endowment effect

 Signal-to-noise ratio

 Availability bias

Moments
4D MEMORIES

People don't remember every minute of every experience, only the essential or interesting moments. Map a visitor's bigger-picture journey (on-site and off-site) to understand their expectations for a product: their mental model. Prioritize the emotional peaks and troughs where they're filled with energy or frustration, as well as the final scene they'll take away. Strong concepts deliver practical, emotional, interactive, or unique value for a user's mindset at a particular time. Successful product design creates moments that matter.

KEY QUESTIONS	EXERCISES
• **Mental models:** What are people's expectations for a process?	Journey map
• **Value:** What unique benefits does the experience provide?	Value propositions
• **Format**: What's the right form for the experience?	Experience model

COGNITIVE PRINCIPLES

- **Peak-end rule**
  People judge an experience based on how they felt at its most intense point and at its conclusion, not the average or total sum of moments.

- **Isolation effect**
  Unique or distinctive things (differing from current alternatives or from past versions) are more readily remembered than common ones.

- **Fundamental attribution error**
  When judging behavior, people usually underemphasize situational and environmental effects and overemphasize personality characteristics.

Map the mental model

To find design opportunities and serve them well, designers must understand the audience's internal idea of a process or experience: their mental model.

Mental models don't exist in a one-to-one relationship with technical models. A mental model for "starting a car" is "press brake, insert key, turn key, shift into drive, release brake, press accelerator." There's a lot more going on under the hood, but the driver doesn't need to think about the mechanical details. They have a mental model that's good enough for them to operate the car.

Mapping existing mental models helps us consider the effort a new process will take to learn; a better process is not necessarily easier at first. Electric cars had to change drivers' mental models from "insert key and turn it" to "push button"—a simpler process, but still a new one. "Intuitive" experiences match a person's mental model for a process; "innovative" experiences create a new model. Consider both options.

> "[P]eople's views of the world, of themselves, of their own capabilities, and of the tasks that they are asked to perform, or topics they are asked to learn, depend heavily on the conceptualizations that they bring to the task."
>
> Don Norman, "Some Observations on Mental Models," in Dedre Gentner and Albert Stevens, *Mental Models*

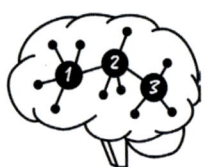

Mental models for an experience include certain steps and associations.

List the steps or phases

The steps in a mental model for an experience are more than just clicks; they usually include many related off-site or offline tasks. A mental model for "buying a bicycle" might include phases of consideration, research, comparison, trial, selection, and purchase; it might also include post-purchase phases like receipt and service. Some models are more technical; others are more social.

COMPARE
Models for product interaction

Don Norman's "seven stages of action" model identifies two major phases of interaction with technology, each involving several stages. The process may occur once, or in loops.

Execution
1. Set goal
2. Plan
3. Specify
4. Perform

Evaluation
5. Perceive
6. Interpret
7. Compare

Lance Bettencourt and Anthony Ulwick's "job mapping" model lists nine "jobs" that people try to complete with a product or service. The order and importance of the jobs may vary.

1. Define
2. Locate
3. Prepare
4. Confirm
5. Execute
6. Monitor
7. Modify
8. Conclude
9. Troubleshoot

Interview the intended audience, and ask them about their processes. Find the consistent steps in the journey, and the higher-level phases. Make sure to consider the opening moment (why they first get triggered to act), their unique approach (specific environments and tools), and the ending (what makes the scenario feel successfully resolved for them).

| Consideration | Research | Comparison | Trial | Selection | Purchase |

Sticky notes are a great way to quickly outline and refine a model. List one phase per note so they can easily be rearranged or replaced.

- **Look for leverage points**

Next, find the highlights. Experience design requires a constant prioritization of efforts. Of course, we want every single moment to be designed beautifully, but a sustainable business has to start with the efforts that will fund later work. Similarly, all minutes are not equal in the user's journey. It's tempting to fixate on home screens, but they're often not the first, most frequent, or most important stop. A "forgot password" experience is essential but banal; it's wise to focus design energy on things that make the biggest difference.

System analysts look for leverage points, where small changes can tip much larger shifts. Leverage points can go beyond UI edits; they may change systemic rules and rewards, functional access and feedback, or psychological mindsets and beliefs.

Product designers should look for the most difficult points in a process—these are the moments where the product can be a must-have, not a nice-to-have. As designer Erin Nolan told me: "It seems obvious but it's incredibly easy to forget, from what I've seen, in product cultures that value high-fidelity mocks and constant shipping of features."

A fun inspiration is Joseph Campbell's "hero's journey"; the twelve phases he proposes have symbolic relevance for many products. "Meeting the mentor," "Tests, allies, enemies", and "Return with the elixir" speak to the social phases in various processes, when people get advice or share successes with friends. "Crossing the first threshold" and "The road back" highlight times when people often need additional help. Find the pivotal points for your hero.

"The silver bullet, the trimtab, the miracle cure, the secret passage, the magic password, the single hero who turns the tide of history. [...] Leverage points are points of power."

Donella Meadows, "Leverage Points: Places to Intervene in a System"

The hero's journey, from Joseph Campbell's *The Hero with a Thousand Faces*, is a fun inspiration for key points in an experience.

- # Create moments that matter

  "Moments that matter" are the valuable, memorable, shareable interactions people have with a product. Jaime Levy's *UX Strategy* calls them "key experiences"; Dan Saffer's *Microinteractions* emphasizes "signature moments." These are the best places to prioritize design energy.

  A key moment may last only seconds, but create memorable spikes of feeling between boring and forgotten flatlands. Products are structured architecturally but experienced emotionally; a clock ticks blindly on, but our perception of each day distorts with its drama.

  Imagine someone buying a new phone: purchasing the device, waiting for delivery, unboxing it, setting it up, discovering features, receiving a first bill, dropping it, considering repair options, contacting customer support, and resolving the issue. Those moments are not equal. Unboxing moments are so special that entire channels are devoted to people sharing them; a moment of bad customer support can be so terrible that it turns a customer off forever.

  Moments don't have to be standard steps; they can also be arbitrary celebrations (like signup anniversaries) or creative insertions. Google is known for its easter eggs, where certain search terms have unexpected results (try googling "askew").

  Don't forget the finale; the peak-end rule reminds us that people judge an experience based on their feelings at its most intense point and its final conclusion.

Plot the phases in the process horizontally. Stretch or shrink them to show duration or focus. Add a vertical dimension showing enjoyment. Examine the moments visitors enjoy least or most.

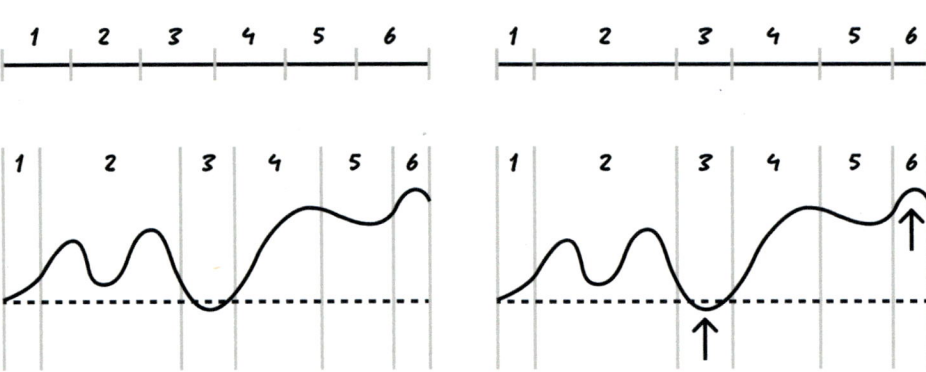

EXERCISE: Journey map

Journey maps communicate the emotional arc of a person's experience and reveal times when they most need service. Have user research close at hand to keep you user-centered; remember *their* preferences and habits, not your own.

1. Title a page with a specific audience, job to be done, and motivation.
2. On the top half of the page, create four rows: phase, activities, environments, and barriers. Fill in each row with notes that could or should inspire design choices. Start from a specific trigger, and go step by step until the job is "done" in the audience's mind. (See the AEIOU research exercise if you need more inspiration.)
3. On the bottom half of the page, draw a horizontal dashed line underneath the timeline; this is a baseline for the user's emotional journey. List each major step in the journey, and how the person feels at that moment, putting an emoji above the line if it's positive or below if it's negative. Connect the dots with a smooth line.
4. In the graph, highlight the dots farthest from the baseline or pivotal for completion. These are the moments that matter; this is where to focus design energy.

Note: Journey maps need to be detailed enough to provide inspiration, but high-level enough to be skimmable. If the journey has 25 steps, you may need to zoom in.

Find the emotional highs and lows to serve.

 Researcher

 Strategist

ALT: *Service blueprint.* For complex business scenarios, consider adding the behind-the-scenes processes as additional rows. Interactions with data, employees, software, and third-party vendors may be excellent opportunities to improve user experiences.

budget-minded senior trying to get vitamins in order to follow doctor's orders

PHASE	TRIGGER	RESEARCH		SELECTION		PURCHASE		USAGE	
ACTIVITIES	annual physical	listening, trying to remember	searching for vitamins	searching for coupons	choosing brand, other details	checking out	waiting for delivery	first taking the vitamins	continuing to take them
ENVIRON-MENTS	doctor's office	public transit (phone)		home (computer)			home (kitchen)	out and about	
BARRIERS	lack of energy, health anxiety	forgetting the rec	tech anxiety	hard-to-read websites	choice overload	budget	fear of scams	starting a new habit	maintaining new behavior

EMOTIONAL JOURNEY:
- gets doctor's advice
- sees prices
- finds a coupon
- fills out forms
- places order
- waits for delivery
- forgets to take vitamins
- gets a reminder

THINK IN 4D // MOMENTS // 201

• Define unique value

> "If your team doesn't agree on why the product is interesting, it's going to be hard to market it."
>
> Nicole Fenton,
> "Words as Material"

Once you've identified the moments that matter in an experience, brainstorm the best ways to serve them. How can the product provide the most value to its audience?

Tim Sheiner's "digital machine" framework calls this part of a product the *value model*. Strategists generally call it the *value proposition*. Value props help teams remember why a feature or product matters for the audience: the larger achievements it enables.

To create brilliant products, we work backward from an idea that's most valuable to the target audience: a strong value proposition implies a user experience strategy that then implies certain features and content. Product value can be practical, interactive, or emotional—but it must be clear.

Be very clear on the value of the product (to a specific audience at a certain time).

• Practical value

> "The secret to building great products is not creating awesome features, it's to make your users awesome."
>
> Kathy Sierra,
> *Badass: Making Users Awesome*

At a base level, the concept must serve the practical needs of the moment. Ride-sharing apps provide on-demand transportation. Weather apps help people decide whether to pack an umbrella or an extra layer. The most beautifully drawn and animated map lacks value if it doesn't solve someone's practical need.

Remember that the audience, not the design, is the star. The value is not in the feature, it's in what someone does with the feature. Find the exciting use cases. Practical value could include organization, education, entertainment, or reference.

Does the practical value of the experience stand out enough to be memorable?

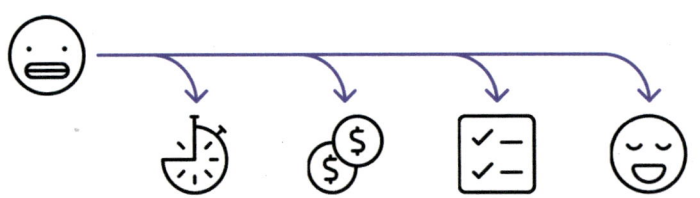

Practical value helps people save time, money, stress, and hassle.

- ## Interactive value

A differentiating part of the product's value might be *how* you serve user needs. Even the earliest stages of design may include interface ideas that define strategy.

Using GPS to get someone's location instead of requiring data entry is a form of interactive value. So are audio interfaces that serve harried moments better than thumb typing, or swipe-right UIs that quickly indicate preferences (a novel pattern that has become a defining experience). Interactive value could take the form of one-click checkout, augmented browsing, shake-to-refresh, or voice navigation.

Literal descriptions or analogous metaphors can help convey a product's interactive value (for example, this page is your news feed, your desktop, your journal, your album). Each one will imply certain features and usage patterns; a weather ticker seems like a hands-off feed to watch, but a weather journal sounds like something to write in. Try some creative metaphors and see how they inspire different designs.

> "[P]retend the interface is magic. If your persona has goals and the product has magical powers to meet them, how simple could the interaction be? This kind of thinking is useful to help designers look outside the box."
>
> Alan Cooper, Robert Reimann, and David Cronin, *About Face 3: The Essentials of Interaction Design*

Could an interaction's format be its core value?

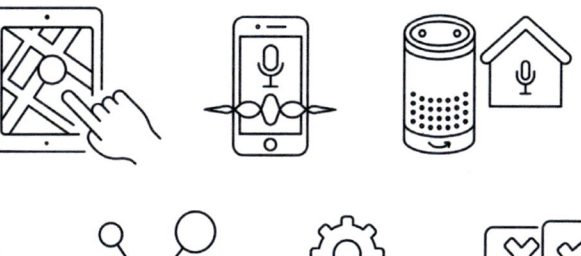

Interactive value could mean wireless connection, touchscreen control, voice control, browsable formats, maps, diagrams, settings, chat, and more.

- ## Emotional value

A higher-level, less-obvious type of value is emotional. When you use a ride-sharing app and step out of a car without paying, the feeling of freedom is part of the product experience. When you're at the grocery and the credit card reader starts buzzing loudly with a message in all caps, you feel as though you're being yelled at. Emotional value is not an add-on to be considered once we've launched functionality; it's an essential part of the experience.

Aarron Walter's *Designing for Emotion* turned psychologist Abraham Maslow's famous hierarchy of human needs into a pyramid of interface design needs: a product must be functional, reliable, and usable, but also pleasurable. Functionality is the foundation that people pursue in your product (or other options). Reliability is the way to build trust, habits, and long-term relationships. Usability makes it simpler and easier for people to achieve their goals. But emotional connection makes it something people love to do, and will remember later.

> "People will forget what you said, people will forget what you did, but people will never forget how you made them feel."
>
> Maya Angelou

Could emotional impact be the most valuable piece of the product?

Designer Jussi Pasanen encourages us to work not in ascending layers of this pyramid, but in vertical slices. The goal is to find not just a minimum viable product (MVP), but a minimum lovable product. Emotional value could be excitement, peacefulness, intrigue, or warning. (See the Relationships chapter for examples of product metaphors that create emotional connections.)

👁
Emotional value is important even in MVPs.

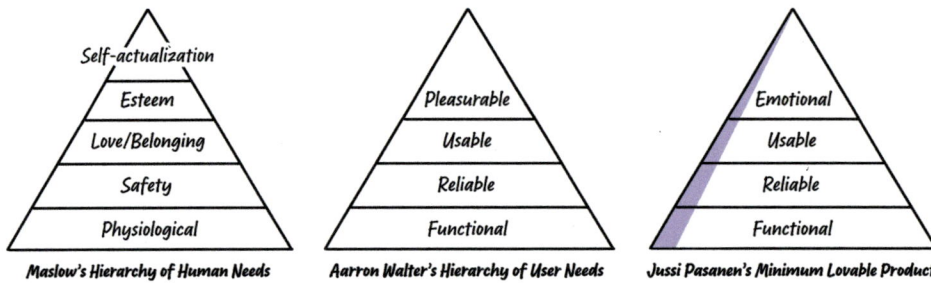

Maslow's Hierarchy of Human Needs   *Aarron Walter's Hierarchy of User Needs*   *Jussi Pasanen's Minimum Lovable Product*

• Differentiated value

"Flashbulb memories can arise from brand-related experiences [...] this may be especially likely when a brand is well-differentiated from competitors and when an encounter is [...] a first-ever interface between a consumer and a brand."

Harper Roehm and Michelle Roehm, "Can Brand Encounters Inspire Flashbulb Memories?"

Could an experience's uniqueness be its value?

Don't forget the element of surprise. In the clouds of memory, it's the novel and meaningful encounters that linger.

Imagine a jaded visitor who's seen everything before. How can you surprise them? Make something about the functionality, interactivity, feeling, or relationship new and different. Differentiated value could be a playful experience when everything else is serious, a luxury experience when everything else is minimal, a fashionable approach when everyone else is functional. In an increasingly crowded digital world, you can't be boring.

Define the reason for using the experience.

🧭 Strategist
✖ Writer

EXERCISE: Value propositions

Get really clear on the value proposition of an experience. Make sure to consider the specific audience and their particular goals. Answer their core question of *What's in it for me?*

1. Try this sample format: "Product provides unique value for specific audience."
   e.g., "Circle Tours provides safe ride buddies for casual cyclists"
2. Try other word choices. Thinking and writing is design; don't rush to the visual part.
3. Put the options in front of the intended audience (in the form of headlines or multiple-choice questions) and get their reactions. Ask why they prefer one over another.

• Turn value props into UI

Shaping a product experience requires an understanding of the audience's mindset: what they want, what they notice, and how they tend to react. Different tasks and mindsets require different forms: doing data entry is very different from playing a game; managing security settings for employees is very different from making a collage of bedroom decor.

I worked on one product that served both IT professionals and salespeople; they could not have had more different mindsets. IT people wanted all the details to appear on each screen; their job was to check every number and noun. Salespeople just wanted attention-getting benefits and dramatic stories; their job was to inspire conversations and action. Usage patterns were also a dichotomy: IT people wanted to go heads-down and figure things out themselves, salespeople wanted to pick up the phone and talk to someone. We ended up creating "lite" and "full" versions of the product for the different mindsets, and splitting the shared homepage into a skimmable top plus an information-rich bottom.

While mental models and journey maps help us understand a visitor's internal and external experiences, and value propositions help us define the reason the product exists, experience models make sure we provide service in the right form. Choices include a product's platform, content, and structure.

> "what if the customer doesn't want to go on a journey. i think they're just trying to chill rn"
>
> Christopher Reath, on Twitter

• Platform: Where you meet them

Value propositions often imply a certain platform; products designed as apps or as websites will be more or less able to deliver on certain promises.

For example, native apps can deliver great personalization and flexibility. Products that are only used out in the field, on a phone or tablet, can leverage mobile-specific features and interactions like camera integration and voice inputs. But apps may fail to deliver on promises of immersion or insights; small screens can be too limiting.

Responsive websites, on the other hand, provide great accessibility and space; they can take advantage of big screens and stable internet. But they might not deliver personal experiences or polished designs as nicely as dedicated apps; UI patterns vary by platform, and disparate screen sizes put layouts to numerous tests.

Platform decisions must consider both audience and business needs. Make sure the capabilities of the platform match the product's value proposition.

Where does the audience want to use the product?

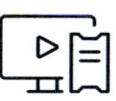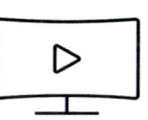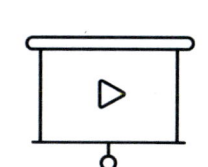

Platforms vary not only in typical screen sizes, but also in other qualities.

COMPARE
Platform benefits for apps versus websites

		Native apps		Responsive sites
Audience benefits	Access	Only available on specific devices		Available on every device
	Display	Constrained screen sizes		Large-screen capabilities
	Interactions	Standard or custom interactions		Familiar search and find patterns
	Recall	Discrete, simple mental model		Hidden/nested within a browser
Business benefits	Acquisition	Downloading creates a barrier to entry		Almost no barrier to entry
	Activation	Easier to access wallet, contacts, data		Often harder to link other app data
	Revenue	Less shopping cart abandonment		More shopping cart abandonment
	Retention	Built-in push notifications		Fewer notifications built in

• Content: What you show them

What type and amount of content does the audience want?

Value propositions must be expressed in content: what people see, and what they can do with it. A concept whose value is "meeting other smart people" would probably lead with faces or blurbs that show a community and demonstrate each person's intelligence (plus ways to connect). A moment whose value is "getting a big task checked off my list" would probably lead with text or an image representing the task, and a checkbox to mark it complete.

Don't assume people pay attention to the same things you do. Visual people may jump from image to image and ignore all the text; heavy readers often do the reverse. I like to judge layouts in "looking mode" and then "reading mode" to see how they're serving each type of attention. User research will often reveal surprising areas of focus or gaps in attention. Choose content that serves the audience's learning style.

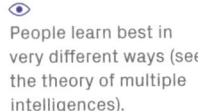
People learn best in very different ways (see the theory of multiple intelligences).

Visual   *Auditory*   *Tactile*   *Social*   *Numerical*

Also consider the right amount of detail for the chosen audience. If people love videos, that doesn't mean they love long documentaries. If people want a comparison chart, they may be expecting every spec or just an overview. Understand the visitor's appetite for information—scanning to find a few particular facts, skimming to get the overall idea, or studying to check all the details—and support that level of attention. In general, remember the principle of *progressive disclosure:* start with simplicity, then provide more depth as requested.

Searching — *Skimming* — *Studying*

◉ Consider the level of detail the use case implies.

• Form: How you serve them

Value propositions become interactions, and their design should suit the visitor's mood or mode. Designers spend hours at their desks, poring over product content and design details, so there can be a natural bias to design for a focused, intentional, "getting things done" mode. But visitors may be in "urgent quick fix" mode, "sleepy commuting" mode, or "drunken retail therapy" mode. They may be enjoying a learning process, or they may be in a hurry to finish something.

How could the interface serve the mood and expertise of the visitor?

Interfaces could be comforting, silly, or snappy to suit a mood. Imagine that checking your email was designed as a game, versus a tutorial, versus a control panel. Understanding the audience's emotions will help us understand what propels them forward and what holds them back in the moment.

Think about energy levels. If visitors are low energy, consider ways to do the work for them. They may want to lean back and passively watch a video or skim a list. If they're high energy, consider how you can best channel that energy. They could actively put together their own plan, or help others.

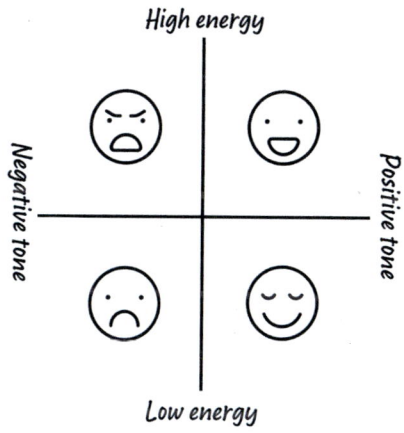

Also consider the tone. If there's a possibility that people might be stressed, use more predictable patterns; consistency is comforting. If you think people are more likely to feel positive, you can have fun sharing a joke, surprise, or celebration. Memorable moments are emotional.

◉ Consider the visitor's energy levels and mood for the product experience.

Lastly, consider the amount of control the audience wants; it should match their proficiency at the required tasks. If the audience is full of beginners, simplify the interface to the most essential parts. If the audience is full of experts, consider full control like custom dashboards. Do visitors need to customize every detail, get some guidance, or do as little work as possible? Could the experience be passive, one-touch, or customizable? Find the right spot between DIY and TMI.

All these considerations should give you some ideas for an experience model for the moment. The Relationships chapter also talks about interaction metaphors—spatial, prosthetic, or human. Think about a metaphor that matches the value proposition and the user's needs, and how it might create an innovative interface.

Find the right form for the moment for the audience.

 Visual designer
 Engineer

EXERCISE: Experience model

Find forms of interaction that deliver the promised value to an audience.

1. Outline the technical constraints: When and where might a visitor act? On what devices?
2. Understand the energetic spectrum: Is the activity more solitary or social? Are visitors more active or receptive (lean-forward or lean-back)? How much detail and control do they need?
3. Shape the experience model: What format might suit their needs? Revisit interaction metaphors—the product could be a reading *friend,* a reading *environment,* or a reading *tool*—and explore correlating interfaces (a tool could be a map, an X-ray machine, or a psychedelic drug).

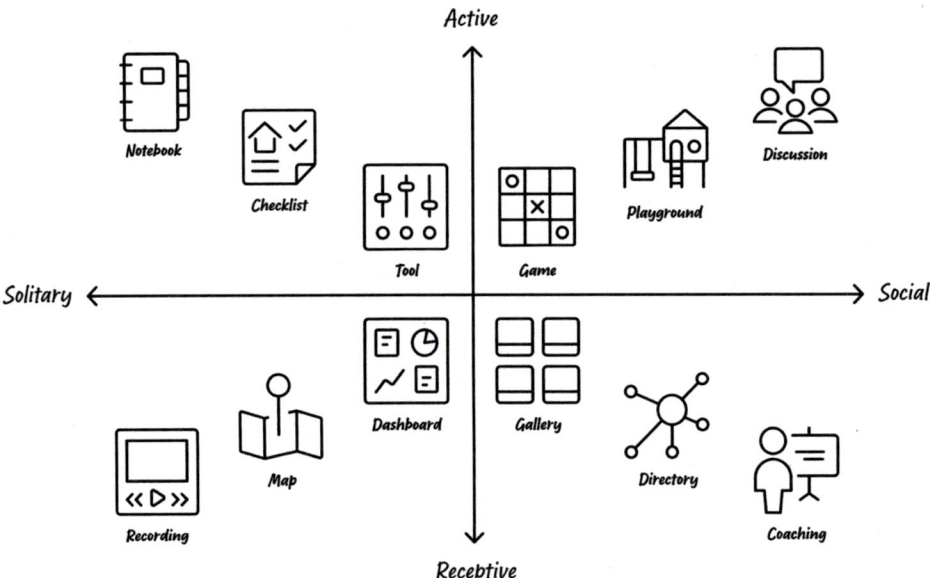

REMEMBER: MOMENTS

Map the mental model —  Journey map — Peak-end rule

Create unique value —  Value propositions —  Isolation effect

Turn value props into UI —  Experience model —  Fundamental attribution error

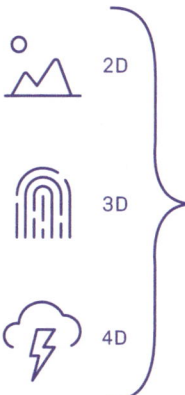

2D

3D

4D

CREATE: Concepts

Concept sketches are a core practice; they can be done after every single section in this book. Do them yourself, but also ask teammates and client partners to sketch (even and especially non-designers). Sketching gathers key information and aligns key people earlier. Stay loose; sketches need to be clear enough to facilitate conversations, but unfinished enough that you're not wasting time figuring out layouts for low-value ideas.

1. **Prepare a list of sketching prompts.** Return to the various questions in this section for inspiration, and see the Thinking chapter for guidelines on framing "How Might We" questions.

2. **Prepare sketching materials.** In person, cut printer paper in half to make sizes that are easier to pin up, and use markers, not pens, so the sketches are visible from across the room. Online, set up a digital whiteboard for people to type and paste into.

3. **Pick a framing question** and set a timer for 5–10 minutes.

4. **Sketch!** Do one idea per page. Think about where the audience is and what they need at that moment. Concept sketches can be more like an ad for the product than the design for it: just a simple, skimmable moment or sketchy wireframe.
   - Big title or headline: What is this?
   - Visual of key value or action: Why bother? What do you want me to do?
   - Supporting details: What else should I know? Why should I trust you?
   - Omit navigation and details unless they're essential to the idea.

5. **Pin up** all the sketches and have each person talk through their ideas. Cluster similar ideas together, and give each group a new name.

6. **Repeat** this for as many prompts as you can; 3–5 key prompts will give you a great spread. Refine the strongest groups into concept sketches to take into research.

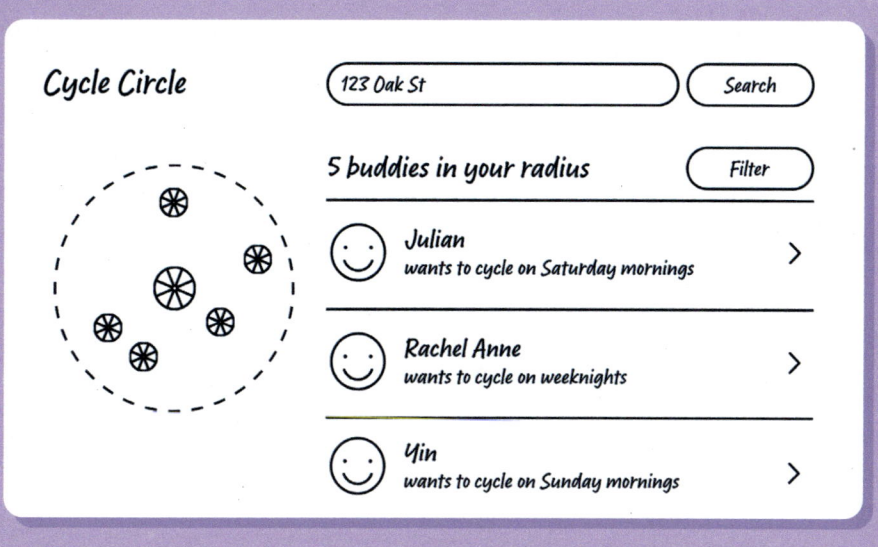

Brainstorm ideas for a memorable moment.

CRITIQUE: Value

Ok, so you have some ideas you like! Who cares? Analyze them according to the success metrics of the project, and then take them out to the intended audience to do the same. Concept research is a form of generative user research that helps us find and focus on the most valuable, differentiated ideas. We see if internal ideas have real-world resonance.

See what people remember and care about.

☑ Impressions

Present a concept sketch, along with a pre-prepared name and short description. Ask for initial thoughts and impressions on those first few words.

"What's your first reaction? Is the idea useful to you? Why?"

☑ Utility

Probe on specific details that participants like or dislike. Don't get derailed by shallow comments on visual things; keep redirecting the conversations to underlying value.

"Why is that part important? What would you want to see?"

☑ Distinction

Have participants rate the value of each idea, and force-rank them against one another (or against the competition) to double-check their qualitative answers.

"On a scale of 1 to 5, how valuable is this concept? Of all these ideas, which are most valuable? Why?"

☑ Memorability

Also consider uniqueness and differentiation within the marketplace. See what's memorable (if anything).

"What do you remember from that page? What was the name of the product? What does it do? What was most unique about it?"

"Practice safe design: use a concept."

Petrula Vrontikis

REMEMBER: MEMORIES

To summarize: product experiences float in an ocean of other options. Ideas must be valuable and memorable to stand out and succeed. We need to think about 2D images, 3D personalization, and 4D moments to create compelling, differentiated concepts.

• CRAFT •

CRAFT

• CRAFT •

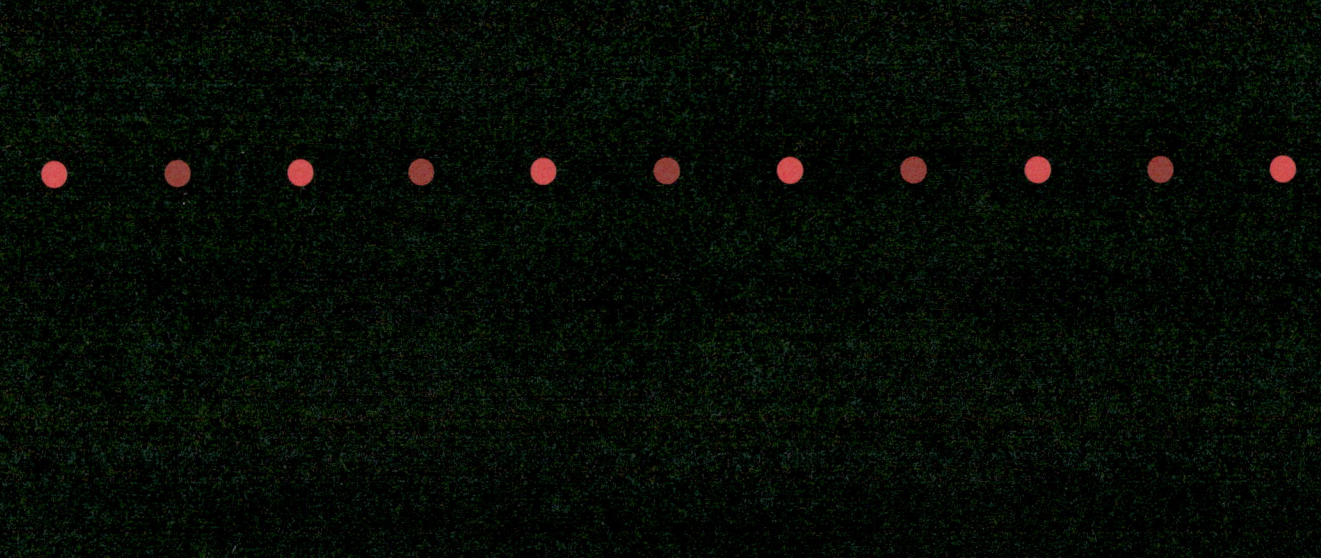

Prototyping

The FRAMEWORK and PRACTICE parts of this book provide conceptual structures for product experience design; this part provides tactical tips. The Method chapter talks about *why* we prototype; this chapter gives a bit more detail on the *how*. But the craft of prototyping is a funny thing: with generative, strategic design approaches we often work in low fidelity, so it's not about how beautiful the mockups look or how well the code works. Well-crafted prototypes are those that generate accurate, valuable insights. Four key skills will improve product prototypes: writing, sketching, wireframing, and playing.

"If a picture is worth a thousand words, a prototype is worth a thousand meetings."
Tom and David Kelley, IDEO

• Write better

> "[Writers] are the fastest designers in the world. They're amazing at boiling down incredibly abstract concepts into tiny packets of cognition, or language."
>
> Matt Jones, "Jumping to the End—Practical Design Fiction"

Writing is designing at its most abstract. Word choices imply product features; writing styles imply design styles. Well-chosen words are key.

Clear writing is a valuable asset in all parts of a design practice, whether you're generating concepts, drafting product strategy directions, or creating interfaces to put in front of research participants. It's also extremely valuable in all stages of a career, whether interviewing for a position, choosing the words to use in critiques, or reporting progress to investors. So any investment you make in your writing skills is exponential.

Even if you're not a professional writer, you can be a better one. But "great" writing depends on the context: a great poem and a great research paper use very different words and styles. In product design, language gets better when it's more visual, active, brief, human, and real.

• Be visual

Which phrase best communicates an image?

Strong words that create clear mental images transport readers into their own imaginations and feelings; abstract descriptions are much harder to understand and remember. Imagine "an antiques marketplace" versus "a B2B sales portal." One is an experience; the other could mean anything. We could label a section of our app "Address Book," "Community," "My Team," or "Faculty Lounge"; each label would conjure different things, people, or places. Specific and colorful characters, settings, actions, and outcomes can create more powerful and memorable experiences (as long as they have the same connotations across a diverse audience; different people have different visual backgrounds).

• Be active

Which words might be more energetic?

Products are built for interaction; consider verbs instead of nouns and directions instead of descriptions. Verbs are shorter and stronger than nouns; they add extra energy to the tone of a page *(achieve* versus *achievement, rely* versus *reliance)*. Active voice is more exciting than passive: the subject acts ("the doctor shared a file") instead of being acted on ("a file was shared by the doctor"). And present tense can be more gripping than future tense; the subject feels close ("the event starts at noon") rather than distant ("the event will start at noon").

- ## Be brief

Product design definitely trains you to edit; less text means easier layouts. Brevity is the soul of wit and web text. Try to simplify complex language; journalism generally writes at an eighth-grade level, and accessibility guidelines recommend a sixth- to ninth-grade level. Delete any filler words or redundant language, and look for phrases that could be shortened. Then give each layout a squint test, or thumb through it on a mobile device, and see if the key ideas pop.

What words could I delete?

- ## Be human

Read text out loud, and notice any stumbles. Skimming visitors need simple language; the text in interactive designs is part of a conversation, not a monologue. Brand personalities will differ from your unique one, but compelling interface writing sounds like a human, not a robot or a drone. Practice using the tools of great storytellers: clarity, emotion, humor, and drama.

What personality do we want to convey?

- ## Be real

At low fidelities, words are a much larger part of the design, and so research participants are easily distracted by errors in example text: incorrect math, changing names, or unclear language. Every time I leave *lorem ipsum* text in a mockup, multiple people spend valuable minutes trying to understand it. Participants want to be helpful, and it's easy to feel confident correcting typos, so they love to point out small errors and inconsistencies. Use real text, real data, and real descriptions so you get feedback on the important words and ideas, not the inconsequential ones.

Do all the details add up?

EXERCISE: Writing style

Writer and strategist Nicole Fenton's Tiny Content Framework shares a number of attributes a brand could embody. Pick five, and rewrite a headline in five different ways.

Accurate • Alive • Articulate • Calming • Challenging • Clear • Clever • Compelling • Concise • Confident • Conversational • Crisp • Direct • Eloquent • Engrossing • Fascinating • Fast-paced • Fluid • Flowing • Friendly • Generous • Heartfelt • Honest • Illuminating • Incisive • Informal • Insightful • Inviting • Joyful • Layered • Light • Lively • Luminous • Moving • Nuanced • Open • Organized • Precise • Provocative • Purposeful • Readable • Resonating • Rhythmic • Riveting • Simple • Slowing • Solid • Straightforward • Strong • Thoughtful • Transcendant • Trustworthy • Useful • Vibrant • Vivid

Create text options that vary in personality.

Strategist
Writer

• Sketch more

> "Sketchbooks are not about being a good artist. They're about being a good thinker."
>
> Jason Santa Maria, "Pretty Sketchy"

Sketching gets ideas out of your head and into a shareable format. It helps designers, teammates, and audiences work together in much more productive ways—visual thinking is a totally different muscle than verbal thinking. Sketches help simplify complex or abstract ideas into relatable and approachable visuals. They also make low-fidelity prototypes feel more tangible and interactive.

"Great" sketches are ones that clearly communicate great ideas; it doesn't matter if they're ugly. If you "can't draw" or it makes you feel anxious, just use rectangles and smiley faces. Sketches are not drawings, they're thoughts; they're not illusions, they're symbols. Many product design interviews ask applicants to do a sketching exercise on a whiteboard (for example: design an alarm clock that has only one button) so they can see a candidate's logical skills and creative process.

Frequent, uninhibited sketching keeps the visual parts of your brain in shape and encourages the habit of continually exploring many options. (Try *sketchnotes*; they're illustrated notes that give you an excuse to doodle in meetings.) To deepen and refine your product thinking, explore different sketching mediums, formats, and topics.

• Choose a medium that works for you

Sketching should happen in whatever medium makes it happen. Try your hand at concepts, prototypes, UI shorthand, and/or storyboards.

◉ Consider the scale, immediacy, modularity, and remote-friendliness of different sketching mediums.

Easy-to-erase whiteboards
Whiteboards provide a great break from screens. The ephemerality helps you loosen up, the messiness prevents you from wasting time on trivial details, the large scale lets you think big, and the visibility makes it easy to pull in a collaborator. Sometimes a computer screen just isn't big enough; go back to the literal drawing board.

Tangible, tactile paper
Scratch paper lying around the office begs to be reused, and its plainness prevents anyone from seeing sketches as precious art. Strong ideas can be pinned up on walls for extra visibility, while weak ideas can be crumpled up with a satisfying crackle. Simple tricks like overlapping pages can turn sketches into paper prototypes.

Rearrangeable sticky notes

Sticky notes are so small that they force modular thinking, and so easily rearranged that they encourage flexible mindsets. Use real sticky notes to add layers of physical fun (buy them in bulk so they seem less precious), or digital versions for easy copy/paste and remote collaboration.

Remote-friendly software

Software can be efficient and comfortable for sketching, as long as it doesn't trigger premature hi-fi designs or confusing mid-fi work. Like digital sticky notes, such programs provide easy copy/pasting and remote collaboration. You can also link lo-fi digital sketches into clickable "paper" prototypes. Check product-hunting sites for the latest or most popular tools; the crowd favorite changes frequently.

• Try different formats

Different types of sketching can frame and inform product design strategy in different ways. You could sketch concepts, prototypes, shorthand, or storyboards.

Provocative concepts

Concept sketches are the key exercise in the Memories section because they're so valuable. People respond to low-fidelity ideas with different lenses of judgement than they do to polished mockups. I call it the *Craigslist test:* Is the idea so good that people would use it even if it looked like Craigslist?

Useful concept sketches don't have to present the expected design—they're just visual aids for learning conversations, so they can also be provocations. Presenting terrible ideas to a target audience is a fun way to confirm their fears or pain points (and get some dramatic quotes for presentations). Sketch any ideas that will validate or invalidate key needs, goals, behaviors, and mental models.

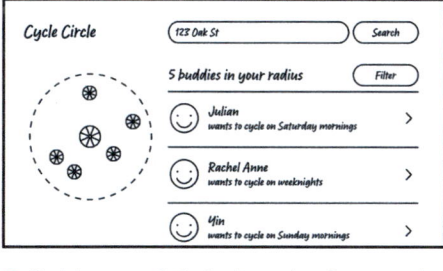

👁 Sketchy concepts test value, not surface appeal.

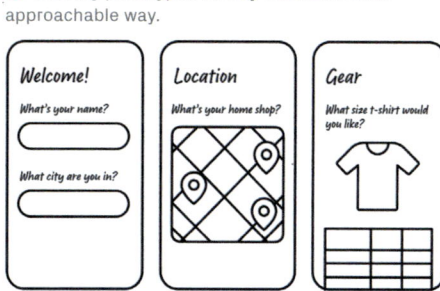

👁 Sketchy prototypes convey interfaces in an approachable way.

Playful prototypes

Sketchy prototypes make serious interaction research possible without the constraints of hi-fi mediums. They convey enough interactivity to spur imaginations, and because they're obviously not visual designs, they force viewers to focus on the content and flow. Functionality issues will show up even at these very early stages, so you can start iterations in minutes, not weeks.

Sketch at or near the actual size of the target device, so that you better understand size constraints for text and UI. Don't scribble; write actual words and try to draw the images or buttons or symbols expected. If you're working on actual paper, consider sticky notes for dynamic elements so you can add or remove them to show a state change. And don't make paper prototypes elaborate examples of handicraft; they just need to communicate content and functionality in a usable way.

Speedy shorthand

UI shorthand is a useful format recommended by Ryan Singer, former head of strategy at Basecamp. Like *breadboarding,* where electrical engineers prototype components and wiring before doing any industrial design, UI shorthand is a simple, streamlined way to plot experience designs (even if it's not the most visual). Go step by step through a process; at each step, list what the user *sees* and *does*. It's a fast, usable, draft of a user flow. Concept sketches can then explore particular moments in the flow with better insight on the surrounding context.

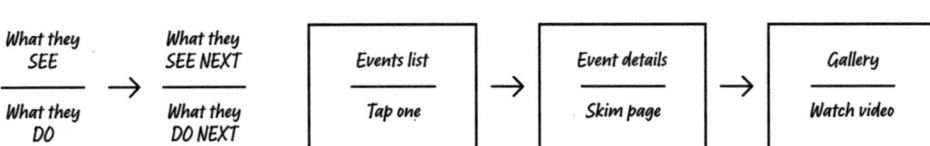

👁 UI shorthand quickly drafts what someone sees and does at each step in a flow.

Empathetic storyboards

Storyboards are great ways to get collaborators in sync with a strategy. I often do these as part of presentation materials to show how a product will fit into and affect someone's life. (For executives, these usually end up in high-fidelity formats, but it's great to practice more quickly and frequently in low fidelity.) Zooming out to show a product's context and environment makes it much easier to empathize with the audience's situation, understand their unique needs, and evaluate the proposed solution.

Illustrate each key scene in a specific journey toward a goal, and caption as needed.

👁 Sketchy storyboards help people understand the context for and value of the product.

Serena is traveling overseas, and missed the last train

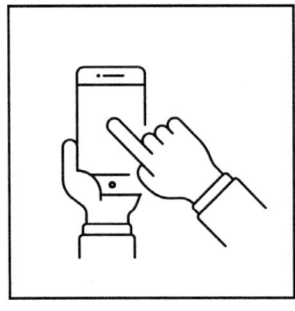
She logs into her QuickDrive account and requests a ride

Within 20 minutes she has a shared ride to her destination

• Explore many options

Sketching lets you quickly explore and discuss a large number of ideas; even tiny sketches can clearly show different experiences. Focus on quantity, not quality; evaluations and refinements will come later.

Imagine you're designing a new movie-browsing experience. Sketches could show a dense list of showtimes, an oversized carousel of images, and a lively feed of reviews—all in a few minutes. Concept sketches don't need to show every element on every screen; the point is to show an idea and provide the feeling of interaction.

Sketches can quickly explore many options.

Imagine you're designing a new fitness coaching service. Sketches could present many different packages and value props to see what parts the target audience values most (e.g., personalized 1:1 sessions, small-group challenges, or 24/7 community connection). The low fidelity helps us get more information sooner, and validates the value proposition instead of the surface appeal.

Even after research validates a concept, low-fidelity work can help you iterate ideas and explore UX/UI options before high-fidelity details suck you into a single choice. Keep exploring.

EXERCISE: Sketching practice

Finding and refining your own shorthand for basic user interface elements will help you generate and iterate ideas faster.

Get comfortable making interface shapes.

 UXer

1. Grab a piece of paper and draw these basic UI shapes a few times. Practice until they're easy and clear.
2. Combine them into a few layout ideas. Grab your phone and trace around it if you want to work at actual size and make a paper prototype.

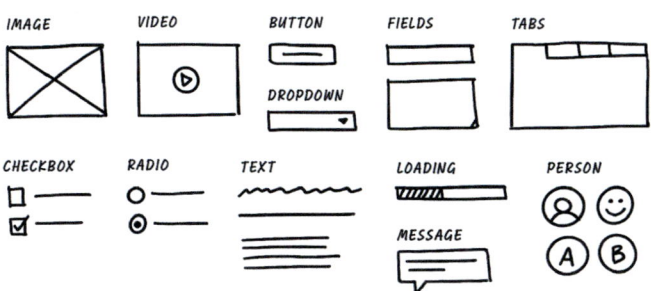

• Wireframe better

Wireframes help resolve decisions about functionality and content, affordances and signifiers. They're a common deliverable, but it's another extremely vague term that can mean anything from an arrangement of gray boxes to a full-fidelity mockup. If someone asks for wireframes, always clarify what they really need.

Some designers say they find wireframes useless. I say they're doing them wrong. Good wireframes enable valuable discussions about the anticipated content and functionality and the possible UX/UI patterns. If done well, wireframes:

 provide simple visual aids that improve collaborators' understanding and make sure everyone is literally on the same page in a discussion;

 force stakeholders to provide input on content and functionality and flow, instead of getting distracted by styling;

 help teammates scope or start their own work sooner (for example, engineers can start evaluating tech and writers can start drafting possible content); and

 allow the huge quantity of layout designs in digital projects (especially responsive ones) to be sketched, not skipped.

If done poorly, wireframes repulse viewers and waste time. Let's not do that.

• Stop making bad wireframes

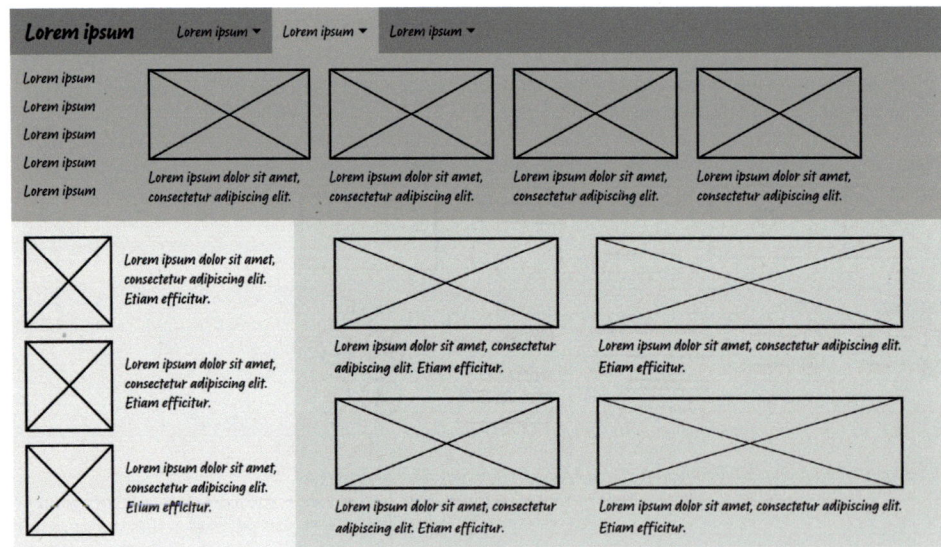

Bad wireframes lack detail, so they answer no questions and inspire no discussions.

Avoid these slips:

Vague arrangements of gray boxes don't answer any questions or prompt any good discussions. Content should serve specific decision-making.

Nonsensical *lorem ipsum* text doesn't put real ideas and messaging up for discussion and doesn't solve the issues that arise with real usernames, headlines, sections, or pages of text. Text should be real for as many elements as possible, even if it's a very rough draft.

Boxy wireframes treated as unalterable design blueprints impede visual design opportunities and create hierarchical issues. A visually trained person should arrange layouts.

Semi-colored diagrams can derail strategic discussions. Symbolic color on interactive elements sometimes clarifies functionality, but decorative color often steals design and discussion time from harder decisions. Learn to work without color and you'll be a stronger designer; grayscale forces you to study contrast and focus on content. Wireframes should omit decoration.

Semi-styled collages often hit an "uncanny valley" of awkward mid-fi mockups. People perceive them as "designs" instead of diagrams and get repulsed by the ugliness. Wireframing with some hi-fi UI elements can feel like a jumpstart on visual design work, but it's a slippery slope into mid-fi confusion. The fidelity should be as low as possible, and consistent.

Make wireframes that serve (or force) the discussion you need to have. For example:

• Boxy wireframes for content strategy

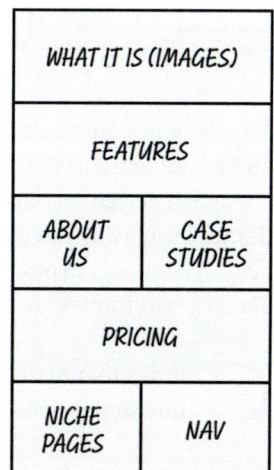

This content blocking for ProPublica lets us talk about what might appear on the screen, and in what order.

Not all gray boxes are bad. For zero-to-one projects, where nothing exists for you to redesign, you have to start somewhere. Discussing spreadsheets or documents makes some people's eyes glaze over; even a simple layout can help them visualize and engage with the discussion more easily. Gray box (or colored box) wireframes can support early planning discussions for content and design. To do this:

- List content sections intended for each screen, using labels and not actual headlines for each box.

- Arrange sections in a rough order corresponding to their priority (knowing that visual designers will refine the actual visual hierarchies later).

• Sketchy wireframes for experience direction

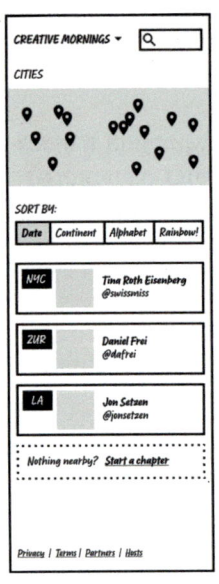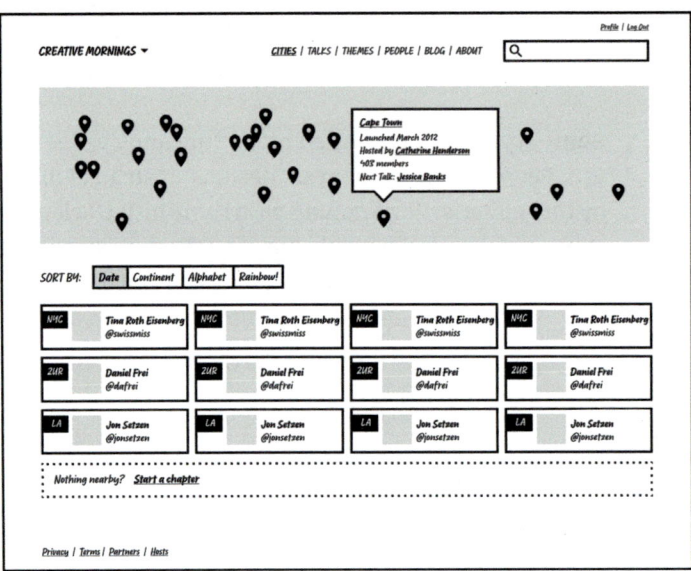

These sketchy wires for CreativeMornings supported talks about the founder's vision and the engineers' plans.

Sketchy wires are a fast and fun way to communicate ideas for content, functionality, and layout without letting yourself spend precious minutes on colors or fonts. (In the age of design systems, final element designs will often come from component libraries anyway.) You can draw them by hand or use software; either way they should be rough enough to be critique-friendly but clear enough for technical discussions. Sketchy wireframes are good when they:

 indicate functionality with clear symbols, to support discussion about interactions and microinteractions;

use real text so you see how it starts to fit or not fit the interface (and it gets as many rounds of revision as possible); and

 organize layouts at realistic scales close to the final deliverable, so spatial issues start to be considered and visual design requirements are clearer.

• Technical wireframes for functional details

Technical wireframes are a visual way to explore more detailed interface or technology options and document the decisions. We don't need to hold up certain user research or technical approvals with high-fidelity design finesse, and we don't want the design team to do a whole photo shoot or the dev team to code a whole framework when big questions have yet to be answered.

Some technical wireframes are so polished they are basically grayscale or outlined versions of the final design; others are still a little boxy. If a large design system exists, technical wireframes might be full-fidelity mockups. As always, it depends on the project, the team, and the audience. But in general, good technical wireframes:

 present usable layouts with thoughtful information hierarchy and realistic typography (a visually skilled person should make them);

 convey functional details (e.g., input types, navigation menus, error states) in clear detail, allowing viewers to experience full flows or scenarios; and

 include annotations for any hidden elements or interactive behaviors the developers need to consider or code.

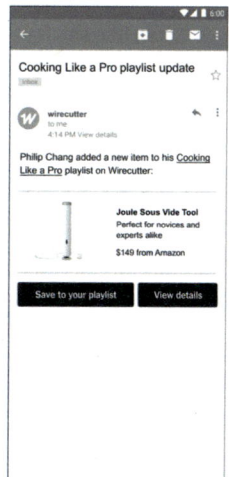

These grayscale technical wireframes done with Runyon for Wirecutter helped research participants react to clear-enough provocations, but saved us many hours of needless design polishing.

• Page description diagrams for forced prioritization

Boxy, sketchy, and technical wireframes should solve most of your experience design collaboration needs, but a final trick in your bag can be even lower fidelity. If you have no visual training or stakeholders can't stop seeing wireframes as literal designs, do a page description diagram. These are old-school design deliverables that remove layout from the equation entirely; they're basically just ordered lists. Good page description diagrams:

 list all the content or functionality planned for the page (with as much or as little detail as you need to discuss); and

 sort elements by priority, usually in separate sections for high, medium, and low priority.

EXERCISE: Wireframes

Make useful representations of functionality and content.

 Strategist
 Writer
 Visual designer
 Engineer

Laying out content and functionality without stylistic distractions can help teams discuss and settle many practical questions.

1. **Remember the flow:** You can wireframe a single screen, but it's hard to be smart about its content without considering the 4D (what comes before and after). Consider the steps leading up to the screen, and where you're trying to get people to go.

2. **Shape functionality.** Add clear symbols for functionality. Find the best design pattern for each moment: not just buttons, but "share sheets" or "drag-and-drop" or something new. Use symbol libraries to broaden your vocabulary and speed up your work.

3. **Craft text.** Draft rough text or get real text from a copywriter. Scale it semantically: Is it a key headline or an inessential caption? Consider using grayscale shades to indicate primary, secondary, or disabled elements.

4. **Clean it up.** Wires don't have to be beautiful, but they should be skimmable. Use the principles of alignment and proximity to reduce noise. Revisit the goal of the screen or flow, and consider hiding secondary information until it's needed.

• Play more

The final element in the craft of prototyping is play. Loosen up and see where the material takes you; dig into sensation instead of theory.

Musicians don't work music, they play music, and connecting all the dots of design requires a similar approach. Design is not an assembly line using the same parts in the same way each time; it's a dance that has to respond to different partners and rhythms. To create more creatively, stop working so hard. Playful mindsets add new dimensions of thought and understanding, no matter our skill level.

When we play with paint or music, we feel how the medium works and see what might be possible. When we play with pixels, we do the same. Higher-fidelity prototypes in visual design or code are out of scope for this book, but worth touching on as mediums for play.

> "We're not playing to win, we're playing to play."
>
> Rick Rubin, *The Creative Act*

> "My work is play. And I play when I design. I even looked it up in the dictionary, to make sure that I actually do that, and the definition of 'play,' number one was 'engaging in a childlike activity or endeavor,' and number two was 'gambling.' And I realize I do both when I'm designing."
>
> Paula Scher, "Great Design Is Serious, Not Solemn"

• Visual design

Higher-fidelity design skills require good taste and a sharp eye. Pausing to play with the visual culture you see will turn you from a consumer into a creator. Some ideas:

- Collect high-quality examples of product design. Some people say that good taste can't be taught, but I think it's just a matter of exposure. Look at both older classics and newer trends to build an aesthetic vocabulary; this is your toolkit.
- Look beyond product design to visual communication in general. Find inspiring elements in art, film, or dance, and convert them into designs.
- Sort a collection of visual elements you enjoy into themes. This is an outline of your individual style.
- Play with existing design system components and principles until you understand their strengths and limitations. Try your own mutations.
- Look for striking designs, and try to recreate them.
- Pick a specific technical topic like RGB colorspace or animation easing, and play with designs that push the boundaries of that technology.
- Learn to draw; it's learning to see. The mystery grids and drawing tutorials in game magazines and cartooning books taught me how to break shapes down into smaller parts and see the relationships among them.

Return to the exercises in this book with this expanded visual vocabulary and enhanced eye. See how the creation and critique processes change at a higher fidelity.

Mystery grid puzzles are fun ways to sharpen your eye.

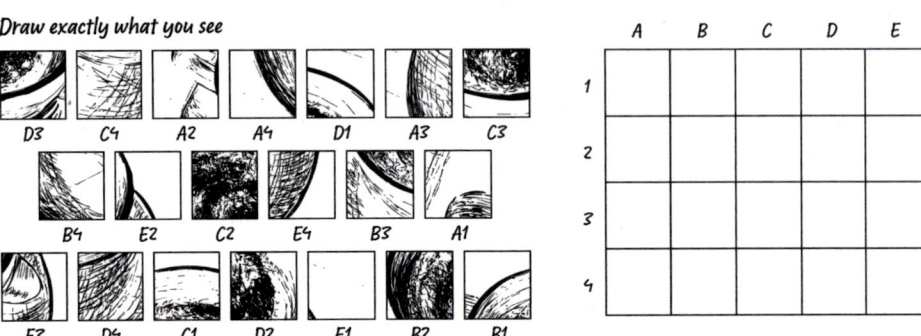

• Code

Code is the real medium for product design, no matter how convincing our mock-ups look. As with visual design, expanding your exposure to code will expand your toolkit and your thinking. Coded prototypes are dynamic and interactive in a way no other form can match. We can play with the raw material ourselves, or with people whose coding skills go beyond ours. Some ideas:

- Fork some existing code (see the exercise below). Tweak some variables, and see how the design changes.
- Play with others: try a co-creative workflow or session with a developer. They'll know resources and approaches you've never heard of. Technologists should be equal partners, not late-stage executors.
- Pick a popular language or framework (e.g., CSS or Python), and finish a tutorial.
- Continue with your chosen technology, and try to build a janky prototype of one interface element. No one is judging you, so have fun.

Return to the exercises in this book with this technically informed eye. See how the design process changes when you think with code.

Edit some actual code!

EXERCISE: Fork some code

Coding can feel intimidating, but the internet has billions of lines to start with (and new assistants popping up all the time). Even when I was a professional developer, coding was more like collage then freewriting. Don't scare yourself with a blank page; fork one.

1. Pick a UI element with layers of interactive or responsive behavior (e.g., a navigation bar).
2. Go to CodePen or another online code gallery and look at some relevant patterns.
3. Fork a pattern, change some variables, and see how the design feels in its real medium.

Thinking

One part of the creative process is execution: knowing how to arrange the text readably or time the animation beautifully. Those tactical, specialized skills are the visible craft of design. Another part of the creative process is strategy: coming up with the idea to add some text or use an animation in the first place. These conceptual skills are the invisible craft of design.

Thinking skills may feel slippery because they're mindsets, not recipes, but they're invaluable and infinitely applicable. Creative and critical thinking skills provide clear first steps when you're overwhelmed and multiple avenues to explore when you're searching for solutions. They help you figure out problems without a teacher or template.

Conceptual skills are not automatic at first. It's easy to see if design software is functioning correctly; it's hard to see if your mind is. Try to notice when you're heading into autopilot worker mode. Pause to think strategically, and *then* decide on next steps. Eventually your brain will naturally switch into these mindsets; they're muscles you can learn to engage.

Some key strategies for strategic and creative thinking are to deconstruct, frame, research, diverge, converge, differentiate, and think in 4D.

"Thinking is a skill, not intelligence in action."
Edward de Bono

• Deconstruct

Deconstruction challenges any structures, assumptions, or vagueness, uncovering underlying priorities and opportunities. To deconstruct, we examine a given element closely and break it down into its component parts.

A common version seen in design kickoffs is to "rip the brief"—to question the assumptions of an assignment and identify the real goals. If a client says they want an app, do they require an iPhone/Android app or just an interactive product? If a stakeholder defines the goal as "great UX," do they mean usable information architecture, pretty layouts, happy users, lots of revenue, or something else? The process can be simple (asking seemingly stupid questions), but the insights can be significant.

Deconstruction is also the skill that helps you make accurate project plans or estimates. "Website design" is impossible to estimate, but "six complex pages and three simple pages with two rounds of revisions each" can be quantified. Look for patterns, structures, or formulas underneath the surface layers.

Deconstruction is also the skill behind diagramming. It's abstraction, reducing the level of detail in an image or system in order to show larger patterns or relationships. If an issue feels too complicated, try mapping its components.

Start any initiative by taking it apart. See what you're actually working with.

> "Do not solve the problem that's asked of you. It's almost always the wrong problem. Almost always when somebody comes to you with a problem, they're really telling you the symptoms."
>
> Don Norman

Deconstruct language to find fuzzy areas and assumptions.

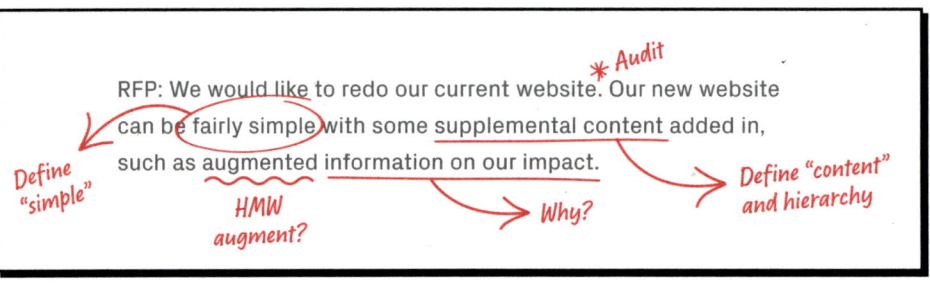

● Frame

Framing is a form of reconstruction: taking all the essential elements of a situation and putting them together in a form that inspires appropriate action. The words and structures we use to describe a situation affect how we think about it. Whether we are choosing research methods, planning design initiatives, or pursuing technical solutions, clear framing of objectives and constraints will help our work go in useful directions.

"How Might We" (HMW) questions are a popular framing technique for creative thinking. The phrase is an "invitational stem" introduced by creativity scholar Sidney Parnes in his 1967 classic *Creative Behavior Guidebook*. Well-written HMWs should inspire solutions but not define them; they should make space but retain a focus.

> "We use the How Might We format because it suggests that a solution is possible and because they offer you the chance to answer them in a variety of ways."
>
> IDEO

HMW criteria	Example		Critique
Identify a goal, not a solution	HMW create new apps for financial education?	✗	Assumes that people want an app
	HMW increase access to affordable housing?	✓	Provides many routes to explore
Be open, but not gaping	HMW end poverty?	✗	So broad it's useless and egotistical
	HMW improve financial literacy in teens?	✓	Realistic opportunity and scope

COMPARE "How might we" criteria

To write a great HMW, include the project's impact, audience, and constraints.

HMW elements	Example		Bring it all together
The ultimate impact desired, tangible or psychological	Eliminate barriers to entering the workforce	✓	HMW eliminate barriers to entering the workforce for technically skilled immigrants in large cities?
The specific audience, defined by behaviors or mindsets	People who've immigrated to large cities	✓	
Any constraints or context for the project or audience	The industry requires technically skilled users	✓	

COMPARE "How might we" elements

If an HMW doesn't immediately trigger a variety of ideas, revise it—the whole point is to inspire creative thinking. Good framing creates good creative energy.

• Research

> "[I]f you wish to develop fresh, groundbreaking ideas, highly varied experiences are critical."
>
> Frans Johansson, *The Medici Effect*

Designs don't exist in silos; each one must acknowledge its environment. That's where *research* comes in. A research practice helps us transition from ignorant dictators to insightful investigators. Research is the mechanics of inspiration.

I like to take "inspiration" in its literal sense: to inhale. We breathe in nourishing elements to breathe out new expressions. Inspiration may be direct, analogous, or user-centered. Triangulating all three forms will provide the most solid foundation for ideas.

• Direct inspiration

> *What makes relevant designs "good"?*
>
> "Imitate, assimilate, innovate."
>
> Clark Terry, trumpeter
>
> "Imitate. Remix. Invent."
>
> Dan Mall, designer

Direct inspiration (looking at products similar to what we're designing) is often a first instinct when doing research; it gives us a sense of current trends and patterns. Many great designers make it a daily habit to browse galleries of new work.

But designers also call people out for creating work that appears to copy the visual designs of others. Where's the line between appropriate and inappropriate inspiration?

The idea of inspiration is strongly linked to the modernist concept of the solo genius creating unique visions from divine insight. This is the simplistic story of great men doing great things to move culture forward, like Jackson Pollock "inventing" action painting.

But even geniuses have to start somewhere. Art students copy the works of celebrated artists to learn how they achieved such a high level of quality. Mimicry is how animals, including humans, learn to live. True creativity is "combinatorial," according to Maria Popova of The Marginalian: "something we all understand on a deep intuitive level, but our creative egos sort of don't really want to accept [...] is the idea [...] that nothing is entirely original, that everything builds on what came before." Pollock's fuller story credits his partner Lee Krasner and others with great influence.

Ideas of originality faded with postmodernism, which credited larger communities and cultures for ideas while freely appropriating and redefining them. And the internet moved us into "remix culture," according to Lawrence Lessig and other media scholars, giving us access to ideas and images from around the world, plus the creative tools to easily repurpose them.

The key point is to remember the remix. Inspiration and imitation teach us the patterns and vocabulary of our field; creativity reinterprets and recombines them. Feed yourself the best inspiration possible, but don't stop at consumption. Credit your sources and go beyond them.

"Creation requires influence."

Kirby Ferguson, "Everything is a Remix"

"Unless you can definitively show that your use of another creator's work is transformative (i.e., you are using it for a new or different purpose while not detracting from or trying to steal its original audience), always err on the side of seeking permission."

Adam Weissman, media and entertainment lawyer

Direct inspiration reveals the landscape; analogous inspiration reveals insights.

• Analogous inspiration

Direct inspiration may show you real-world solutions to the challenge you're exploring, but indirect or analogous inspiration is the route to new ones. Creativity puts existing things together in a new way; it's hard to do something fresh if you're using the same pieces as everyone else. Analogous inspiration is a key progression; unexpected solutions are often found in parallel fields.

What are similar systems? What ideas are transferable?

Start with analogies, a powerful strategy for creative thinking. Analogies transpose a working system into an entirely new area. Imagine we're designing a fitness tracking app. We might see that the process is similar to managing finances, which might lead us to analyze budget tracking apps or interview financial planners to see how they organize their work. We could also say that the goals of fitness resemble the goals of parenting, and look at how people coach, incentivize, or speak to children.

Then go deeper into desk research, visiting the sites, apps, or databases of these analogous experiences. Don't forget old-school libraries that have obscure materials other people may be too lazy to find.

For multisensory inspiration, try field research (doing site visits or community observations). You'll gather richer details and nuance about real-world environments. Look at IDEO's *Human-Centered Design Toolkit* for more methods of field research and parallel inspiration.

Analogous inspiration helps us avoid the muddy, crowded waters of incremental steps past competitors. Go somewhere unique.

• Generative research

The richest form of inspiration often comes from the ground up. User interviews and other forms of generative research expose details you simply can't see yourself; they're like messages from the past and future. And if you've fully embraced the principle of co-creation, research *is* design. It's not an isolated up-front phase; it's a continuous method of learning and creating. The overlap means that even though user research is its own field of expertise, experience designers must understand when and how to do valid investigations.

There are many, many research methods; evaluative tests may be more familiar to most people, but generative research is the focus for strategists. It finds opportunities and creates options; it helps us understand people's habits, needs, and environments; it gives us inspiration rooted in real life.

As a foundational practice, I recommend one-on-one interviews (early-stage ethnographic investigations, not late-stage usability tests). You'll get real empathy, great stories, and many insights. Note that interviews are different from conversations—there are many nuances and methods to avoid bias and find significance. I was lucky to learn the practice of grounded theory from my brilliant friend Jodi Leo; check my resources page online for some helpful books and articles.

Shy people, you can do this. Talking to strangers might seem nerve-racking, but conversation skills are learnable. Thinking of questions, asking them, listening attentively, finding follow-up questions, and interpreting answers each have their own anxieties, but yield huge rewards. The skill of asking questions will help you keep any conversation flowing. The practice of listening deeply to people and trying to understand their perspective increases empathy and connection in all relationships. Researchers are some of the most thoughtful people I know, and the practice has definitely been life-changing for me.

> "In every class, my main advice to students is to ask 'why?' many more times than they did. [...] Don't be afraid to pause and ask 'why?'"
>
> Jodi Leo, professor of user research at SVA

COMPARE
Research methods

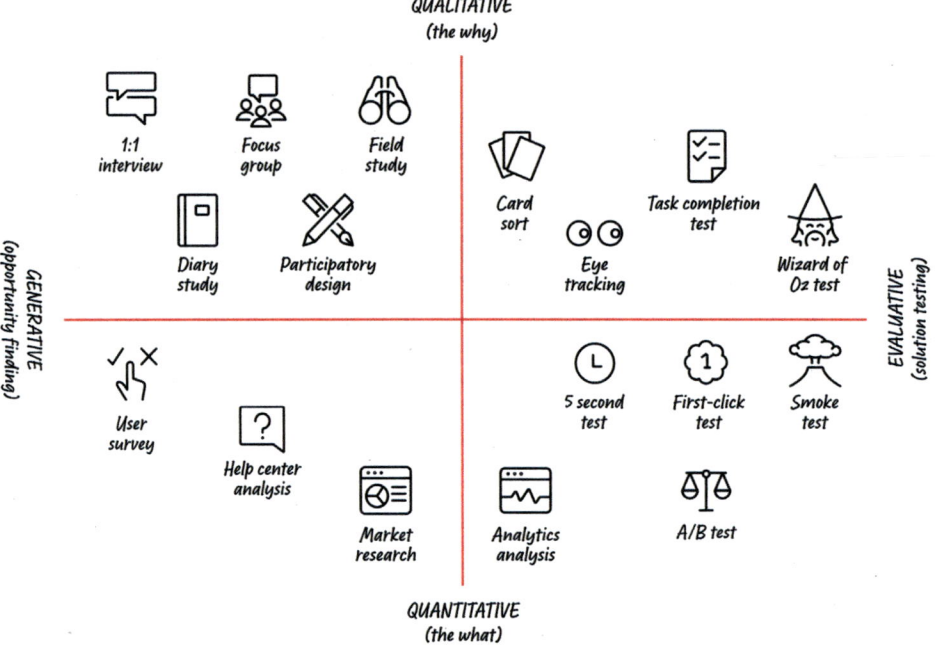

• Diverge

Being creative is often seen as a personality trait, but I like to take it as a verb: to be more creative, we create more. And to create a larger number of ideas, we explore a larger scope of possibility. We take all those inspirations we found in deconstruction, framing, or research, and turn them into new what-ifs.

To diverge means to go wide. We think laterally, not vertically, and pursue quantity, not quality. Don't go straight down the expected path; take detours and scenic routes. (In a literal parallel, neuroscientist Andrew Huberman cites studies saying divergent thinking is enhanced by walking, or even thinking about walking.) Force yourself to try several options, look for many different approaches, get inspired by the details of other worlds. Use the "yes, and" principle of improv comedy: yes to that idea, *and* here's a build. No critiques, only additions; creative mindsets require safe spaces and good moods. Let yourself be silly and playful, even at work.

Beginners tend to stop after one sketch and start refining it. They're infatuated with a first good idea, or uncomfortable with "the messy middle" of design processes, or anxious about returning to the void. But if you converge too soon, you'll cut back sprouts before they bloom. Great ideas combine many smaller ones or push into unexpected areas, so "extra" ideas are never wasted.

Analysis also kills empathy, which is essential for human-centered design solutions. A 2012 study at Case Western Reserve University showed that empathy and analysis fire different networks of neurons, and each one suppresses the other: "we have a built-in neural constraint on our ability to be both empathetic and analytic at the same time." Mute the critic until they're invited; convergence will come next.

Welcome all "bad" ideas; they still have nuggets of insight or creativity. Designer Frank Chimero says to start brainstorming with the stupidest idea possible; it loosens you up and gives you nowhere to go but up. Author Anne Lamott lists "shitty first drafts" as an obligatory step in the creative process. Designer Christina Wodtke reminds us to keep going: "the longer you freelist, the more painful it becomes… and the more productive. More time: weirder ideas."

Put that first idea aside, and generate ten more.

What's an alternative solution?

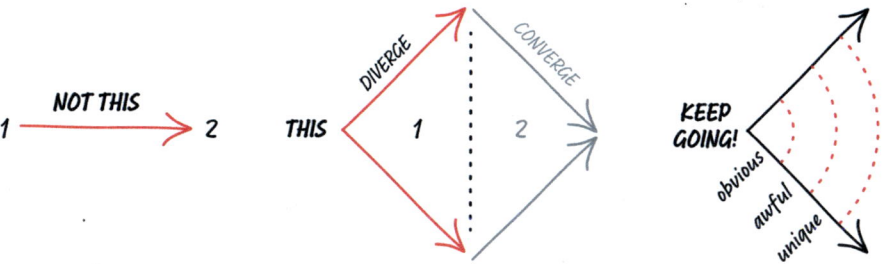

Divergence is not linear; it wanders widely to find more unique elements for ideas.

• Converge

> "The creative process, in essence, is an individual in dialogue with themselves and the work. [...] It is a dance of switching contexts [...] that produces a tight feedback loop between mark-making and mark-assessing. The artist, when near, is concerned with production; when far, he enters a mode of criticism [...]"
>
> Frank Chimero,
> *The Shape of Design*

After (and only after) you're totally spent from brainstorming, it's time to evaluate and refine your ideas. In the classic Double Diamond design innovation process, we go wide, then narrow. In lean startup circles, we think and make, then test and learn. This distinct split between generating and evaluating can't be overemphasized; they are two conflicting mindsets. Keeping them clearly separated reduces mental struggle, and prevents people from limiting ideas to the most practical, obvious thing.

To *converge* means to narrow. We combine ideas, reduce options, select directions.

A good first step is to look for patterns and create clusters of related ideas. Some concepts are small and cute on their own, but powerful partners in combination with others. A cluster may also point to a larger underlying theme or problem.

A key part of convergence is prioritization: we're not picking ideas haphazardly; we're trying to pick them strategically. Start by clearly framing the project's priorities—convergence may use creative, engineering, or business lenses. Are you trying to find the most valuable idea, or the most feasible one? Is the goal about engagement, or more about differentiation? Pick two criteria as the axes for an evaluation chart, and look for ideas that fall in the top right quadrant (e.g., valuable *and* feasible).

Just as we can co-create, we can co-evaluate. It's important to develop your own point of view, but evaluations will be more accurate with input from teammates, subject matter experts, and the target audience. Frame the criteria for convergence and pull in thoughtful analysts, and you can turn any tangle of possibilities into a strategic direction.

Look for patterns in the mess.

👁 Convergence finds patterns, sets priorities, and reveals primary opportunities.

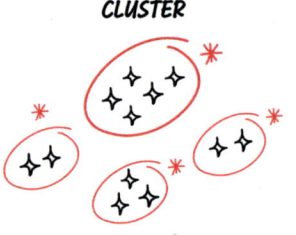
CLUSTER

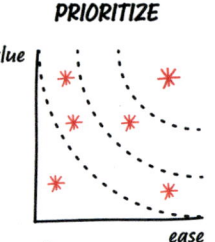
PRIORITIZE

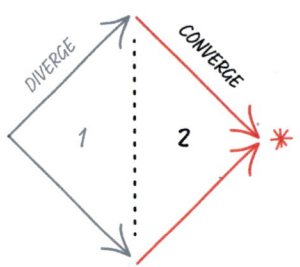
DIVERGE 1 CONVERGE 2

● Differentiate

Differentiation is a constant critique in strategic workflows; understanding a market is an essential part of business design. Audiences have a lot of options available, so designers need a clear perspective on where products or key experiences sit among existing solutions. Boring companies will do competitive research as a form of inspiration, but opportunity-spotting is a better goal.

Define the field you're playing in. Make a list of the products or processes competing for an audience's attention. Competitors aren't always other apps or services—they may be lo-fi tools like pencils and paper, or other hobbies like watching TV. Competitive landscapes can help reveal where marketplaces are crowded, or where "blue ocean" opportunity areas exist. Two-by-two matrices plotting logos along two key spectrums are a common format, but you can also use lists or spreadsheets or whatever format helps teams absorb the information.

Identify each thing competing for an audience's attention, and explain how your product is better. Simple fill-in-the-blank exercises are a great format: PRODUCT is more TRAIT than COMPETITOR.

Where do you see space to stand out?

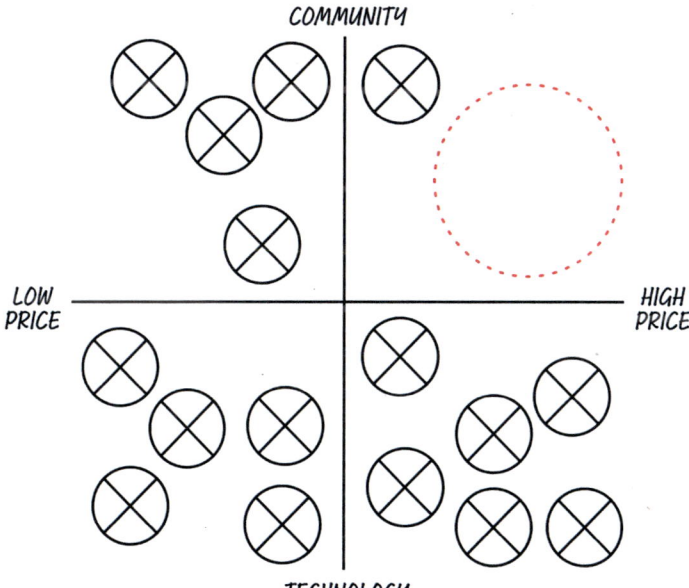

Find the open space in the places where you play.

• Think in 4D

What happens?
What changes?
What remains?

A lawyer must understand logic and emotion, cause and effect. A sculptor must weigh aesthetics, history, materials, and gravity. An experience designer must think about change, time, and people.

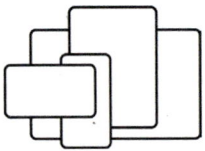

Each screen is flexible, changing to accommodate a variety of contexts and content. There is no solid frame, only temporary impressions and resultant interactions. It's easy to fixate on screens and other spatial artifacts of product design, but the medium is malleable.

Each screen is a single cell in an extended animation; our medium is temporal. We may not sketch every frame, but our scope is a movie, not a snapshot. Zoom out and imagine the entire filmstrip: the leadup, the arrival, the destination, the epilogue. There's always one more step.

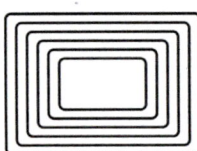

Each screen is a throwaway; what we're really designing is behavior. Our medium is cultural. A design isn't successful if it looks nice; it's successful if it makes nice things happen. Pause to think about the downstream effects of each experience: internal, systemic, or scalar.

At every step in the process, remind yourself to reset your framing from things to events, from nouns to verbs, from objects to behaviors. Let go of screen design, no matter how flexible or dynamic. You're not Frida Kahlo creating the painting; you're Sol Lewitt creating the rules.

Throw away the artifacts and focus on the impacts. Think in 4D.

OUTRO

Acknowledgments

This book came to life because of many generous people. Thank you so much for your input.

- *Inception:* Kat Vellos and her designer-to-author course (with fellow dreamers Max, Ariel, and Viet) turned my itch to write a book into a title, cover, outline, landing page, and production plan.
- *Editing:* Sally Kerrigan's thoughtful developmental editing helped me turn the rambling notes for a book into the structured draft of one, and Caren Litherland's wonderful guidance and line editing helped me communicate all these ideas much more clearly.
- *Industry expertise:* Marquina Marie Iliev provided insider tips and plans for book marketing, while Sarah Dickman helpfully explained book agents and the publishing world. Ben Kiel and Rebecca Leffell Koren helped me set up InDesign to not be a total pain.
- *Subject matter expertise:* Erin Nolan read drafts, tried the ideas with her team, and provided brilliant insights. David Cole, Andy Matuschak, Linda Eskin, Amy Drayer, Ben Bryant, Marjorie Turner Hollman, and Felipe Castro read early drafts and outlines and provided essential encouragement. Sarah Phares, Krystyn Heide, Sam Raddatz, Kate Neely, and Juliette Hainline provided perspectives on product design and UX, while Rob Fitzpatrick and the Write Useful Books community shared valuable insights about nonfiction writing.
- *Professional practice:* Joe Rizk, Anthony D'Avella, Felipe Garcia, and the extended Runyon Design community provided many amazing collaborations and work opportunities that helped catalyze, inform, and test these theories (with additional thanks to fellow team members Becca, Katie, Brenda, Sarah, Shawn, Mat, Erin, Rashina, Belu, Chris, Ali, Jay, Fiona, Mindy, and Gena). Repeat clients Tina Roth Eisenberg, George Eberstadt, and Neil Baptista, plus many other wonderful partners and employers, supported my work over the years. Ed Lane gave a shy teenager her very first job in the field, and Jim Gleason was an inspiring boss.
- *Teaching practice:* Juliette Cezzar, Brendan Griffiths, and Liz Danzico provided teaching and curriculum development opportunities at Parsons and SVA that informed and led to this book.
- *Design education:* Jodi Leo taught me proper user research and synthesis, while Ken Botnick, Sarah Birdsall, and the other excellent professors at Wash U taught me the typography, graphic design, and conceptual skills I still use.
- *Formative years:* My parents put the love for books in me early, and made education a top priority that became a lifelong passion.

• Mentions

Everyone quoted or mentioned in the book (see Acknowledgments for more).

A

Aaptiv 33
Aaron Z. Lewis 71
Aarron Walter 203
Abraham Lincoln 80
Abraham Maslow 203
Adam Weissman 231
Adriana Valdez Young 193
Agile Manifesto 30
Alan Cooper 203
Alan Fletcher 1, 178
Alan Kay 193
Alan Klement 157
Albert Stevens 198
Alfred Lui 147
Amazon 26, 42, 146
Andres Glusman 57
Andrew Huberman 167, 233
Android 97, 140, 153, 228
Andy Hunt 22
Anne Lamott 233
Ann Light 147
Antoine de Saint-Exupéry 138
Anton & Irene 100, 156
Apple 61, 62, 63, 72, 97, 102, 115, 127, 128, 136, 153, 175, 179

B

Bailey Richardson 75
Basecamp 218
Bernard & Sheshadri 149
Bloomberg 130
Bob Ross 67
Bootstrap 131
Brad Frost 105, 109
Braun 127
Brian Chesky 33
Buster Benson 31

C

Canon 182
Card, Moran, & Newell 72
Carl Jung 72
Carlo Rovelli 2
Carl Sagan 245
Carol Bove 134
Carol Pearson 72
Charles S. Carver 157
Chip and Dan Heath 42
Christina Gravert 167
Christina Wodtke 49, 233
Christopher Alexander 108
Christopher Reath 205
Chrome 61, 105, 172
Claire Rowland 147
Clark & Chalmers 69
Clark Terry 230
Claude Debussy 94
Clubhouse 132
C. Northcote Parkinson 25
CodePen 226
Colin Ware 150
Conor O'Sullivan 153
Craig Kistler 126
Craigslist 40, 130, 217
CreativeMornings 222

D

Dan Mall 230
Dan Saffer 200
Dave Gray 59
Dave McClure 32
David Cronin 203
David Hockney 88
Dedre Gentner 198
Disney 115
Donella Meadows 165, 199
Don Norman 17, 139, 198, 228
Drudge Report 130

E

Edward de Bono 227
Elizabeth Goodman 147
Ellen Lupton 89, 94
Erika Hall 24
Erin Nolan 199
Ethan Marcotte 101
Evernote 105

F

Facebook 33, 51, 138
Fiorito & Dalton 46
Frank Chimero 34, 233, 234
Frans Johansson 230
Frida Kahlo 236

G

Gayle Curtis 46
GEICO 179
George Lakoff 45
Geri Coady 67
Gmail 172
Google 32, 48, 61, 71, 72, 97, 103, 118, 119, 175, 129, 133, 136, 169, 183, 200
Gretchen Rubin 163

H

Hannes Seifort 45
Harrington Emerson 31
Harry Roberts 183
HAWRAF 130
Headpace 33
Helen Van Wyk 67
Hilde and Ylva Østby 190

I

IBM 66
IDEO 34, 213, 229, 231
IKEA 46
Instagram 132, 174, 192
iOS 127, 140, 145
iPad 191
iPhone 97, 115, 131, 228

J

Jack Kerouac 176
Jackson Pollock 230
Jaime Levy 200
Jakob Nielsen 45
Jamais Cascio 56
Jane McGonigal 162, 168
Jason Santa Maria 216
Jeff Crossman 108
Jennifer Tidwell 113
Jeremy Keith 101
Jill Butler 31
Jina Anne 109
Joan Didion 50
Jodi Leo 34, 232
John Maeda 167
Jonathan Harris 51, 166
Jonathan Korn 33
Jon Yablonski 31
Joseph Campbell 199
Josh Clark 145
Jussi Pasanen 204

K

Kai Elmer Sotto 75
Kara Pernice 87
Kat Holmes 60
Kathryn Whitenton 149
Kathy Sierra 25, 202
Kat Norton 75
Kelli Anderson 161
Ken Kocienda 115
Kevin Huynh 75
Kirby Ferguson 231
Kohavi, Tang, & Xu 32
Kritina Holden 31

L
Lara Hogan 183
Lawrence Lessig 230
Leah Buley 179
Lee Krasner 230
Lenny Rachitsky 33
Lewis Carroll 14
Liz Danzico 92
L.M. Sacasas 168
Luke Wroblewski 146

M
Marco Suarez 132
Margaret Chan 62
Margaret Mark 72
Margaret Mead 130
Maria Popova 230
Marshall McLuhan 72
Martin Charlier 147
Masonry 131
Matt Jones 214
Mat Yurow 33
Maya Angelou 203
McKinsey 191
Michael F. Scheier 157
Microsoft 63, 128
Mies van der Rohe 128
Mike Kuniavsky 71
MIT 147
Molly Clare Wilson 167
Morningstar 165

N
Naoto Fukasawa 170
NASA 108
Naval Ravikant 30
Netflix 33, 61
Neven Mrgan 127
Nicole Fenton 44, 202, 215
Nike 71

Nir Eyal 73
N.K. Jemisin 176
NoKey 145
Notion 172

P
Paola Antonelli 70
Parsons 12
Pascal Deville 130
Patañjali 150
Paula Scher 225
Peter Morville 46
Petrula Vrontikis 210
Photoshop 131
Pinterest 131, 132, 188
Polestar 191
ProPublica 221

R
Rachel Nabors 116
Rem Koolhaas 129
Richard Saul Wurman 41
Richard Thaler 164, 165, 167
Rick Rubin 225
Robert Bringhurst 90
Robert Cialdini 163
Robert Reimann 203
Rodden, Hutchinson, & Fu 33
Roehm & Roehm 204
Ron Kohavi 32
Rosie Holtom 182
Runyon Design 12, 223
Ryan Singer 160, 218

S
Sahana Foundation 34
Salman Rushdie 42
Sam Raddatz 18
Samuel Salzer 165
Sarah Drasner 116

Sara Wachter-Boettcher 58
Scott McCloud 11
Scrivener 103
Shopify 133
Sidney Parnes 229
Sketch 131
Skillshare 12
Slack 105
Snapchat 138
Sol Lewitt 236
Spotify 62, 172
Stein & Ramaseshan 190
Stephen A. Mouzon 127
Stephen Wendel 165
Steve Jobs 42, 127, 144
Steve Krug 54, 148
Steve Rogers 76
Sunrise 105
Susan Goltsman 60, 68
SVA 12, 232
Synchron 147

T
Tangity 53
Target 191
Theresa Wiseman 58
TikTok 132, 172, 192
Tim Sheiner 202
Tinder 136
T.K.V. Desikachar 150
Tom and David Kelley 213
Trent Walton 91
TripAdvisor 33
Twitter 24, 30, 33, 61, 62, 179, 205
Tyler Tate 98
Typekit 131

U
Uber 33
Umberto Eco 96

V
Val Head 116
Vasilis van Gemert 99
Victoria Young Idol 33

W
W3C 136
Walter Gropius 127
Walt Whitman 246
WCAG 65, 67, 89, 90
Weather Underground 172
WebAIM 67
Wikipedia 31, 40, 45
William James 29
William Lidwell 31
Will Rogers 122
Wirecutter 223

X
Xerox 76, 127

Y
Yu-kai Chou 162

"Do I contradict myself?
 Very well then I contradict myself,
 (I am large, I contain multitudes.)"

Walt Whitman, *Leaves of Grass*